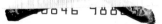

D0935495

DATE			

CULTURAL THEORY AND PSYCHOANALYTIC TRADITION

CULTURAL THEORY AND PSYCHOANALYTIC TRADITION

David James Fisher

Transaction Publishers
New Brunswick (U.S.A.) and London (U.K.)

846 95885

Library of Congress Catalog Number: 90-23582
ISBN: 0-88738-387-4
Printed in the United States of America

Library of Congress Cataloging-in-Publication Data

Fisher, David James.
    Cultural theory and psychoanalytic tradition / David James Fisher.
    p.   cm. -- (History of ideas series)
    Includes bibliographical references and index.
    ISBN 0-88738-387-4
    1. Psychoanalysis and culture. 2. Psychoanalysis--History. 3.
    Psychohistory. I. Title. II. Series: History of ideas series
    (New Brunswick, N.J.)
    BF175.4.C84F57 1991
    150.19'5--dc20   90-23582
    CIP

Dedicated to my loving and beloved wife, Karen L. Fund

Contents

Introduction

I

In September of 1973, I defended my doctoral thesis in the field of European cultural history. I was two months shy of my twenty-seventh birthday. My doctoral defense was hardly of the nightmarish quality, the rumors of which circulate as graduate students move toward the end of their studies. My jury was composed of three inspiring teachers; I knew in advance that they would all show up, read my extremely lengthy manuscript, and that they genuinely wished me well. The trio was composed of George L. Mosse, my major professor and gracious host, the French social historian Harvey Goldberg, and the French literary critic, Germaine Brée. The setting was Mosse's living room in Madison, a comfortable and familiar ambiance to me because my former wife and I had lived downstairs in the Mosse residence for one year and a half during an earlier phase of my training.

I had affectionate, relatively intimate relations with the professors on the committee; each one had influenced me deeply and, as it turns out, permanently. Mosse and Brée were Europeans, although markedly different in cultural training, sensibility, style of intellectual life, teaching methods, and in relating to their favorite students. Goldberg, it should be noted, was from New Jersey, but he lived half the time in Paris and was so knowledgeable about and enamored of French socialist and radical political movements that he had adopted a Parisian

persona. Mosse was a German-Jewish refugee from fascism, highly
educated and erudite, a powerful public speaker with a booming,
trumpet-like voice and beautiful diction; through his example and his
pedagogy, he encouraged his students to learn about the cultural
legacy of the past. He emphasized the convergences of "high" cultural
life with politics, social movements, and popular forms of culture,
which he seldom denigrated as "vulgar." He expected, rather
demanded, that we conduct our research and theorizing as competent
scholars, with respect for the empirical data and primary sources of
history. "Facts and documents!" George would bellow.

The antifascist, liberal Mosse was enlivened by his dialogue with
mostly left-wing male Jewish graduate students in and around the
University of Wisconsin; he had a more difficult time with female
graduate students, quite unlike Brée. He loved to argue and to
disagree, challenging us, teasing us, exhorting us to sharpen our critical viewpoints. Critical analysis was not just an ideal; in his lectures
and discussions with us, he demonstrated it, took pleasure in it. Most
importantly, he was a presence, a vital and vitalizing presence, someone who listened to us attentively, someone who forced us to reexam-
ine our facile assumptions and sweeping conclusions. If he opposed
sloganeering and posturing, he also showed us how to pose tough,
nonsentimental questions about historical reality. Mosse stressed the
ambiguities of historical choice, the finite possibilities of action in
specific historical contexts; his perspective was particularly salutary in
the late 1960s and early 1970s when utopian thinking was prevalent,
when the thought that everything was possible widely proliferated. He
urged us to be skeptical of the moral zeal and revolutionary ardor fuel-
ing the politics, theorizing, and theatrics of the New Left in precisely
the period of my graduate studies.

As soon as it became clear to me that my doctoral defense was
designed to be a conversation about transforming my thesis, *Romain
Rolland and the Question of the Intellectual*, into a book, that no one
wished to trip me up or humiliate me, I relaxed; I even enjoyed
myself. Here I was with three gifted individuals having a civilized,
impassioned, relatively high-powered discussion about a European
intellectual of another era. Not a trial at all, the dialogue was
conducted with verve, with receptivity to the issues I raised, acknowledging that they were worth investigating, that something valuable,

namely a scholarly book and articles might emerge out of this. That book, it should be noted, was published, but not quickly and certainly not without much anguish as to its significance to a post-1960s audience—to a changed environment that I perceived as indifferent to and nonaffirming of my work.

I had developed a powerful, primarily positive unconscious transference to Mosse and to his variety of doing history. He practiced a form of European cultural history which eludes generalizations or distinct categories. It was fundamentally European in that he had inherited an imaginative, learned version of examining how cultural activity converged with politics. He handled ideas and abstractions adeptly, though he preferred to link theoretical developments to more specific historical and cultural contexts; he did not engage in speculation for the love of speculation. He exercised a vast power over me. He exuded a self-assurance, a verbal facility, and a knowledge of what questions really mattered. Some exceptionally bright students found him irremediably arrogant and pompous; I found him stimulating and fascinating; I identified with his outrageousness; I resonated to his intuitions. Mosse was bored by lengthy discussions of historical methodology and historiography, believing that such concerns disguised a loss of creativity on the part of the working historian.

His method was both simple and hard to emulate. Cultural history had to enlighten and to provoke thinking on the part of its audience—whether it was lecturing to undergraduates in a large hall, reflecting on issues in small seminars of pipe smokers, or communicating to one's scholarly readership. When Mosse practiced it, it could also be compelling, entertaining, contentious, even if it was always directed toward the rethinking of established pieties and received opinion. Mosse's cultural history probed the motivations, conscious and unconscious, of historical choice in concrete moments; it also investigated symbolic or emotional modes of thinking, including the impact of the irrational on the historical development of nationalism, fascism, and modern cultural movements.

It was critical in that cultural history went together with critiques, with sophisticated methods of analyzing texts, documents, and a wide variety of cultural artifacts. To engage in a critique implied a capacity to understand relationships and processes. Cultural critique also meant being suspicious of one's self and of one's own assumptions, methods of inquiry, prejudices, and theoretical inclination, especially those which overly estimated the dominance of reason. Mosse's approach was never antitheoretical or anti-intellectual, but theory was subordinated to an inquiry into its uses and abuses, its application and misapplication by particular individuals or groups in particular circumstances. Cultural history was elevated into more than a sterile academic discipline, not some peripheral subspecialty of European history. He practiced it as if it were a legitimate way of life, advocating it as an authentic way of being, a dynamic way of interacting with and making sense out of the world. Mosse, it should be noted, tempered his seriousness with a playfulness and an ironic view of himself; he avoided a spirit of intellectual heaviness and was rarely pedantic, quite capable of laughing at himself.

I was catalyzed by this heady notion of European cultural history and cultural critique, especially by the European dimension of it. I developed a naive, messianic belief in its mission. In the politicized and radicalized atmosphere of Madison, Wisconsin, I, too, had acquired a political and radical consciousness, jettisoning my own family's allegiance to a comfortable liberalism of the FDR and Adlai Stevenson variety. I became convinced that the study of history was not some antiquarian activity involving the exploration of dead issues about dead people from the dead and distant past. Contemporary history, say from the Paris Commune of 1871, or from the First World War, remained close to the anxieties of the present, that is, my own concerns.

Fantasy also played a major role in my "convictions" about history. I had spent a year in Paris in the early 1970s and I immersed myself in the study of French intellectual and cultural life. I resonated to the controversies and I craved the esteem that writers exercised over their public. I desired one day to be a voice heard on the Left Bank of Paris, imagining that I might enter this universe, master its discourses and secret codes, even speak French with an impeccable Parisian accent. In short, I fantasized that I would become warmly welcomed, perhaps find a home, a community, a new family, as well as a sophisticated mode of thinking and articulating myself.

This wishful fantasy was not fulfilled. But it took me several years to recognize it. Meanwhile just weeks after graduating with my doctorate, I returned to Paris in the fall of 1973 for another two years of advanced studies at the Sixième Section of the École Pratique des Hautes Études, now known as the Research Institute for Higher Studies in the Social Sciences. There, under the generous tutelage of Georges Haupt, an astute scholar of socialism and communism of Romanian origin who had trained in the Soviet Union, I entered a post-doctoral seminar. It was conceived of as the "Geography of Marxism," investigating the penetration and diffusion of Marxism into the "space" of Europe and the world since the 1880s. At first it was an intimidating then a marvelous learning experience.

Haupt brought together a colorful rogues gallery of international post-1960s Marxist types, ranging from Gramscians, Lukacsians, Karl Kautskians, dissident French Communists, Austro-Marxists, Althusserians, critical theorists, anarcho-Marxists, worker self-management Marxists, dissident Catholic Marxists, academic Marxists, independent scholars of Marxism, porno-Marxists—a kitchen sink of Marxists. Many of these scholars had completed the prestigious state doctoral thesis in France, usually consisting of a minimum of ten years of work and the production of a tome of over one thousand pages; several had published numerous books on Marxist themes or had contributed to the history of Marxism.

Haupt gathered these diverse thinkers together. Besides his considerable charm and knowledge, the glue was the seminar meetings every second week, usually to explore work in progress. And what discussions they were: incisive, contentious, well-informed, rigorous, partisan, unsparing. After two years of serious debate and contestation, very little consensus emerged. In fact, the seminar could not even agree on a definition of Marxism, except to acknowledge that Marxism was a dialectical method of analysis and a variety of social movements that developed in Europe during the 1880s that had something to do with a commitment to reason and to the understanding of the class nature of society and history. I mention this absence of consensus within Parisian Marxist circles in the period 1973 to 1975, shortly before the crisis and perhaps total collapse of Marxist inspired regimes, prior to the demoralization and defeatism among those committed to forms of Marxism analysis.

The absence of agreement did not then trouble me for I was uninterested in consensus; I embraced conflict. It was exhilarating to be in the company of these historians and theorists; I was awed by their command of the literature, envious of their abundant skills with an abstract and ideologically loaded French language. I tried to emulate their ease in expressing brilliant perceptions about the past as well as their articulation of insightful, often stinging parallels with the present. What I failed to notice was that the 1960s was over, at least in the United States, and that a discouraging and lengthy period of depoliticization was underway. I had to think about the unpleasant prospect of earning a living.

Living as an outsider in Paris, feeling marginalized in terms of my relationship to French circles, either academic or avant-garde, freed me up to lead an exciting, semi-bohemian life. I became a consumer in a city specially designed for cultural consumption. I became a cultural *flaneur*, frequenting concerts, plays, museums, galleries, cafes, walking the streets and parks of Paris, reading *Le Monde* and *Le Nouvel Observateur* as if it were required. I took in all I could. Meanwhile, I was very much unaware of significant changes in the American academic marketplace, including the steep decline in any jobs for historians, and the dramatic shift from intellectual history in favor of social history.

I was oblivious. I was in a state of denial. I did not care. I cared too much. I was happily and romantically alienated from America. I regarded myself an unappreciated outcast, a neglected man of talent. I equated a certain form of personal misery with authenticity; those who were successful I automatically saw as opportunists or sellouts. I was unaware of my own considerable envy for them. I was identified with a distinctly French cultural attitude that saw things American, above all American cultural products and the American political system, as distinctly mediocre and shallow. I simultaneously overestimated all things French, from the drinking water of Paris, to the aesthetics of everyday life, to French cuisine, to French movies and literature. I erotized an already erotic civilization, dramatized a society that already thrived on its own tradition of dramatization; my language became inflated and grandiose, a bad imitation of French rhetoric. The irritations of French society, the backwardness of its bureaucracy, the formality, rigidity, and anachronistic codes of ordinary French life, I recognized but minimized or discounted. I hated French nationalism and ethnocentrism, while espousing all things French. Being committed to being committed, or at least to transmitting and perpetuating a

French style of engaged intellectual life, I lost contact with a number of sober realities about the American scene and about myself.

When I returned to the States in the late summer of 1975 with my seemingly high level of consciousness, I was rudely awakened. Jobs in modern European history were few and far between. Competition for the small number of positions was keen. The old club network that I had scorned and never belonged to reasserted itself. Social historians increasingly enjoyed a privileged position in history departments and in the profession at large. They were aggressively attacking old-fashioned methods in the history of ideas and intellectual history, including traditions and research strategies that I still found legitimate.

Actually I was ill prepared to be a "professional" historian in that professionalization was anathema to me. My graduate training at Wisconsin and post-doctoral studies in Paris had failed to professionalize me; I unfairly equated professionalization with careerism, typified by a memorable aphorism from my Madison days: "A 'colleague' is not a person but a disease." Without seeing how harsh and foolish that dismissal was, I considered myself immune to this bourgeois disease, I thought. Disdain for American academics, contempt for American culture and materialism, a need to devalue prevailing American values, particularly American patriotism and militarism, a summary dismissal of political opinions local and national, a tendency to blur the distinction between conservative and liberal, a pleasure in pontificating about third parties and third ways in America, all converged with a number of deeply ingrained personality problems to produce a terribly lonely situation and an impasse in my career.

I became the proverbial gypsy scholar, wandering from university position to position, employed for six consecutive one-year jobs. My dispersion began in Paris and shifted from the midwest to the east coast to the west coast. My persistent anxieties and ambivalence about the university caused my scholarly productivity to suffer; I was not always able to maintain the highest levels of competent teaching in the classroom, even though I valued teaching and found it a highly rewarding activity.

My character problems, an outspoken argumentative style, an apparent arrogance and self-confidence masking persistent uncertainty and a need to be loved and admired, a recurring tendency to attack the personalities that I wanted to like and respect me, a need to dismantle the ideas and methods of older authorities in the field (usually tenured professors or influential up and comers) did not easily lend itself to job renewals or to the continuity of employment. It seemed that I scorned the esteem of the colleagues; in truth, I valued their estimation too much. Nor did the yearly academic ruptures work to heal my unanalyzed inner turmoil nor my ideological hostility to America. A visceral conflict emerged toward that peculiarly medieval institution, the university and centers of higher learning.

I became a gypsy scholar without much taste or aptitude for the gypsy side of life. I developed grave doubts about my scholarship, given my chronic employment anxieties and deep-seated worries about how I would support myself. I became obsessed with finding some job stability and continuity, as if an external structure might center me. As I doubted the value of my own research, my confidence in my writing became shaken; after all, if my scholarship was any good, I would have landed a tenure-track job. I blamed myself. I blamed the profession. I was caught up in a vicious cycle of blame and self-blame. I became angry and disillusioned with intellectual history, resenting some of my former professors, wondering why they could not intervene and make a job happen for me, as it they were capable of making miracles. When the negative transference kicked in, it did so with a vengeance, leaving me feeling terribly weakened and vulnerable.

I moved from one-year position to one-year position. Job would actually be a more accurate description. I would start teaching in September of an academic year, usually responsible for a large load of courses. By October of that same semester, I would have to gear up for the shame-inducing and almost always frustrating job search. My messianic thoughts about European cultural history, alternating with a residue of bitterness at the profession and anger at myself, my presumption about bringing "culture," "reason," and a "critical perspective" to the American campuses were doubly out of touch with the anti-intellectual and increasingly specialized and conservative climate in and around university campuses in the middle and late 1970s.

I judged the people evaluating me to be uncultivated and mediocre; I was unable to disguise signals of contempt for them. I was terrible at academic politics; I never acquired the skills of becoming deferential and of making the correct alliances. I was too honest. I was ambitious and unable to take a process oriented view of university life. I was aggressive. I was tactless, abrupt, insensitive, abrasive; I used my awareness of the narcissistic investments and wounds of my fellow academics to attack or undermine them. I hid a friendly, accessible, caring, and charming part of my personality. I used my knowledge and understanding for destructive purposes. In short, I engaged in repeated acts of self-sabotage.

Furthermore, one of my fantasies of bridging the specialties of intellectual and social history, of maintaining a respectful dialogue, proved to be a wrong-headed illusion, a swindle. Perhaps I was unprepared for the dialogue; perhaps the climate was not ripe for it. Upon returning to America in 1975, I discovered that social historians dominated most history departments and that they exercised an increasing hegemonic influence on employment searches, determining the direction that the discipline was moving. For the most part—obviously there were some exceptions—social history positioned itself against intellectual history. Whatever their methodological orientation and whatever their watchwords were, social historians sharply dichotomized history into black and white categories, expressing a sharp hostility toward those doing intellectual history. In my experience, there was no dialogue in those years, only isolation and a feeling of beleaguerment if one practiced any version of intellectual history. When a given department was able to secure a tenure line in history, it almost always went to a "new" social historian.

This professional impasse ended for me during the academic year 1978-79, while teaching at UCLA. I had moved to Los Angeles from Brooklyn Heights for a one year replacement job with the expectation that a tenure track position in my field would open; I was assured that I would be a serious candidate for such a job. A tenured position in Modern European intellectual history did, in fact, open, and a national search was conducted. After a promising beginning, I was abruptly eliminated from consideration. I was devastated. Wounded. Deeply humiliated. And depressed.

During the early months of that search and under the influence of Peter Loewenberg, a historian and practicing psychoanalyst, who incidentally had been on the original committee recruiting me to UCLA, I applied to the two psychoanalytic institutes in Los Angeles for full psychoanalytic training. This was not the first time I had considered analytic training. My appetite had been whetted after I had organized a seminar on psychoanalytic theory (actually to study Freud's texts) and on the psychoanalytic application to literature and history while still in graduate school. During the previous year in New York City I applied and had been accepted by the National Psychological Association for Psychoanalysis (NPAP), originally founded by Theodor Reik. I had made an overture to the prestigious New York Psychoanalytic Institute as well, but had been advised that they did not train individuals with nonmedical backgrounds.

Loewenberg gently persuaded me to apply to the two psychoanalytic institutes in Los Angeles, urging me to begin therapy. I was hesitant, frightened, "resistant." I figured I would be leaving Los Angeles in August, on to my next academic job, who knows where. In a caring voice he told me that no one would be able to take away from me the insights I gained, even after only a short period of therapy. I had been given the names of two psychoanalysts in Los Angeles by a trusted New York analyst. I asked Loewenberg for his recommendations. Of the three names he provided, one was identical to my New York source. I made the plunge, not without trepidation. I called for an appointment.

The psychoanalyst, Rudolf Ekstein, had some time available for me, especially if I could be flexible about the scheduling of our appointments; he had been informed in a letter that a "candidate" might be contacting him for a possible training analysis by my friend in New York. At that first appointment I brought with me, needing to impress him and hoping to receive some reassurance from him, an essay I had published on Freud. I also began to tell him the story of my life, beginning with my current mess. He was an older Central European with a distinct Viennese accent, then in his middle sixties. I was struck by three things about him: his decency, in agreeing to work with me for a rather low hourly fee; his excellent and subtle listening skills; and his ability to combine an astute intelligence with kindness. We began our work together, first meeting twice a week, gradually shifting to four times a week for a full analysis.

I did not then realize that this relationship would last for another nine years, nor how essential and powerful an instrument it would become in learning about myself and in learning how to be a psychoanalyst. I was somewhat astonished that he permitted himself, despite a comfortable reserve, to be warm, charming, and fully engaged in the process from our first meeting; this contrasted with a caricatured image I had of the psychoanalyst as cold and detached, distant and scientific, a blank screen or surgical instrument.

I mention this article on Freud. Actually it addressed the relationship and debates of Freud with Romain Rolland. It had been written in my last months in Paris, the spring and early summer of 1975. Retrospectively, I was moving not exactly from Marx to Freud, but from Romain Rolland to Freud; that is, from an immersion in a French intellectual tradition of idealism, vitalism, mysticism, and of political engagement to one more firmly grounded in Freudian psychoanalytic practice. As a graduate student and in my post-graduate seminar on Marxism, I had read Marx mediated through the perspectives of Sartre, Marcuse, Lukacs, and George Lichtheim. This was a humanistic, anthropological Marx interpreted in a distinctly New Left flavor; it was one that rejected Marxist dogma, the economistic Marx, and which utterly refused the Soviet style or Leninistic Marx.

In uncovering rare and beautiful letters from Freud to Romain Rolland in the Archives Romain Rolland in Paris, I became intrigued with the nature and depth of their friendship. I endeavored to understand how two intellectual figures who were so different could have established such a profound bond. Actually, the essay articulated my own developing convictions about the interpretive power of psychoanalysis as a method of inquiry. At the university I had discovered Freud, where he was situated as one of the seminal thinkers of twentieth-century intellectual history. Freud was depicted as the revolutionary who had synthesized then surpassed the medical, psychiatric, and cultural approach to mental illness as conceived in the nineteenth century. If he invented a new discipline, he also created a subversive approach to modern man's anxious and depressed state.

My first contact with Freud—once again in Mosse's lectures on European cultural history—came through reading *The New Introductory Lectures on Psychoanalysis* (1933) and with the magisterial *Civilization and Its Discontents* (1930). In the sixties I encountered Freud through the lenses of Norman O. Brown, R. D. Laing, Herbert Marcuse, and Erich Fromm; I had also been influenced by Frantz Fanon's *The Wretched of the Earth* (1966), which questioned psychoanalytic universalism. I first encountered Freud suspicious of psychoanalytic reductionism and determinism, open to psychoanalytic metaphor and its theory driven methodology, receptive to its utopian and liberating possibilities. The early experience of reading Freud disturbed me, despite the clarity and eloquence of his writing. To discover his mordant insights into defenses, into the power of early childhood, into the conflictual realm of the subjective world, into the psychological modalities of the mind was like opening up vistas about *my* family, *my* self-protective maneuvers, *my* inner world.

Scholarship, I subsequently learned, often disguises autobiographical quests. What I uncovered in the Freud-Rolland relationship, incidentally, became core themes in my own analytic relationship with Dr. Ekstein. Having daringly analyzed Freud's psychodynamics, I now needed to turn to my own both to work them through and to transform them into instruments of understanding others.

II

I was accepted by the Los Angeles Psychoanalytic Institute for full psychoanalytic training approximately nine months after I had applied. It seemed like an interminable wait. I was beginning my education in psychoanalytic time, which is slow, laborious, needlessly bureaucratic, and not particularly attuned to the desires and anxieties of the novice.

My formal psychoanalytic training occurred between 1980 and 1988. It was an incomparable adventure. In *A Movable Feast*, Hemingway aptly described his youthful experiences in Paris as an unending, slightly perilous quest in search of creativity, above all in finding his own self-confidence and distinct voice. For me, Paris had represented a blend of sensual experience and high powered intellectual inquiry; my youth in Paris mingled the sights, sounds, smells, and tastes of France with the unusual and original characters of the city. If I imagined that nothing could compare to my expedition to Paris, my foray into psychoanalysis proved to be an equally fabulous source of discovery and self-discovery. It also placed a high value on memory and the return of affectively charged memories.

There were a number of external difficulties that made training a hardship: it required the sacrifice of time; it was expensive (above all, the cost of a long and comprehensive training analysis); it exposed one to a series of seemingly endless scrutiny by local and national committees; and it opened one to the relative miscomprehension of others, many of whom had strong opinions about psychoanalysis as a profession, to biases about it as a therapy.

Psychoanalytic training at the analytic institute is structured to provide the candidates with a heightened emotional and intellectual immersion into psychoanalytic ways of thinking and of doing therapy. Candidates are required to begin their training analysis at least one year before formal seminars begin; they are allowed to select the analyst of their choice from a list of accredited training analysts; this particular analyst must be certified a training analyst and he may not already have three or more candidates in analysis. I later learned that these "rules" were not always strictly enforced. Rule was one of those slippery notions that depended on one's perspective; rule almost always meant guiding principle.

After one year of his own analysis, the candidate usually began seminars; between six months and one year into seminars, the candidate was encouraged to begin analytic work with a patient, for not less than four hours a week, with one hour a week with a seasoned supervisor to discuss difficulties with the case. After another six months, one was eligible to begin a second analytic case with a second supervisor. Candidates were free to select from a pool of available supervisors. The same guidelines operated for the third analytic control case and for the third supervisor.

By the end of the second year or beginning of the third year of seminars, the analytic candidate would be somewhere in the middle of his own psychoanalysis as a patient; he would be well along in his first control case as an analyst. Simultaneously, he would be working with supervisors and thinking about significant psychoanalytic texts on theory and technique. For most candidates it is an all-encompassing undertaking; one receives a powerful dosage of psychoanalysis; in terms of time, energy, intellectual and emotional involvement, the training has a built-in geometric progression. Regression is also built in.

The training analysis slowly transformed itself into an in-depth experience about the psychoanalytic process in practice. Here one explored, inquired, probed, doubted, projected, resisted, and reflected upon buried psychic meanings as they emerged in a strange, undefinable dialogue structured around the free flow of associations. Even though the training analyst was an integral senior member of the psychoanalytic institute, appointed because of his knowledge, experience, and clinical acumen, he would not be reporting to institute committees on any aspect of the analysis. This non-reporting guaranteed confidentiality, helped to promote trust, and thus allowed the candidate to delve into forbidden aspects of his psychic life and fantasy world. These areas might remain hidden if they were to be exposed and scrutinized by some formal committee with a nontherapeutic agenda.

In my experience at the Los Angeles Psychoanalytic Institute, most training analysts conducted their analyses with tact and restraint so as to maximize its therapeutic efficacy; they carefully attempted to avoid leakages, gossip, and injurious casual remarks about a given candidate. Despite the efforts to be abstinent, I learned that there could be no "purity" in such a training program, for one might meet one's analyst at a scientific gathering, a committee meeting, or even at the annual Christmas party. Such encounters, usually quite charged, were grist for the analytic mill. For many and at moments for me, the training analysis also served a safety valve function; I used many sessions to take up complaints, some imaginary, some real, about the formal aspects of psychoanalytic education—whether about instructors, supervisors, advisor, committees and so on.

Candidates were obliged to take four years of seminars consisting of two courses meeting four hours a week. After the fourth year, the seminars continued in the form of electives, typically clinically oriented, for two hours a week until graduation. The seminars were taught by the faculty of graduate analysts. The faculty was composed essentially of unpaid, nonprofessional instructors, who primarily had expertise in the clinical applications of psychoanalysis; in my experience the quality of teaching varied widely, as did communication skills, scholarship, and knowledge of the literature. Seminars were either theoretical or clinical in orientation; only rarely were the two blended. In terms of pedagogical orientation, the curriculum was designed to lay the clinical and theoretical foundations of Freudian psychoanalysis by thoroughly familiarizing the students with key texts by Freud and subsequently by a selected canon of his heirs. The concept "heir to Freud" frequently became a battleground of contending theories.

In the first two years of seminars, candidates studied a number of converging aspects of Freud's thinking: his fundamental hypotheses about the mind and his assumptions about a psychology of unconscious mental process; his revolutionary approach to dreams; his emphasis on early childhood development; his thinking about psychic energy and sexuality; his contribution to the understanding of resistance and transference; his case history method; his metapsychology and his structural model; his formulations about character, psychopathology, and anxiety. In the seminars, we encountered Freud as he was discovering, elaborating, then revising the psychoanalytic paradigm. As we were experiencing the difficulties and pleasures of overcoming internal resistances in our own psychoanalyses, the candidate's seminars promoted a historical, critical, and clinical overview of Freud's trajectory over forty-five years of theorizing and fine-tuning his new discipline.

Psychoanalytic seminars also alerted the candidate to contemporary forms of psychoanalytic thinking; here he could ruminate on certain post-Freudian texts and modes of working with more disturbed patients and extreme forms of psychopathology. At the Los Angeles Psychoanalytic Institute, we studied the contributions of the English object relations school and the writings of Melanie Klein and her followers with a number of analysts who were committed "Kleinians." Some of my teachers were trained in England and were knowledgeable practitioners of Kleinian techniques.

Kleinian psychoanalysis revised classical Freudian and ego psychology by placing great emphasis on innate, murderous aggression and on the earliest phases of infant development. Their technique returned to an early stage of development marked by the infant's relationship with his mother, or parts of his mother's body, dominated by severe splitting of the personality. This splitting was caused by primitive defenses against deep-seated aggressive urges. The Kleinians are persuasive in understanding borderline and psychotic personalities and extremely disturbed children; they also subtly grasped the early and primal role of the superego and of severe self-punishing forces in the personality organization. Since the Kleinians placed so much emphasis on destructiveness and self-destructiveness, I observed that their theories angered people, often provoking extreme agreement or disagreement; many Kleinians were themselves transparently angry and envious individuals, incapable of genuine dialogue, unwilling to tolerate opposing points of view. In the name of "science" they claimed a privileged access to the primary process, as if they alone were capable of offering deep insights into the unconscious.

My training began in the years immediately following acrimony and a serious threat of a breach between the Kleinians and the classical psychoanalysts at the Institute. Such a split never occurred. Nevertheless, there were some scars and much resentment underneath an atmosphere of rhetorical tolerance and respect for differing points of view. I soon discovered the power of transference to a school of thought or method of inquiry: it almost inevitably happened that the candidates became loyal to the psychoanalytic school of their training analyst and favorite supervisors. Unconscious identification proved more powerful than independence of thought, more persistent than the mature cogitating on clinical and theoretical issues.

Furthermore, certain charismatic teachers and public speakers rallied their followers and generated excitement, zeal, and sometimes faith among the young, less experienced analysts. Having studied debates and ruptures within the European left and within the Socialist and Communist internationals, I now reexperienced some of the same tensions within my local psychoanalytic domain—all conducted ostensibly in the name of science, clinical efficacy, and "true" psychoanalysis. If it was at first disheartening, then deidealizing, to see that psychoanalysts could posture, distort, misrepresent, and overvalue the claims of their own theory while belittling the theories of their competitors, it subsequently humanized my view of analytic practitioners. I eventually learned that analysts were imperfect and fallible, subjected to the same uncertainties as the rest of the population. They mollified their anxieties by attaching themselves to some all-encompassing theory. I slowly began to modify my grandiose expectations about psychoanalytic theory and practice.

Besides the classical Freudian-ego psychological theory and the Kleinian approach, the 1980s brought the emergence of self-psychology, a form of psychoanalysis associated with Heinz Kohut and his followers. Self-psychology seemed particularly resonant to the narcissism and consumerism of America in the late 1970s and 1980s, to what Christopher Lasch felicitously called "the culture of narcissism." Kohut's psychoanalysis captivated therapists because it was clinically grounded and because it elevated empathic understanding and the emotional attunement of the therapist into fundamental "rules," guiding principles of clinical work. Self-psychologists offered a way of grasping the subjective world of narcissistic personalities, of individuals suffering from a variety of disorders of the self, ranging from fragile self-esteem, to repeated feelings of depletion, to loss of meaning in their lives, to fantasies of omnipotence and grandiosity accompanied by emotional coldness and inaccessibility.

My seminars on narcissism and on the self-psychological perspective were highly significant to me, assisting me to feel my way into the mental and emotional world of the patient; it also helped me to grasp the dynamics of transference of severely disturbed patients, whose ways of relating and whose psychopathology did not seem to fit the classical theory. When practiced sensitively self-psychology permitted the therapist to gain close access to the subjective world of the patient, without presuming to read the mind of the other in the light of superior scientific or objective knowledge. It was respectful and caring toward the other and it was experience near, that is, positioned as closely as possible to the perceptions, sensations, fantasies, and affects of the subject himself.

What I find off-putting about self-psychology is its messianic spirit and its own exaggerated claims of therapeutic success. The theory tends to be soft and lacking in rigor. Self-psychologists often misrepresent and polemicize against earlier psychoanalytic thinkers—in short, to distort the history of psychoanalysis to give their stance a preeminent place. There was an irony that many former Kleinian analysts had converted to self-psychology; it was paradoxical that they underwent such a dramatic theoretical reorientation, as if they stood their previous theory of technique on its head.

Such was the diverse theoretical climate at the Los Angeles Psychoanalytic Institute during the 1980s. Without getting caught up in any of the vituperative sides of these controversies and without being invested in one theory over another, I found the atmosphere to be remarkably alive and stimulating. Being a research candidate also permitted me to hear out all sides, to maintain some impartiality, to be critical toward all, to distance myself from the parochial spokesmen, and to cut through the cant while incorporating what was valid in each perspective. This might be called an eclectic and pluralist approach; I found it to be well-suited to learning, an antidote to orthodoxy or counterorthodoxies.

I was uninterested in party-line partisanship, in dogma of any variety, realizing that most of these disputes disguised personal or economic motives in the name of alleged scientific disagreements; sometimes they were simply about control of turf, about power. I, like many others, found myself skeptical toward the official position of the American Psychoanalytic Association, which prided itself on representing and bearing the standard of classical Freudian psychoanalysis. Through selected contact with instructors and supervisors, I came to respect all three theoretical positions, recognizing that there were astute, decent, and committed practitioners in each school.

If the curriculum compartmentalized seminars into four distinct categories of metapsychological theory, psychosexual development, psychopathology, and technique, it also offered explicitly clinical opportunities—the continuous case seminars. At the continuous case presentations, a candidate would report detailed process material, sometimes verbatim notes, from an ongoing psychoanalytic case in the presence of the other candidates and a senior instructor. These were demystifying learning experiences, at first because of my nonclinical background. One finally saw how other people worked and approached the material; I observed what was actually said and not said. I learned how my fellow seminarians processed the data and responded to their patients. I watched how a seasoned analyst listened to and assigned meaning to the same material. These continuous case seminars, while anxiety-provoking for the presenter, opened up fascinating discussions on the intricacies of the psychoanalytic process, from the various dimensions of understanding the transference and countertransference, to ways of addressing the resistance in terms of grasping defensive maneuvers. It underscored strategies of phrasing and timing interpretations, refining tools to develop insight and to remove barriers interfering with the free flow of associations.

I was struck by a number of features in every continuous case seminar: how incredibly intricate and elusive each case history was; how, even after years of diligent work, one only scratched the surface in exploring the intra-psychic realm; how impossible it was to pin down a personality; how every session contained multiple possibilities for interventions, that there was not necessarily one "correct" way; how providing a safe and nonthreatening atmosphere was a significant aspect of the therapeutic process; how vital the therapeutic alliance was with each patient and how it needed to be maintained and strengthened; how analytic listening tapped into the analyst's emotional and fantasy world more powerfully than it did into his intellectual and cognitive faculties. These converging factors could make analysis an exhausting experience until one developed self-discipline and technique.

The continuous case seminars made me aware of the endless possibilities of psychoanalytic clinical method, especially if the rules of free association and interpretation were carefully followed and if the process were left open-ended. The most textured form of analysis was oriented toward the exploration of clusters of meaning about a life history as they unfolded in the analytic relationship. If I began naively and enthusiastically, and if I entered training without clinical experience, I soon realized that no definitive truth or scientific consensus existed regarding what was happening in any hour, or in a particular case, despite the years of experience of a given clinician.

Not surprisingly, those from different theoretical schools had widely divergent ways of assessing, accenting, interpreting, and integrating the material. There were distinct views on what constituted a genuine psychoanalytic therapy, although most analysts agreed that it had something to do with an analysis of the transference, with an introspective dialogue, and with the creation of a fantasy-driven, evocative, and shifting relationship between two individuals. Similarly, analysts disagreed if psychoanalytic therapy was a science, an art, a humanistic discipline, or something entirely distinct from science, art, and the human sciences. Psychoanalysis was impossible to objectify in words.

I discovered that there was a relative atmosphere of acceptance of different languages and theory, although on occasion that ambience of mutual respect could be disrupted. At moments, expressions of faith might be expressed; at times, parochial notions would be asserted as scientific or empirical truth; old-fashioned formulations would be reiterated with an authoritarian tone. And, on occasion, new and fashionable ways of thinking might stir an ardor not unlike those in religious cults or political sects. For the most part, however, the psychoanalytic institute encouraged freedom of thought and relative freedom of expression; it was structured democratically if a bit hierarchically. It tended to be generous and tolerant toward non-"main-stream" positions. It was paternalistic in the best and worst sense.

In general, the optimal learning of psychoanalysis takes place in one's own training analysis and secondarily in the years of supervision; most analysts regard the knowledge gained in formal seminars to be peripheral and vicarious, something akin to an intellectual superstructure built on the infrastructure of the analysis and controlled supervisory work. Thus, psychoanalytic training sharply contrasts with graduate school and is closer to the educational structures of art institutes, where one works intimately and for long-term periods with one or more masters. Freud argued that the most reliable way to learn about psychoanalysis was not through reading theory, but rather through undergoing an analysis (or through interpreting one's own dreams). There is a potential danger of anti-intellectualism if this approach is abused; much of contemporary psychoanalytic education tends to denigrate the acquisition of an authentically philosophical approach by the practitioner in favor of creating a training environment more akin to a technical school. Psychoanalytic education at its best combines the heart and mind, lived experience and the capacity to cogitate on it, the expression of affectively charged memories and the ability to express coherently one's lived history.

After undergoing analytic training, I came to realize that only intuitive and exceptional individuals can grasp the subtlety and magnificent explanatory power of the psychoanalytic instrument, if they have not had analysis. At times philosophers and literary critics comprehend core psychoanalytic ideas and insights by immersing themselves in psychoanalytic theory without the practical experience of training or of undergoing an analysis. Even with the most distinguished of them, with a Marcuse, Adorno, Habermas, or Ricoeur, their writing about psychoanalysis always seems distant from the actual give and take, the dramas and plateaus, of the clinical hour; their writing remains detached from the emotional and fantasy-driven aspects of the work; they are inclined toward overestimating the intellectual aspects of analysis to the detriment of other features. Most high-powered theorists without training failed to emphasize the features of the analytic relationship itself, the nonverbal factors, the role of affects, the predominant significance of fantasies in the subjective lives of individuals.

I slowly realized that interpreting was not some dazzling intellectual operation revealing the mastery and brilliance of the interpreter. Rather it was a small but crucial step in an ongoing, laborious process. Deft interpretations worked when they illuminated internal conflict, when they permitted the analysand to realize his own defensiveness, to understand the underlying, unconscious forces causing the defenses.

For me, supervision became a unique learning experience, situated somewhere between a tutorial and an analytic therapy session. I was permitted to select all of my supervisors. Because of an old psychoanalytic ethic about providing service to the community, my supervisors agreed to work with me for sharply reduced fees. For those cases screened by the psychoanalytic clinic and approved for analysis, the supervisors pooled the clinic fees. To be sure the hourly fee for such supervision could be reduced as much as one fifth of their usual fee. This piece of generosity set the tone for the supervisory process. For me the experience began and ended as a collaborative venture; it was not structured around an imitative process of learning what to say or do as if one were mimicking a great master. Supervision evolved into a highly focused, richly textured clinical conversation about specific clinical issues.

I chose supervisors who were invested in disseminating relatively sophisticated psychoanalytic modes of thinking about the clinical material. None wished to develop a coterie of disciples or loyal apprentices who did analysis exactly as they did. I began by meeting with a supervisor once a week. These relationships often lasted years and became quite intimate. Styles of supervision were markedly different. Emphases were not the same.

In my first supervision, the primary focus was on recognizing and interpreting the defenses. Defenses were to be understood within the framework of a life history and with particular attention to early childhood and to patterns of upbringing in the family. Great stress was placed on the interpretations of transference, how older self-protective patterns were reenacted in the patient's relationship with me, often reexperienced in feelings, fantasies, desires, and thoughts about me. In the relative safety of the supervision, I explored not only problems in understanding the patient's dynamics, but my own anxieties, resistances, disappointments, and unrealistic desires in dealing with my analytic patients. I realized that my own reactions and feelings were legitimate, profoundly real, and not necessarily neurotic or beside the point; my supervisors encouraged me to trust my own subjective reactions to patients and various situations, to use myself as a reliable instrument of understanding the psychoanalytic process. This opened up many alleys for me. It also prompted me to develop my own style of doing analysis, one which enabled me to be myself, to be spontaneous, and not to be bound by a rigid externally superimposed set of rules.

I mention the term "relative" safety. It was relative because my supervisors were evaluating me, writing reports on my progress; their assessment of my work was crucial in graduating from the local institute and in gaining certification from the American Psychoanalytic Association. I learned bit by bit to be candid within a framework of reserve; I was free within a well-defined structure. Sustained self-disclosure and self-analysis most appropriately took place in the training analysis. Furthermore, too much honesty with one's supervisors, including too much affection for them, was often considered inappropriate. At analytic institutes, pedagogy and supervision easily cross over into presumptuous attempts to psychoanalyze rather than assess the educational growth of the candidates; thus, one risked being labeled diagnostically, even pejoratively, as loose, labile, metaphorical, flamboyant, or exuberant. These labels, if thrown in your direction, could be hurtful; they often inhibited creativity and efforts to forge one's own analytic style. I was fortunate. Labels used to describe me were noninjurious and not without merit.

Other invaluable aspects of supervision were the importance placed on clinical empathy and emotional sensitivity; both were highlighted in the theoretical orientations of the English object relations school and in self-psychology. Before beginning my training and personal analysis, I mistakenly believed that psychoanalysis cured through the analyst's incisive interpretations, his heroic efforts to transform the unconscious into consciousness. I was determined to emerge as an imaginative and razor-sharp interpreter. In practice, however, the analytic process required great patience, tact, and restraint; it was oriented toward allowing the analysand to arrive at insight himself or herself, toward forging a mode of self-analysis. It was not a pedagogical or pedantic enterprise; and it was not about impressing patients with the interpreter's virtuosity.

More significantly, I learned that sensitivity to the patient required a new mode of listening and of feeling oneself into the inner world of individuals who appeared very different from my self. I quickly discovered how similar I was to many patients, how easily blurred the spectrum of mental illness could be and was. Craziness was not easily demarcated; it was a question of degree and of intensity and of adaptational capacity. Normality became a mythical construct.

One of my supervisors pressed me to discuss my emotions toward my analysand with him, to consider my affective responses as valid ways of understanding the dialogue; through affects one entered into the patient's intra-psychic world. He urged me to imagine what it would be like to be my patient at a very young age, what it might feel like to be helpless and dependent, to permit myself to be attuned to the effects of repeated traumatic events; he, at first, jolted me in order to break through my defenses, to alert me to the terrors of this patient. He advised me to abandon my interpretive position of safe distance and authority, of apparent objectivity and impartiality, to feel myself intimately into the actual inner universe and psychic struggles of this suffering individual. To relate affectively to patients was to resonate to their conflicts and deficiencies respectfully and without condescension, without manipulation, and without presuming to know one's conclusions in advance; it transformed the analytic process into one of open-ended discovery and mutual recognition.

This mode of supervision was surprising, irritating, and immensely rewarding. It pushed against some of my own most stubborn defenses and rigidities; it opened me up. I found that working analytically with close attention to affects—both my patients' and my own—radically expanded the psychoanalytic process, while intensifying and clarifying the dialogue. It also enabled me to experience and learn things about myself from my patients that proved invaluable; it became an indispensable way of being helpful to them.

III

The thirteen chapters comprising this book do not claim to synthesize nor disseminate the results of scholarship in its three overlapping areas: the history of psychoanalysis, psychoanalytic culture criticism, and the psychoanalytic application to history. I prefer to think of these writings as starting points, touching on significant themes and ambiguities in various arenas of psychoanalytic tradition. The culture of psychoanalysis has many traditions, multiple perspectives. The most penetrating method still seems to be a historical and critical one; here my training in psychoanalysis complements my prior formation as a cultural historian. I do not offer a tightly-knit or unified conceptual approach to psychoanalytic theory and practice, in part because such unity has not existed since the 1950s. Furthermore, I have not elaborated that coherent unity, in part because of my doubts about the legitimacy of such a totalizing stance.

I have attempted to provide balanced evaluations of various representative authors and themes in the psychoanalytic literature; my perceptions are based on a broad understanding of the psychoanalytic movement and its complex history, including its interaction with the wider context of European cultural and political history. By tapping into my knowledge of the philosophical and clinical origins of psychoanalysis, I try to map out and assess its subsequent evolution. I have tried to maintain a sensible and critical point of view throughout without flooding my reader with an overabundance of detail and without asserting the primacy of theory. I have resisted the temptation to tilt the book toward philosophy or philosophizing; therein lies my former bias and my current ambivalence toward increasingly abstract discourses not grounded in clinical experience. If these essays serve as thought experiments, if they serve as reliable introductions, if they become springboards for subsequent reflection and research by interested readers, then they will have served their purpose.

In Part One, I explore the history of psychoanalysis with a number of assumptions about this legacy and its importance. Most analysts do not know their own history, either locally or internationally; the educated public has only recently begun to develop a historical perspective on the ninety-five year history of the analytic movement. I view psychoanalysis as part of the larger cultural, political, and social history of its time; analytic practitioners and thinkers were not hermetically removed from sociopolitical, cultural, and economic forces of their times, even if they work in a seemingly artificial environment—the analyst's office—with a high degree of confidentiality and an ethical vow of privacy, even if their object of inquiry is the individual and his subjective world. History has always impinged on analysts and on psychoanalytic tradition, which is markedly distinct in the various countries and cities in which it has taken hold.

I have tried to discover the fundamental inspiration of psychoanalysis by returning to the origins of the discipline in its own time and place; I pay close attention to what analysts meant when they wrote, or think they meant. As a way of retrieving their original impulses in becoming analysts, I have tried to uncover some of the motive forces of psychoanalysis. Not surprisingly, I learned that new ideas and departures often occurred as a result of debates within and confrontations outside the psychoanalytic movement. Dialogue, then, sometimes cordial, sometimes acrimonious, was not only crucial in the elaboration of psychoanalytic clinical theory and technique, but significant in the creative extension of the theory and its diverse applications. Thinkers in the psychoanalytic field have always exchanged ideas and contested with one another; they have engaged in fertile arguments with interlocutors who have encouraged them to demonstrate, not just assert, the proof of their propositions.

The history of psychoanalysis is intimately related to Freud and to Freud's authority as an initiator of discourse, a writer of charm and theoretical power. Freud looms over this history as a prodigious discoverer, a synthesizer, a master of stunning detail and illustrative example, as one who blended the sparkling *aperçus* with the breathtaking power to systematize. Freud's twenty-four volumes of writings dominate the psychoanalytic movement; these writings have shed great light and cast deep shadows on all subsequent analysts. While it may be an exaggeration to see all of analytic literature as a commentary on Freud's texts, certainly the way he worked, rethought, maintained, and modified his ideas has kept psychoanalytic scholars busy and humbled. I have yet to meet an analyst without a powerful transference to Freud. (This seems true of any person involved in a therapeutic profession, even if from a competing, nonanalytic perspective.)

To resolve my own interminable transferences to Freud, including dismissal and devaluation, idealization and exaltation, and everything in between, I pictured his life and work in its own historical milieu. Freud's significance as a thinker could be recaptured outside of the framework of contemporary affinities and divergences. Freud's thought could be restored, at least partially, if his thinking was studied as it emerged in his own circumstances. I imagined Freud as he tackled problems and devised tentative solutions to these problems.

I also looked to the second generation of European analysts to retrieve their original motives for becoming psychoanalysts. In examining a Frenchman (Lacan), a Central European (Fenichel), and a Russian (Spielrein), I gained an insight into the multi-dimensional and creative personalties who were drawn to Freudian psychoanalysis and who either gathered around Freud, or drew energy from his ideas. I came to view these personalities in their contexts as cultural revolutionaries and subversives; I inquired into the factors that drew this second generation of radicals and mavericks in to the movement. I resonated to their nonconformism, felt some longing for their noncompliance with certain bourgeois and professional standards. I wondered about the precise nature of their passions and commitments; how an immersion in the psychoanalytic universe changed or reinforced their free-thinking and iconoclastic natures. In investigating some of the questions they posed, I grappled with their conflicts with their contemporaries and older generation. I realized how pressures on their lives may have altered their views of the psychoanalytic process. Many of the second generation identified with visibly left-wing or avant-garde causes in their political and cultural orientations; many sympathized with or joined the Socialist or Communist parties of their own countries.

I discovered that politics always played a decisive role in psychoanalysis, though sometimes a hidden and not always a well-articulated role. Even if denied or disavowed, it operated in the internal affairs of institutes and in the International Psychoanalytic Association. The birth and victory of political and social movements like fascism and Stalinism radically shattered the practice of psychoanalysis in Central Europe and the Soviet Union. If that political culture changed and if it were replaced by dictatorial regimes, psychoanalysts were forced into exile or into underground situations. It was intriguing to see how earlier commitments to Marxism and left-wing ideologies were transformed as a consequence of emigration and the need to establish a psychoanalytic practice in America.

Chapter 1 is designed as an introductory overview of Lacan's practice and basic assumptions against the background of post-1945 Parisian cultural politics. While not a searching conceptual analysis of Lacan's ideas, it is intended to capture the flavor and style of his version of psychoanalysis. My own ambivalence about Lacan's histrionics and a good deal of his theory intrudes into the chapter as a subtext, providing some critique and irreverence; perhaps the reader will share my uneasiness about Lacan without diminishing my regard for the "French Freud's" originality and genius, without denigrating his substantial and continuing influence on academic American literary theory and social thought. The clinical practice and efficacy of Lacanian analysis still remain shrouded in mystery to me, even ten years after the master's death.

Chapter 2 treats the relationship and debates between Freud and Romain Rolland from 1923 to 1939. While narrating the story of a unique, epistolary friendship, it analyzes the private and public dimensions of their dispute over the "oceanic sensation" that Freud takes up in the opening paragraphs of *Civilization and Its Discontents*. This debate extended Freud's project of uncovering the neurotic origins of religious belief, of applying psychoanalytic method to decode cultural phenomena. The chapter is built around previously unpublished archival material, mostly letters and journal entries. To explicate Freud's style of intellectual life, I detail a controversy that produced new ideas and theoretical suppositions on an elusive issue, the origin and nature of religious feeling. The chapter also views Freud and Rolland not only as two different individuals, but as representatives of conflicting, central strands of modern European thought. Rolland exemplified the stubborn effort to hold onto a humanism grounded in nineteenth-century idealism, feelings, and intuition. Freud's world vision remained terrestrial, that is, aimed toward a disenchantment and desacralization of that world through the deployment of his corrosive rationalism and analytical skepticism.

Chapter 3 addresses the drama and intricacies of the Freud-Jung-Sabina Spielrein relationship. This strange analytic triangle introduces the reader to the startling intellectual and emotional trajectory of

Spielrein, a creatively disturbed female personality in the early psychoanalytic movement. It also sheds light on some important factors causing Freud to rupture relations with Jung in 1913, in particular aspects of Jung's anti-Semitism and his unethical behavior in the Spielrein affair. The chapter raises but hardly resolves the complicated issue of the meanings of Jewishness both for Freud and members of the psychoanalytic movement, as well as complicated reactions to Jewishness on the part of opponents.

Chapter 4 makes psychoanalysis and sociopolitical commitment its central theme. Otto Fenichel and his circle are its representative sample. As a critique of Russell Jacoby's *The Repression of Psychoanalysis: Otto Fenichel and the Political Freudians*, I underline Jacoby's strengths while pointing out the inherent failings in his polemical and present-centered approach. The core problem pivots on whether a Marxist sociological view is compatible with the liberal, individualistic, and humanistic foundations of psychoanalysis. The chapter questions the Frankfurt School's tendency to dismiss clinical work and the commitment to building clinical theory in favor of privileging psychoanalysis as a philosophical instrument. This results in a distorted understanding of early leaders in the analytic movement such as Fenichel, who remained committed both to the perpetuation of psychoanalytic technique and to the implementation of socialist, even revolutionary, politics.

In Part Two, I examine a number of themes involving psychoanalytic culture criticism. The psychoanalytic component of this critique extrapolates the symbolic meanings and psychological themes from a variety of written works. The chapters experiment with a psychoanalytic version of hermeneutics, the application of psychoanalysis to explicate clusters of meaning in the text. Psychoanalytic hermeneutics may be a royal road of decoding texts, of performing an exegesis of latent elements at play. Although currently connected to the works of Habermas and Ricoeur, Freud initiated psychoanalytic hermeneutics by underscoring the centrality of interpretation in all psychoanalytic investigations, not just in dreams, symptom formation, the psychopathology of everyday life, but also in the understanding of written works.

By hermeneutics, I mean those interpretive strategies employed to discern hidden and inaccessible meanings in texts. To decipher secret meanings, the text is examined from a double position of trust and suspicion, just as an analytic therapist might address a patient's transference and resistance. The psychoanalytic critic focuses on a text's symbolic content and its emotional tonality; the critic must display a sensitivity to the feeling-tone of language, as well as resonate with the formal designs and sounds of the written word. Traditionally, psychoanalytic culture critics tend to place more emphasis on content than on form; this may be shifting as analytic authors have digested various perspectives on language derived from Lacan and from French structuralism. Because they are attuned to unconscious dynamics, these critics are sensitive to the associational chains, to the unpredictable, wandering, flowing aspects of language, in addition to the pauses and breaks in that flow.

Psychoanalytic hermeneutics presupposes the centrality of language in all human endeavors. If analytic therapy began with Anna O. and Breuer's version of the talking cure, psychoanalytic hermeneutics continues the tradition of dialogue; it develops a method of investigating underlying dimensions of a text, of deepening the levels of interrogation. The close attention to language is consistent with a theoretical interest in narrative; some psychoanalytic critics argue that something liberating occurs when unconscious conflicts are addressed when a person tells another a coherent story of his life; this telling of a personal history is often painful, nonlinear, and full of gaps; it is mediated by unpredictable linkages and implausible events and situations. Expressing the story to a caring and attentive listener seems to be therapeutic. Rendering the latent language of that story intelligibly to a reader is the task of psychoanalytic criticism.

In chapter 5, I experiment with a psychoanalytic reading of a seminal essay by Freud, *Civilization and its Discontents*. Quite distinct from the historical and contextual methods of chapter 2, I attempt to use psychoanalysis as a way to account for the multiplicity of meanings in the text. The text can be comprehended as the relatively random free associations of an analysand, either addressing his analyst or undergoing self-analysis. This provides some insight into Freud's method of writing and his various discursive strategies; it demonstrates the plurality of genres and rhetorical forms at work. I argue that the figure of Romain Rolland is pervasive throughout the text, as symbol, muse, opponent, stimulus, adversary; in short, as someone who provokes wide-ranging speculations on the nature of civilization and on man's unhappiness inherent in that civilization. Besides discussing Freud's theoretical attempts to comprehend the elusive, narcissistic dynamics of the "oceanic sensation," besides advancing my own interpretive elucidation of the oceanic, I also show how Rolland functions in the text as Freud's repressed Other and his Double. The disguised doubleness may be particularly astonishing, given Freud's manifest declarations of how different he was from the French writer. Freud's deep but unacknowledged identification with Rolland reveals Freud's yearning to share the idealism and perpetuate the optimism of the nineteenth century that his skeptical thrust did so much to undermine.

Chapter 6 sketches an overview of Bruno Bettelheim's life and work, with close attention to the soulful nature of his hermeneutic orientation. Bettelheim subordinates theory to analytic strategies of reading texts, to empathic understanding of the writer, to emotional resonances of ordinary spoken language. His criticism assigns meaning to the psychological components of myths, images, and assorted cultural references. His argument about the mistranslations of Freud's work in *The Standard Edition* is less a mean-spirited polemic against translator Strachey then an articulation of an alternative view of psychoanalytic humanism. Bettelheim's version of psychoanalysis is not distancing, pseudoscientific, jargon-ridden, or ostensibly objective as is Strachey's, but persuades us to reverberate to the wonders of our own subjective world. He approaches Freud in the ways a clinician attends closely to the clinical data. Always echoing his experience as a concentration camp survivor, Bettelheim urges us to courageously tap into our own desires, fantasies, unconscious conflicts, and narcissistic hurts to vibrate sensitively to Freud's writings. Bettelheim's interpretations delight in the multiple emotional, intellectual, and imaginative possibilities of understanding a text, or an individual. While rejecting the scientific claims of psychoanalysis as a general psychology, he practices interpretation as an artist-clinician, attuned to the psychological underpinnings of introspective dialogue, demonstrating how analysis opens up the inner world to deeper human understanding.

Chapter 7 is a final, intimate conversation with Bettelheim in which he sums up some significant themes from the corpus of his work. This dialogue reveals Bettelheim still preoccupied with the wounds and shattering impact of the Holocaust, still ruminating on the meaning of the concentration camp experience. He locates himself in a direct line from Freud, but emphatically sees himself as an independent and somewhat marginal figure in the history of the psychoanalytic movement. Here Bettelheim permits himself to reflect poignantly and bravely on his own wishes to commit suicide.

Chapter 8 is a eulogy to Bettelheim after his suicide. It condenses some of my feelings about him and our friendship, as well as some of the grief I experienced after learning of his death. Perhaps the psychoanalytic memorial is a text which subsequent critics will decipher.

In chapter 9, I compare Foucault's *History of Sexuality* to Freud's perspective of psychosexuality. For Foucault, sexuality is historically constructed, always emanating from linguistic codes and institutionally sanctioned usages. Foucault argues that the naming of sexual phenomena, the giving of specific words to certain acts or practices, allows the philosophical historian of sexuality to understand the interlocking grid of sex, knowledge, and power. His writing is particularly strong at explicating the ways in which the languages of psychiatry, law, religion, and morality infiltrate various dominant discourses on sexuality, influencing Western attitudes toward the body and sensual pleasure. His libertarianism sheds a light on how these discourses impinge on daily sexual practices and perceptions. As a radical skeptic and Nietzschean, he discloses how dominant modes of conceptualizing sexuality have attacked deviant and excluded nonconformist sexual practices.

Chapter 10 transforms my ambivalence about French structuralism and post-structuralism into a nondismissive but irreverent critique. In looking at the flamboyant theorizing of Lévi-Strauss, Barthes, Foucault, Lacan, and Derrida from 1966 to 1986, I discuss the structuralist thrust toward shattering unities, toward disputing the possibility of textual or the desirability of personality integration. These thinkers deployed a sophisticated linguistic analysis to dissolve texts into contradictions. Structuralist hermeneutics strike me as more excessive and exaggerated, less respectful of texts and of individual subjectivity, than psychoanalytic forms of exegesis. They also appear less grounded in concrete empirical, historical, or clinical frameworks. They reflect an intoxicated and intoxicating attitude of anything goes. Yet French structuralism deftly punctures disciplinary arrogance and softhearted humanistic pieties; its elaborate decentering strategies can be refreshing. Its radical relativism, its refusal of supreme values, and its unrelenting skepticism can result in intellectual nihilism.

Part Three takes up a number of methodological issues in the area of psychoanalytic history. In the past twenty-five years, historians have started to look to psychoanalysis for its insights into personality dynamics and for its explanatory assistance in areas where conventional history reached dead ends. A number of imaginative intellectual historians boldly responded to the crisis of their discipline, recognizing the need for an injection of another dimension of inquiry that addressed the unconscious and its ubiquitous impact on personal lives and collective life. They realized that psychoanalysis could fertilize history, that the vertical history of ideas maintained a naive and antiquated view of the mind, which severely underestimated the impact of unconscious conflict, representation, and symbolization on cultural life. If history could descend below the belt, if it could integrate some of the findings of psychoanalysis about the problems revolving around love and hatred, work and play, then historians might extricate themselves from reliance on ordinary and nonrigorous forms of psychology. Once psychoanalytic perspectives were ingeniously injected, historical inquiry might breathe new life.

When historians turned to psychoanalysis as a theory of the mind and as a method of investigation and of gathering and evaluating data, they also did so for subjective reasons. Freudian psychoanalysis touched a deep part of them. Reading analytic theory and the clinical literature, applying it to personalities or situations from the past, allowed them to address issues of their own inner worlds. Some historians underwent analytic treatment to sharpen their clinical skills; others underwent partial or full psychoanalytic training and became practicing psychoanalysts. Motivations for applying psychoanalysis to history were mixed; defensive reasons alternated with reparative reasons. Historical objectivity could combine creatively with psychoanalytic perspectives on sexuality and subjectivity. Psychoanalytic theories about theory, about character formation, neurotic repetition, childhood development, patterns of child rearing, all could provide the historical researcher with breathtaking possibilities for understanding the world of the past, but also his own world and himself.

The historiography of psychohistory has been notoriously uneven, varying in degrees of distinction, from its earliest inception say in 1910 with Freud's essay on Leonardo da Vinci, to its takeoff phase a half century later with Erikson's pioneering book on Luther. The discipline has provoked its share of denigrators, generating a subliterature of pugnacious and polemical opponents. There have been more than a few egregious abuses of the analytic method in the historical literature. A number of researchers have failed to digest the analytic tool of inquiry; they have consequently produced shoddy examples of scholarship, varying in degrees of wildness, heavily tilted toward pathologizing figures from the past, unable to balance the rightful place of psychology in the broader context of cultural, social and political history. In contrast, the three chapters included here are by innovators and practitioners who respect the traditions of historical modes of thinking and writing, who are in tune with contemporary historiography, but who apply psychoanalytic history with differing shades of nuance and subtlety. They are aware of the boundaries of a psychologizing approach, yet they attempt to push the method to its limits.

Chapter 11 focuses on the writing of Peter Gay and Peter Loewenberg. It approaches psychohistory as a still unsolved problem and as a challenge to historians. Because Gay and Loewenberg have undertaken professional psychoanalytic training at reputable psychoanalytic institutes, they bring to their psychohistorical writings a rich body of insight deriving from their clinical knowledge. They know experientially what it is like to be a patient; they have immersed themselves in a universe of analysts to appreciate how analysts think and work; Loewenberg practices analysis and teaches it as a faculty member at a psychoanalytic institute. This chapter, then, assesses the contributions and ambitions of these two veteran psychoanalytic historians, with close attention to their underlying theoretical assumptions, language, relationship to Freud and to ego psychology, and to the dazzling large range of materials upon which they draw to establish their cases.

Chapter 12 sets up Serge Moscovici's *The Age of the Crowd* as a pretext for a discussion of the history of seminal crowd thinkers, LeBon, Tarde, and Freud. These political philosophers developed contemporaneously modes of analyzing the impact of unconscious collective dynamics on a wide ranging spectrum of mass activity. I explore the possibilities and limits of the psychoanalytic perspective on mass behavior, or group psychology. Knowledge of the intellectual origins of crowd psychology points up a number of conservative and problematic features of this critical theory; it also underscores the degree to which these modern Machiavellis can illuminate the group dynamics of modern mass movements in urban industrial societies, as well as in industrializing and developing third world countries.

Chapter 13 shifts direction by turning to the magnificent psychoanalytic biography of Newton by Frank Manuel. Here psychoanalysis is married to history, more specifically to the evocative, careful, and skeptical exploration of narcissistic themes in Newton's life. A psychobiographical approach to Newton helps to humanize our view of scientific genius and the mind of the great scientist. I hope to retrieve Manuel's book from its relative neglect by historians and analysts (historians of science have appropriated it). The chapter explicates his text in order to follow his argument and his rich illustrations of his theses; I also indicate some unresolved issues in his use of psychoanalysis as an instrument of understanding. Manuel sensitively balances his portrait of Newton between an appreciation of the pathological and creative features of Newton's narcissistic dynamics. In my critique, I address the potential additions to psychoanalytic history if inter-subjective factors could be integrated into the historian's narrative and critical armory.

Acknowledgements

My psychoanalytic training was made possible by a full tuition scholarship offered by the Los Angeles Psychoanalytic Institute which lasted throughout the years of my education. I would like to thank Seymour Bird and Morton Shane, who were the Directors of Education during these years, for providing me with that subvention. My father, Dr. Martin Milton Fisher, always an advocate of higher education, always delighted about my connections to any medically trained group, generously gave me money to help cover the costs of my training analysis; my dad's altruism was especially crucial in the early 1980s when money was tight and expenses steep. The Lederer Institute of Chicago granted me a fellowship stipend in 1983 for research in psychoanalysis.

My gratitude goes to my supervisors and I would like to underline my appreciation of their perspicaciousness and influence on my clinical thinking: Jeffrey Trop, Melvin Lansky, Morton Shane, Maimon Leavitt, and Melvin Mandel. Joe Natterson, from the Southern California Psychoanalytic Institute, was a trusted colleague and savvy clinician I sometimes turned to when I ran into difficulties with patients. My advisor, Seymour Friedman, worked to guide my passage through the Institute toward graduation; I could always count on him to be a genuine ally. Ms. Pamela Underwood, the Executive Director at the Los Angeles Psychoanalytic Institute, saw to it that I received important information and vital ways of negotiating my way through educational requirements; her tips and her wit were always useful to me.

My psychoanalytic training was immensely supplemented by ongoing discussions with three colleagues, all of whom became intimate friends: Peter Loewenberg, Robert Stoller, and the late Bruno Bettelheim. Above all in private conversations, but also in study groups and seminars, I was extraordinarily stimulated, perplexed, and enlivened by these candid exchanges. All three emanated a sense of intellectual and emotional excitement about the ambiguities of psychoanalytic research, writing, education, language, and institutional structures; all brought their vast experience and erudition to bear on the practice and transmission of psychoanalysis. If they were all recognized as university professors, all remained independent-minded, unsparing in their honesty, and never self-congratulatory. Psychoanalysis without a critical perspective and self-analytical stance could easily dissolve into an esoteric sham or smug world vision. In distinctly different ways, these friends urged me to risk going further in my thinking and clinical work. They assisted me to realize how little we really knew, how much there was to learn.

Mike Sigman, the discerning publisher of the *L.A. Weekly*, sacrificed his valuable time and lent his talent to edit my text; he was been a magnificent friend over these years. I have benefitted from conversations and written exchanges with three dear friends, Robert Rosenstone, Robert Nye, and Russell Jacoby. Alain de Mijolla and Michelle Moreau-Ricaud, two French colleagues, each fascinated with the intersection of psychoanalysis and history, supported me in my scholarly efforts and were generously available for dialogue. Henri Vermorel was receptive to my work on Romain Rolland.

Laurence Mintz did a superb job of copy-editing the manuscript.

Jim Frerichs from XL Associates lived up to his firm's reputation for speedy and excellent word processing; it was a pleasure working with him.

Preliminary version of the manuscript appeared in the *Los Angeles Psychoanalytic Bulletin,* the in-house organ of the Los Angeles Psychoanalytic Institute. Chapter 3 appeared in volume 2, number 1, 1983; chapter 4 in Summer 1988; chapter 6 in volume 1, number 4, 1983 and Summer 1989; chapter 7 and 8 in the fall of 1990; chapter 11 in volume 3, number 2, December 1985; My appreciation to Samuel Wilson, editor of the *Los Angeles Psychoanalytic Bulletin,* and to the editorial board for their encouragement and good will.

Chapter 1 was previously published in *Contemporary French Civilization,* Fall-Winter 1981. Chapter 2 appeared in *American Imago* in the spring of 1976. Chapter 5 was issued in an anthology called *Modern European Intellectual History: Reappraisals and New Perspectives* edited by Dominick LaCapra and Steven L. Kaplan and published by Cornell University Press in 1982. Chapter 9 was originally published in *The Journal of Psychohistory,* Winter 1978. Chapter 10 appeared in *Telos,* Summer 1981. Chapter 12 was published in the *Journal of the American Psychoanalytic Association,* volume 38, number 1, 1990. Chapter 1 was originally dedicated to Peter Loewenberg; chapter 5 was inscribed to my father, Dr. Martin M. Fisher. Paul Roazen originally suggested that I submit the manuscript to Transaction Publishers for his series on the History of Ideas; he has been supportive throughout the publishing process. Irving Louis Horowitz, the president of Transaction Publishers, has been nothing less than a soul mate; be has seen this manuscript through miscarriages and assorted disruptions, allowing it to be born. I am particularly moved by his combination of patience, receptivity, toughness, imagination, and intelligence. I am proud to be associated with him and with his publishing house.

The book is dedicated to my wife, Karen Fund. She has been a warmhearted and loving companion throughout these years. As I became immersed in the psychoanalytic universe, she has developed a deep love for all things Parisian. She has taught me never to underestimate Romanian women and to treasure the passionate care of a fellow-traveling wife.

Part I

The History of Psychoanalysis

1

Lacan's Ambiguous Impact on Contemporary French Psychoanalysis

Theory is good, but it does not prevent things (facts) from existing.

—Charcot to Freud

For twenty weeks in the fall and winter of 1885-86, Freud visited Paris. He came not as a tourist, but rather to absorb contemporary French discoveries in neuroanatomy, particularly the innovations in research on hypnotism, suggestion, and hysteria. Freud's work with Charcot at the Salpêtrière clinics in Paris left a significant scientific and personal impact. Charcot represented for him a model teacher and an exemplary scientific observer of mental illness. During one of Charcot's lectures, a precocious theory builder asked the French master how he could reconcile his factual findings with the theoretical constructs of contemporary German physiology. Charcot replied: "La théorie, c'est bon, mais ça n'empêche pas d'exister" (Theory is good, but it does not prevent things [facts] from existing). The questioner was Freud. And he valued this thought throughout his life as an injunction to integrate theoretical postulations with clinical material, conceptual constructs and observable data.[1]

Freud was fascinated and irked by the city of Paris. He called Paris a "magically attractive and repulsive city." We know impressionistically from his letters that he felt secluded and estranged in the French capital, that his moods shifted between feelings of exhilaration and depression. Scientific knowledge alone seemed insufficient to bridge the cultural gap between the provincial Austrian Jew and the cosmopolitan Parisians. Like so many short-term visitors before and since, Freud judged the Parisians inaccessible and mysterious; they were cold, detached, and difficult to engage in human contact. Yet there was something about Parisian life that was theatrical and passionate. He found the Parisians irresistibly appealing, and he longed to be intimate with them. One senses that, despite his penetrating insight, Freud had trouble figuring out the French. He felt "gobbled up," eerie, weird, not quite able to fathom the intricate secrets of the city and its inhabitants. To plumb its unfathomable depths, he relied on literary works, above all, on nineteenth-century novels, such as Victor Hugo's *Notre Dame de Paris*. Before departing in February, 1886, he exclaimed: "What an ass I am to be leaving Paris!"[2]

Freud's ambivalence toward Paris anticipates the twentieth-century French reaction to his historic discovery, psychoanalysis. It is cultural ambivalence that characterizes the history of psychoanalysis in France during Freud's life and after his death. The full story of the penetration of and resistance to psychoanalysis in France will have to account for the slow, uneven, and partial transmission of Freud's ideas and techniques. These narratives have attempted to explain the transformation of Freud's thought into an idiom comprehensible to contemporary Frenchmen.[3] Sherry Turkle's book, *Psychoanalytic Politics*, was the first English volume to address these issues; she concerns herself primarily with developments in the recent past, that is, since World War II, and more specifically, since the events of May-June 1968. Her thesis is that the resolution of French collective ambivalence toward psychoanalysis has been revolutionary, and she cleverly subtitles her volume, *Freud's French Revolution.*[4]

Jacques Lacan was the revolutionary figure of French psychoanalysis. This essay will focus on his theory; his oscillation between genius and buffoon; his style of intellectual life, particularly his borrowings from French surrealism; his megalomania; his innovative approach to psychoanalytic technique and to psychoanalytic training; and finally, his ambiguous impact on contemporary French psychoanalysis.

In some respects, Lacan's theory began where antipsychiatry ended. Like Laing and Cooper, Lacan admitted no essential difference between the normal and the pathological. He was more deeply pessimistic than Freud about relieving or even ameliorating man's neurotic misery; for him, it was absurd in the late twentieth century to be sanguine about mental health, happiness, or fortification of the ego. He was more optimistic than Freud (and close to the surrealists) in designating desire, sexuality, symbolism, self-expression, and language as potential agencies of personal gratification and self-knowledge.

To his great credit, Lacan attempted to fill a key gap in Freudian theory. Many orthodox psychoanalysts accept Freud's dichotomy between the individual and his environment. For Lacan, the psychological and the social were inseparable, interdependent; the realms "interpenetrate." The social cannot be excluded or bracketed out from an analysis of character. He held that the family and early childhood were the individual's first experience of society, and that the mind had powerful mechanisms to internalize society. Given these internal psychic mechanisms, most of which are outside conscious control, Lacanian psychoanalysis tried to decode the psycholinguistic modes of social and cultural discipline. Thus, Lacanian inquiry focused on the perspective of how society and law entered the individual, with particular reference to the role of language and symbol for conferring social meaning.

Through language theory, Lacan provided a conceptual understanding of the multiple ways we carry law in our heads: either through shame, guilt, and morality, or through metaphorical mechanisms of internalizing culturally acceptable limits. Lacan saw the "I" as "decentered," "entrapped," that is to say, as permanently fragmented. Because the subject emerges out of an alienated environment, even the deepest needs and impulses of the individual are products of, formed and deformed by, society. This radically shifted the therapeutic burden of psychoanalysis away from Freud's commitment to increase consciousness, individual autonomy, and mature interdependence. Lacan saw the subject as divided, facing irreconcilable conflicts;

wholeness was a utopian wish, inappropriate to an individual who lived in an estranging, post-industrial society, inaccessible given the everyday anomie of modern social life, hopeless given the permanent pressure of the unconscious on our psychic structure.

In the Lacanian framework, the subject never existed in isolation, was always defined in relationship to "Others." These "Others," particularly the mother and the father, remain permanently unreachable for the child, symbolic objects of temptation and seduction, desires that remain eternally unfulfilled. Lacanian psychoanalysis rejected the goal of building coherent, fully centered egos, just as it insisted that normal people experience the same splits and inner discontinuities of the mad. Lacan and his disciples had nothing but contempt for ego psychology, for those analysts who studied the ego's capacities for defense and adaptability, for those who posited adjustment, autonomy, freedom from conflict, and even creativity in the secondary process. For Lacan this Anglo-Saxon deviation from Freud muted the revolutionary spirit of psychoanalysis, and represented the smugness, mindless optimism, and social engineering of contemporary psychotherapy. For him, the ego was conceived almost as if it were the enemy: the goal of treatment was to clear it out of the way, to break down the misrecognitions which reside there.

Lacan postulated a dramatic moment in the development of the ego at the "mirror stage." The mirror stage occurs between the ages of six and eighteen months before the infant has acquired full motor coordination, mastered language, or separated himself from his mother. It is a period of life marked by the baby's insufficiency and dependency. Upon seeing himself reflected in a mirror, the child achieves a form of self-recognition which has both a positive and negative component. It is positive in that he views his body as a whole, jubilantly recognizing that his body is not fragmented or mutilated. It is negative in that the child's image of himself is registered in an inverted, symmetrical mirror image, frequently alongside of his mother's image. The mirror stage is bound up with his primal identification and blending with "Others"—that is, with other children and above all with his mother's body and desires. According to Lacan, the mirror phase allowed the subject to pass into the "imaginary" realm.

The mirror stage is linked to Freud's writings on the pre-Oedipal stages of the child, particularly primary narcissism. It coincides with the child's fusion with his mother. But Lacan argued that this merger with the Other is fundamentally alienating because the subject cannot distinguish its own body and desires from those of the mother; in fact, the mother's body and desires are often imposed on the infant. In short, Lacan connected early ego development to identification with the child's double (other children) or with his mother (the Other). This devalued the ego, leaving it in a nonautonomous, highly subordinated position. Moreover, the ego was trapped in this fictitious situation because the process of the mirror stage was almost completely unconscious. Thus, the subject remains not only ignorant of his condition, but misled, a victim of faulty knowledge. The "I" is formed by the loss of the subject in others. The process of objectification consists of imitation and erotic identification with the introjected images of the bodies and desires of others.[5]

The unmediated, misleading entry into the imaginary, however, is only a precondition for the "symbolic" stage—a Lacanian idea which coincides with Freud's Oedipal stage of psychosexual development. The mirror stage confuses and distorts the subject's awareness of himself. The symbolic stage is fundamentally social and triangular. It is mediated by the father. When the father intervenes the child has reached the age of three to five. The symbolic stage prepares him for the restrictions and regulations of life in society. Just as he is the one who has the phallus, so too is the father the carrier of speech. Through a fearful identification with the father—he is at once a rival and a love object—the child internalizes the norms, values, interdictions, and laws of society. By passing to the symbolic, the child's sexuality is tamed, subjected to socially acceptable limits and taboos.

Thus, Lacan's variation on the Oedipal complex implied a social and linguistic dimension: when the child takes on the father's name and the father's no (a word play in French: *le nom-du-père* and *le non-du-père*), he is taking on a socially acceptable identity with clear rules and prohibitions. Yet the child pays a price for access to the symbolic. He is permanently separated from his mother, deprived of his earliest and deepest object of desire. Symbolically castrated by the father, deprived of his sexualized and narcissistic identification with the mother, the child gains passage to civilization through the agency of language and through his identification with his father.[6]

The social implications of Lacan's teachings made it acceptable to a post-1968 Parisian audience of intellectuals and students, who were politicized and temperamentally left-wing. Lacan may, in fact, be viewed as a theoretical and poetic bridge between the social and the psychological, who attempted to introduce nuances in the stages connecting character and milieu. Lacanian psychoanalysis surely fueled the fashionable but amorphous notion of the politics of the personal, an idea now current in French feminist-psychoanalytic circles, just as it resonated in existential-Marxist circles from the late 1960s until 1975. Lacanian psychoanalysis was primarily a cultural force, a sophisticated pedagogy. Thus, what was "liberating" about contemporary Lacanian psychoanalysis operated on the level of consciousness, perception, and education, not in concrete shifts in individual autonomy or health, certainly not in changes in political constellations. It may even be seen as an instrument of order given the privileged role of the father in his teachings. Lacan, likewise, subordinated psychoanalytic technique and clinical praxis to theoretical and even literary considerations.[7] Science for him revolved around theory building, the postulation of a radical and persuasive theory of knowledge.

Lacan polemically rejected the idea of an autonomous ego, viewing it as an illusion. For him the ego was the realm of deep resistance, the repository of absence, incompleteness, and spurious knowledge. Lacan's writings on the subject posited a permanently fragmented ego, decentered, empty, mobile; he practiced psychoanalysis with no expectation of providing coherence, cure, or reliable strength to the ego.

If the unconscious is structured like a language (according to Lacan's famous dictum), then that structure is coherent and universal only if one grasps its endless displacements, its disobedience, and its untamable quality. The unconscious is the discourse of the Other insofar as we carry gaps, incapacities, permanently unfulfilled longings in us all the time.

Lacan claimed that contemporary psychoanalytic theory mistakenly attempted to discipline or unseat the primary process by rendering it a closed universal system. He asserted that the unconscious cannot be bottled up, categorized, domesticated, immobilized. Part of Lacan's project was to extricate psychoanalytic discourse from the arbitrary constraints of Freud's followers and codifiers. Returning to Freud meant returning to the unconscious at the level of language. It was here, supposedly, that one thinks dangerously, that one's ideas oscillate between symbolic absences and presences. By language Lacan was referring to the signifier, or to the sound realm of speech. The signifying chain was the best guide to the unconscious, along with the study of metaphor and metonymy. In Lacan's theory, consequently, there was an abundance of word play, jokes, puns, and witty reworkings of speech patterns. This approach was consistent with his postulation of the unconscious as plural, layered, involuted, uncodifiable, and unstoppable. Lacan's id, following his surrealist precursors, was poetic, polyphonic, and overdetermined. Because the unconscious does not recognize negations, much of Lacan's theory played on contradiction and self-contradiction. Many readers are dismayed by his style, without realizing that for him nonsense is neither simply nonsense, nor accidental, but rather that it represents a form of abundance. The unconscious is our home, yet it knows no limits, no destination, no conclusion. Here, indeed, everything is possible, including the senseless.[8]

Lacan took seriously the linguistic component of Freud's "talking cure." His clinical and theoretical stance privileged the realm of speech and language, while deemphasizing that of affects and drives. For him the analytic situation was incomprehensible unless the analyst became aware of the prime determining role of language in all human exchanges. Language was for him everything, the technique and cure nothing:

> And how could a psychoanalyst of today not realize that speech is the key to that truth, when his whole experience must find in speech alone its instrument, its context, its material, and even the background noise of its uncertainties.[9]

Lacanism was neither a scientific theory, nor was it terribly original. Lacan was essentially a philosopher of psychoanalysis, a psychoanalytic culture critic, who creatively borrowed ideas from linguistics, Hegelian and phenomenological philosophy, structural anthropology, aesthetics, surrealist modes of perception, and classical Freudian theory. If an historian of ideas were to treat him, he might trace his roots back to Hegel, Kojève, Heidegger, Merleau-Ponty, Jakobson, Mauss, Lévi-Strauss, Breton, and above all to Saussure and to Freud. It is perhaps too early to determine if his theory and innovations cohere. Given the fragmentary nature of his writings and his lecture style, one must remain cautious in speculating about the synthetic wholeness of his thought.

Lacan can tentatively be approached as a combination genius and imposter. First, let us examine the genius. Historically, he both stimulated and popularized the French intellectual and academic interest in psychoanalysis; certainly, Lacan's insistence on a return to Freud's texts helped to make available the original writings in French. However, Lacan's interpretation of Freud was highly selective and arbitrary. He prized the early psychoanalytic texts, those products of amazing theoretical fecundity, in which Freud mixed self-analysis with unrelenting dissections of sexuality, jokes, dreaming, and the dynamics of the therapeutic relationship. Lacan identified with Freud's writings where he is most autobiographical, most in touch with his own primary process, most insightful about the psychologically meaningful events of everyday life. Lacan loved Freud's case studies—the Wolf Man above all—where Freud is imaginative and poetic, as well as theoretically brilliant, technical, and elusive.

What attracted Lacan to the early topographical Freud were not so much the revolutionary implications of the discovery of the unconscious, as the subversive and evocative nature of Freud's method. Thus, Lacan's Freud was not a systematic scientist, but a perpetual questioner, an interminable analyst, one who overthrows old pieties and received ideas, a practitioner of radical doubt. Unlike Descartes, Freud's radical doubt does not turn on the deification of reason; and Lacan aphoristically urged his audience to "read Descartes like a nightmare." With *Group Psychology and the Analysis of the Ego* (1921) as the exception, Lacan seemed indifferent to, if not hostile toward, Freud's metapsychology, his sociological and cultural texts, his biological presuppositions, and his writings on ego psychology.

Nor does it detract from Lacan's significance to say that what was strongest in his writings is already present in Freud; Lacan repeatedly said as much himself. He audaciously accented certain aspects of psychoanalytic thought, while muting or omitting others. He investigated the mediations between the lines of Freud's conceptual apparatus.[10] Even the sensitivity to language is explicit in Freud, who as early as 1910 urged analysts to integrate linguistic modes of research into their own.[11] Moreover, Lacan built theory artistically. He aestheticized or poeticized ideas. This was partly what made his style seductive and unpleasant simultaneously.[12]

But the genius in Lacan coexisted with the charlatan, "the clown." There was much in Lacan's theoretical repertoire which smacked of imposture, of intellectual swindle, of language games, of nonredeeming nonsense. Even those who write from a pro-Lacanian perspective judiciously refuse to judge the validity of Lacan's claims about the "matheme"—an attempt to represent psychoanalytic teachings in a precise mathematical mode.[13] The effort to reduce psychoanalytic theory to a meticulous value-free notation had an element of grandiosity about it; it reflected a nostalgia for empirical and predictable certainty that scientists of the mind have not been able to attain—a return to pre-Freudian scientism. At its very worst it may illustrate Lacan's involuted and desperate longing for positive truth, a leap abruptly from surrealist intuition into irrefutable scientific symbolism.

Lacan claimed that his theory could best be understood by an audience outside of the medical or orthodox psychoanalytic community. He did not hide his opposition to the standardization of psychoanalysis in modern Anglo-Saxon countries and in France. Verification of the theory, by implication, must come from nonclinical sources, from mathematicians, poets, philosophers, with the qualification that these people be intimately familiar with Lacan's texts. In Lacan's major writings there was a conspicuous absence of therapeutic material, an omission of case studies. He never grounded his theoretical insights in clinical specificity. This raises large questions about evidence, proof, and the empirical validity of his discoveries. Thus, part of the Lacanian revolution was the reintroduction of idealism into the French discussion of depth psychology. It departed from Freud's technique of combining theory building with empiricism, conceptual insight with detailed observation of clinical material, disciplined intuitions with lucid prose.

As a philosopher of psychoanalysis, Lacan tapped into the contemporary French longings to connect Freud's discoveries with spiritual, anthropological, and even metaphysical concerns. One reason for Lacan's popularity among Protestant and Catholic clergy and among Communist intellectuals was his subtle message of philosophical idealism. Lacan's idealism was made palatable by something deliberately perverse about his discourse. The point was not that he preferred the oral to the written form of communication, but rather that he spoke obscurely. This obscurity was entirely willed and calculated. His early texts were clear, concise and accessible. Lacan's mature texts appealed to contemporary Parisian audiences because they were unclear and speculative. Nor can his deliberate opacity be tactically justified by claiming that the unconscious was by definition dark, unclear, dialectically complex, and confused. Lacan's profundity was associated with his esoteric and inaccessible formulations—abstract formulations that resisted scientific verification.

If we compare the careers of Jacques Lacan (1901-1981) and André Breton (1896-1966), we will be able to situate historically Lacan's theory and practice, as well as disentangle the creative leaps from the dead ends in his thought and intellectual style. As a medical student, Lacan had connections with the Parisian coteries of surrealists. In the early 1930s, he wrote surrealist verse, published essays on the links between crime and paranoia in surrealist journals, and knew writers and painters in and around the French avant-garde and surrealist movement, including André Masson and Pablo Picasso. Much of Lacan's reputation as a cultural radical stemmed from his imitation of many surrealist postures, whether they were anti-institutional, or whether they were in support of libertarian or occasionally bizarre causes. Let us remember the outrage which the first generation of surrealists created when they wrote the pamphlet "A Cadaver" to dishonor the death of Anatole France; when they chanted "Long Live Germany" at French nationalist gatherings immediately after World War I; when they published articles in favor of convicted murderers, or writings which advocated political terrorism. Breton and his supporters set precedents for speaking out on unpopular issues and for challenging preexisting avant-garde artistic and political movements.[14]

The historical link between Lacan and surrealism may also illuminate the unexpected upsurge in interest in psychoanalysis in the 1960s, clarifying the meaning of Lacan's impact. For many Parisians, the cultural revolution of May 1968 converged with Lacanian psychoanalytic teachings, updating the surrealist commitment to play, fantasy, desire, poetry, and the marvelous, reasserting the surrealist call for a revolution of instinct. Lacan and the Lacanians supported the events of May 1968 and French psychoanalysis contributed to the radical requestioning of life, which this student and worker uprising triggered.

Lacan's emphasis on language, on the absolute freedom of the word, the injunction to say what comes to mind, his insistence on the unstoppable flow of speech, was not only consistent with Freud's views, but also corresponded to the explosion of free expression during the May revolt. This festival of creativity proved to many politicized Parisians that psychoanalysis could still be scandalous and that it still operated as a powerful instrument of questioning many of the most stable aspects of daily life: one's political and ideological allegiances, one's profession, one's marriage, and one's relationship to authority.

Lacan and Breton shared a certain sensibility: both made careers of being professional dissidents; both were unclassifiable and shocking; both acted as leaders of movements opposed to elitist, antidemocratic, and hierarchical institutions, yet within their own circles behaved tyrannically and capriciously. Like Breton, Lacan established a cult of personality. Even as an old man, he still demanded unconditional loyalty on the part of the membership, expelling the nonfaithful with a kind of religious fanaticism. Lacan and Breton were notoriously hostile to criticism. For fifteen to twenty years, Lacan enjoyed his role as self-appointed spokesman, as combination antichrist and superstar, of French psychoanalysis. Breton played a similar role within the surrealist movement.

Lacan, like Breton, had a subtle appreciation of literature, poetry, painting, and an affinity for nonrealistic modes of artistic representation. Both delighted in offending the bourgeoisie (for Lacan that included the increasingly insular and self-congratulatory psychoanalytic establishment). It is hard to discern a real difference between Breton's rhetorical advocacy of "dashing down into the street, pistol in hand, and firing blindly, as fast as you can pull the trigger, into the crowd"[15] and Lacan's lecture at MIT on "elephant turds."[16] The effect was to baffle, confuse, throw one's audience off, as well as to discharge some aggression in a public forum. Both Breton and Lacan wrote effectively, and polemically; both could be intentionally obscure. Both experienced the joys and humiliations of being excommunicated from Internationals as renegades; both were slightly paranoid, experienced real persecutions, and had formidable enemies. Both played prominent roles in purging dissidents from their own ranks. Like Breton, Lacan relished his public image as outrageous, silly, unorthodox, delirious, as the eternal rebel. And although he opposed obsolete rules and reductionist thinking in terms of psychoanalytic education, Lacan intransigently imposed his own ideas and methods on his followers. Like Breton, Lacan appeared to sympathize with the left or ultra-left, even with its most outrageous and desperate posturings.

Lacan, like Breton, valued creativity and self-expression above all other human activities. Language was elevated into more than an imaginative device to make art; it was also man's chief tool in self-reflection, in knowing about himself and others, and in perceiving the world. Language made man irreducibly human. Lacan's reading of Freud sprang from the assumption that man was a "speaking being"— a creature with language. Lacan revived Breton's 1924 challenge to explore the imagination,[17] and in the process he proposed a major reinterpretation of psychoanalysis.

Lacan's seminars in Paris were reminiscent of surrealist happenings. At these public lectures, Lacan reversed roles with his audiences, improvising the patient's discourse before up to 1000 spectators, who were themselves transformed into surrogate analysts. The public lecture became a form of sexual discharge. Lecturing becomes identical with the pleasures of copulation. "In other words—for the moment, I am not fucking, I am talking to you. Well! I can have exactly the same satisfaction as if I were fucking. That's what it means. Indeed, it raises the question of whether in fact I am not fucking at this moment."[18] In the context of these seminars, he attempted not to interpret the deep structure of the id, but to speak the language of the unconscious. Here elucidation gave way to simulation of the primary process, discursive prose gave way to symbolic and imagistic discourse—to speech closer to poetry. "I am not a poet, but a poem."[19] Lacan offered free associations to his audience in the form of automatic speechifying: nothing was censored, nothing withheld, nothing was orderly. Puns, word plays, jokes, errors, and theoretical *aperçus* replaced the classical, architecturally constructed, eloquent French lecture.

Lacan was purposefully creating a new form of poetic language, a language based on knowledge of the unconscious, and in this sense certainly belongs to the French literary tradition. But he also belongs to the elusive middle ground between high and popular culture, between art and science. Critics described Lacan's seminars and his one television appearance as virtuoso performances. It is irrelevant that what he says was often incomprehensible, even for those who could decode the jargon. In contrast to Freud, who was an able and compelling public speaker, yet one who eschewed exhibitionism and all forms of demagogy, Lacan enjoyed performing and received stimulation from the public spectacle. Lacan was a narcissistic speaker, a high-powered entertainer.

Ironically, he evolved into a monologist. This is ironic for two reasons: first, because psychoanalysis was invented as a continuous, long-term, open-ended and candid dialogue between analyst and analysand; and second, because Lacan, prophetically, warned the insurgent students of May 1968 to beware of discussions or compromises with untrustworthy university figures or deceptive government officials, by implication with father figures. He advised the students that such "dialogue was a swindle."[20] It is unclear from reading Lacan's writings that the master was capable of real give and take, that Lacan was in fact a good enough or sufficiently patient listener, that he himself remained open to dialogue. Unless, paradoxically, the one best equipped to advise on swindling was a swindler himself.

Before an audience composed of patients, protégés, and disciples, Lacan poured out his ideas, mixing his conceptual formulations incongruously with self-praise, self-pity, and theoretical fireworks. He identified with the great male artists of modernism, and he once quoted Picasso to underscore his mission: "I do not seek, I find."[21] Like the jester in Shakespeare's *Twelfth Night*, one wonders, at times, if he is a foolish wit, or a witty fool. Since the show was part of his mystique, it is not surprising that his lectures became one of the in-places for the intellectual *tout-Paris* in the late 1960s and 1970s. This development coincided with the *spectacle* touching many parts of the contemporary French culture scene, where the late Rolland Barthes, the late Michel Foucault, and Emmanuel Le Roy Ladurie became familiar faces and voices on the French television. Sociologists of knowledge have often remarked about the intellectual star system, and French receptivity to changing fashions, to celebrities, and to theater.

Lacan's popularity may be explained by the unusual cultural ambience of Paris. The Parisian cultural sector is notoriously agile, open to innovative ways of thinking. This versatile and faddish avant-garde can quickly devour, master, and abandon radical techniques of analysis. Just as the social and economic gains of May 1968 have faded or been co-opted in the past decades, so Freud's putative "French Revolution" may be evanescent. What remains to be seen is the staying power, the long-range implantation of Lacan's theory. Since 1968, Lacanism has reached a wider public because of the unprecedented fluidity in Parisian cultural politics. The French have been uncommonly open to iconoclastic, yet personal philosophies, philosophies that promise a grand synthesis of the psychological and the social. With de Gaulle's retirement and death in 1969, Frenchmen reluctantly recognized France's political and historical eclipse; within the left the incessant quarreling between Communists and Socialists in the 1970s and the disillusionment with Mitterand in power in the 1980s has led to a temporary receding of pragmatic political concerns. Lacanism partially filled this political vacuum.

Lacan's arrogance, conceit, and theoretical megalomania certainly made good theater. But to describe him merely as a product of Parisian "radical chic," or as an invention of media hype, would be a gross misapprehension. For beyond the shock appeal and beyond the show-manship, he, following his surrealist forerunners, was attempting to link knowledge to liberation; that is, he formulated a theory which combined sustained insight and a consistent free associating method, which, working together, would function to subvert conformist attitudes and all varieties of conformist psychology. From this point of view, his ideas moved from living theater to direct challenges to personal freedom. And here, it is germane to insist that some of Lacan's ideas deserve a hearing.[22]

Rather than revolutionary, Lacan may more aptly be described as a cultural outsider. For decades, he stood in a marginal relationship to official forms of French cultural life and to the French medical and academic establishment. Lacan's strong empathy with the outsider may explain his lifelong resistance to the institutional and ideological forces of xenophobia and anti-Semitism, both of which obstructed the dissemination of Freud's ideas in France.

If psychoanalysis is revolutionary in the contemporary French context, Lacan played the ambiguous role of a Freudian Bonaparte. The next generation of French analysts and intellectuals will have to decide whether Lacan perverted or extended the liberating techniques and the dialogic spirit of psychoanalysis. This choice may turn on their ability to reconcile his libertarian methods and his verbal exhortations to freedom with his authoritarian personality and his dictatorial style.

For what was subversive in Lacan's teachings may ultimately be neutralized, perhaps shattered, by what was narcissistic and egomaniacal in his life and work. Within the universe of French psychoanalysis, until his death in 1981, Lacan emerged as not just a prima donna, but as the *maître*. He frequently played the role of living god. He and his close followers trained many of the leading personalities and clinicians in the movement. He dominated several French psychoanalytic journals, the prestigious series, *Le Champ Freudien*, published by Le Seuil, and psychoanalytic institutions. He was hailed by philosophers and thinkers outside of the psychoanalytic domain.[23] His quarrels and controversial career split the French psychoanalytic scene for thirty years. Many of his most gifted analysands and disciples broke with him. His son-in-law, Jacques-Alain Miller, increasingly plays an important role in canonizing, diffusing, and deciphering Lacan's writings; Miller, himself, has been accused of being a guardian of dogma. Before he died, Lacan alone signed published articles in his association's journal, *Scilicet: tu peux savoir ce qu' en pense l'École Freudienne de Paris*; all others were anonymous. His theory enjoyed a hegemonic place in the Parisian intellectual milieu in the early and middle 1970s; his death gave rise to sharp attacks, further splintering, and acrimonious polemics.[24]

On 5 January 1980, Lacan declared that he was dissolving the Freudian School of Paris. With one stroke of the pen, Lacan fused the processes of structuralist undoing and surrealist flamboyance. Of the 3000 practicing analysts in France, 600 are members of the Freudian School. Another 900 belong to three other schools; 1500 are independent. This dictatorial dissolution triggered an enormous crisis in French psychoanalytic circles and typified the way in which the desires of a severe father could be transformed into policy. Lacan's will seemed above constitutions, rules, norms, checks and balances, despite the 1901 Law on Associations which required a two-thirds majority to dissolve an association.[25] Perhaps because of the eclipse of his prestige and the decline of his creative powers, Lacan dramatically provoked an affair which became a national event with political repercussions. Having split the movement for the fourth time (earlier schisms occurred in 1953, 1964, and 1969), Lacan demonstrated again how self-love is inextricably linked to blindness. Rather than retire quietly, he revealed how psychoanalytic institutions are subject to the identical tensions of other social organizations, how they are composed of inquisitors, propagandists, functionaries, dissidents, and, occasionally, charismatic figures who erect personality cults.[26]

Lacan's personal idiosyncracies multiplied complications inherent in transference relationships to powerful thinkers within psychoanalytic associations. Lacan's moodiness, his inability to separate personal motives from theoretical issues, his memory of past hatreds and betrayals, his capricious and arbitrary behavior, all made him a target of reverential love or exaggerated hatred. French psychoanalysts in the 1970s and early 1980s had to decide either "for or against Lacan."[27] This choice may ultimately have been a false one, or certainly the wrong question to pose. That this question was debated with so much emotion must remind the historian of psychoanalysis that supposedly well-analyzed individuals can behave in petty, competitive, vindictive, and childish ways, that personal issues frequently cross over into professional conduct and into theoretical disagreements. The massive acting out of the Lacanians and anti-Lacanians was not only symptomatic of immature behavior, of unanalyzed transferences, but more significantly interfered with a dispassionate discussion of French psychoanalysis.

When form overwhelms content, the revolutionary nature of Lacan's methods may prove to be destructive, an impediment to the application of his discoveries and insights. Historically, Lacan struggled for decades against cultural resistance to psychoanalysis in France, frequently against downright stubbornness and ignorance. Yet because of his personality and perhaps because of archaic, unresolved emotional problems, he introduced psychoanalysis as a form imprinter: his intention was to astonish his audience, to proselytize, to initiate loyal and adoring students. As the revolutionary Lacan aged, he developed into an "all-too-human" cranky old man who was overidentified with his disciples and with his scientific discourse, who created extensions and mirror images of himself. Nor did the aging master seem more tolerant, or to be moving in the direction of simplicity or luminous prose.

Rather than stressing the psychoanalytic method of independent inquiry and free, irreverent thinking, rather than insisting on steady growth in knowledge, insight, and in rethinking established pieties, Lacan demanded that one point of view prevail—that his way of doing and thinking psychoanalysis be the way. Even Lacan's apologists have criticized him for appointing himself guru, for injecting a religious tonality into the movement, for substituting intellectual gamesmanship for actual problem solving. Lacanian psychoanalytic politics recapitulated pragmatic power relations; the young playful revolutionary came to power and evolved into a heavy-handed autocrat.[28] Lacan's previous dominance of the Parisian scene, his role as prophet and leader, may have barred the extension of French psychoanalysis as a valid way of knowing, as an adult method of play, and as a way of penetrating hitherto incommunicable realms of the human mind.

In discussing his modifications in psychoanalytic technique, we do not have enough solid evidence to determine if Lacan's experiments were subversive or simply irresponsible. Once again we must disentangle the charlatan from the innovator. Lacan claimed that analytic training was his basic concern. And he challenged two of the three components of classical psychoanalytic training: the personal analysis; and the didactic training in theory and technique at a psychoanalytic institute.

The standard psychoanalytic session lasts for approximately fifty minutes. Freud felt that this time allotment permitted a sustained amount of attention to be given to an individual patient, enabling both analyst and analysand to structure their day. Lacan, allegedly, experimented with the analytic session, occasionally lengthening it, but more typically shortening it. At times it lasted only ten minutes, sometimes he reduced it to three or four minutes. He justified this radical departure by stressing the intensity, quality, unpredictability, and spontaneity in the clinical relationship; risk and astonishment replaced predetermined safety and routine during treatment.

At the heart of Lacanian theory was the question of why the analyst chooses psychoanalysis as a vocation. By making a distinction between career and calling, it is arguable that Lacan's insistence on the analyst's "self-authorization" undermined the professional notion of technical training in the field. To authorize oneself an analyst, to choose psychoanalysis as a calling, implies the rejection of middle-class careerism, and the refusal to buy a ticket into a comfortable bourgeois lifestyle. In a certain sense, Lacan's dictum that "only the analyst can authorize himself as an analyst"[29] is close to the spirit of Freud's writings. Yet Freud was much more traditional in his approach to training than Lacan; he felt psychoanalysts had to learn their specialty like surgeons, that is, from rigorous training, experience, and supervision. Declaring oneself a surgeon was not enough.

Lacan, again, transposed surrealist doctrines about poetry and imaginative creation into a psychoanalytic idiom. Since poets cannot be produced in official institutions or in formal writers' workshops, it was naive to expect that psychoanalysts can become mature after four or five years in a psychoanalytic institute. What Lacan stressed was that analysts be in touch with their own unconscious, not that they receive fancy but meaningless credentials. Just as a great deal of poetry is about poetry, or the creative process, so the analyst develops his analytic imagination as he becomes aware of his reasons, conscious and unconscious, for becoming an analyst, by unraveling the "analytic knot." Resolution means untying this knot by the analysand during the training analysis. Structurally, all Lacanian analysis becomes a self-reflection within a self-reflection: it is the process of analysis with the subject watching itself, while analyst and patient conquer through language the layers of resistance leading to the unconscious, moving toward and reinvoking the realm of symbolic representation.

Orthodox opponents of Lacan, both in France and in the International Psychoanalytic Association, violently contested the idea of self-authorization. It smacked of certain forms of anti-institutional religious practice, of prophecy; and it suggested a rather casual attitude toward granting a license to practice psychoanalysis to people with an inner vision. Lacan's establishment of the Freudian School of Paris in 1964 further outraged his enemies. At the Freudian School, membership was open equally to medical men and lay analysts; training was conducted informally without course requirements or the necessity of fulfilling prerequisites. Study groups replaced hierarchical and authoritarian seminars. Candidates were not regarded as inexperienced pupils or apprentices. Lacan viewed self-knowledge and self-clarification as continuous processes neither to be imposed from above, nor filtered through committees. If training were not designed to infantilize the candidate, then the entire curriculum of the training institute had to be reevaluated. It was no longer acceptable to teach psychoanalysis as an integrated body of scientific truths, an established canon of texts, or as a fully developed model. Here Lacan's method takes direct aim at the normalizing trends he detected in psychoanalytic practice in contemporary France, which he argued polemically reflected the Americanization of psychoanalysis.

To be sure, Lacan's assault on institutional psychoanalysis led to a counteroffensive. Opponents accused Lacan of being irresponsible, dangerous, demagogic, arguing that he was attempting to flood the profession with his own disciples, insinuating that the practice of self-authorization reflected his "cult of theory."[30] Some French groups diverged from Lacan precisely over this issue.[31] Serious questions were raised about the possibility of French psychoanalysis being dominated by poorly trained, poorly analyzed practitioners. Existing analysts wanted to guard jealously the still limited marketplace against competitors; after all, it was in their economic self-interest to keep rivals out of the profession. Moreover, the medical branch of psychoanalysis traditionally opposed the introduction of humanists into the practice of psychoanalysis, although the French have been more open on this issue than the Americans.[32]

Given Lacan's iconoclastic approach to training, it was not surprising that he repeatedly ran into difficulties with the International Psychoanalytic Association. Historians of Internationals have long recognized the almost inevitable patterns by which second and third generations harden the revolutionary fertility of original discoveries. Creative impulses become transformed into legalistic and elitist institutions. Bureaucratic mechanisms and petty political maneuvering replaced audacious thinking. Here the history of Marxism parallels that of Freudianism. (One might also remember Marx's therapeutic response to his orthodox French followers: *"Ce qu'il y a de certain, c'est que moi, je ne suis pas Marxiste."*) In its approach to Lacan in the 1950s the International Psychoanalytic Association acted in an altogether dogmatic and perfunctory fashion. Lacan was not only censured, but ultimately kicked out in 1953. By 1963 the International demanded that Lacan and his colleague, Françoise Dolto, refrain from all further training of candidates. Being purged meant that the French society lost some of its global credibility and legitimacy. Lost also was its self-confidence and perhaps its need to take responsible stands.

Lacan's theoretical and practical innovations were dismissed as "unhealthy"; he was required to follow unconditionally nineteen rules for readmission. Paradoxically, just when the International Psychoanalytic Association could have most benefited from Lacan's theoretical originality, and when internal discussion and self-criticism could have regenerated the discipline, Lacan's challenge was treated summarily. The troublemaker was disciplined. No discussion, rather exclusion. No toleration of dissenters, only a reassertion of orthodoxy.

Lacan was most *sympathique* as a martyr. Without in any way condoning the heavy-handed behavior of the International Psychoanalytic Association, one reads their critique of Lacan with mixed emotions. They found Lacanian analysis wanting in four ways: 1) that it was overly intellectualized, focusing on theoretical concerns rather than on emotional problems, problems that ought to be "worked through" in classical analysis; 2) that it tampered with the time of the analytic session, thus raising questions about the competence and reliability of Lacanian analysts; 3) that it manipulated rather than analyzed the transference, the result being the creation of loyal disciples around an omnipotent cult hero, rather than autonomous, critical clinicians; and 4) that its theoretical preoccupations were suspect, overly weighted toward the early Freud, and neglecting subsequent advances in psychoanalytic theory and technique.[33]

Historians of mass culture know that the popularization of psychoanalysis can result in trivialization and that institutionalization of the science in France can produce excessive professionalization, bureaucratization, and centralization. The deeper problem is how to sustain the revolutionary thrust of Freudian discourse within the framework of an organization founded to perpetuate the theory and technique. That problem is further compounded by the larger context, namely that contemporary psychoanalysis is practiced in a society that resists change and that resists having its citizens look at themselves trenchantly. Lacan addressed this dilemma seriously by attempting to open up psychoanalytic training and discourse to the nonmedical community. Such an approach continued but democratized Freud's support for lay analysis. Lacan claimed to overcome elitism by emphasizing calling and not technical training, by attacking routine, and by jettisoning anything predictable. The vituperative assault on Americanization, sometimes incisive, sometimes nondiscriminating, meant that his theory emphasized challenge, not adaptability, risk, not accommodation, that it rejected the uncritical optimism and conservatism that he saw as characteristic of the American and English versions of psychoanalysis.

Because of the bizarre mixture of Lacan's theory with his surrealistic style, his autocratic behavior, and problematic innovations in technique, one remains skeptical about the extent of the triumph of Freud's infiltration into France. Even the marvelous slogan of May 1968—"We are all German Jews!"—underlined the sharp antagonism to non-French ideas, Freud's as much as Danny Cohn-Bendit's. A 1980 survey indicated that 80 percent of the French population did not know Lacan's name, that despite the Lacanian phenomenon only 13 percent could identify him as a psychoanalyst. The same poll revealed that 65 percent of the French would refuse to enter analysis even if it were offered free of charge.[34]

It is perhaps too early to determine the final impact of Lacan's theory and practice.[35] What does Lacanian self-clarification consist of? And how does it address Freud's injunction to reexperience, reconstruct, and recollect past experience in order to arrive at more self-reflection, more self-mastery, and more self-gratification? Lacan disregarded therapeutic success or cure, but instead concentrated on teaching his epistemology. Thus, theoretical self-understanding replaced changes in the clinical picture of the neurotic patient, the play of analytic interpretation helped the patient restore his own speech to the language of his unconscious.

Having eliminated all reference to factual or clinical data, Lacan's "return to Freud" violates the spirit of Freud's writings, his efforts to fuse theory with observable facts. Lacan deliberately eschewed the humility of the scientific or philosophic inquirer, he refused to distinguish his own sympathies and antipathies from what is real in the world. However, this was consciously part of the Lacanian assault on old cultural and scientific traditions, namely to redefine the "real" from the "imaginary," particularly within our psychic makeup. Like the surrealists, he was arrogant, prejudiced, his thought was suffused with value judgments. Like the surrealists he was neither receptive to realistic modes of perception or representation, nor embarrassed by his ingenious discourse, which fluctuated between childish play, fantasy, desire, neologisms, and adult theoretical acrobatics. Single-handedly, he wanted to reverse the decline of psychoanalytic discourse, purging out all platitudes, all received ideas. Lacan, in this sense, resembled other typical French "men of letters" whose ideology depended on their feelings, whose oral texts sprang from their personal methods of reflecting on their emotions.

Perhaps, in the long run, what was most subversive about him was his surrealistic sense of humor. He was a sensitive soul with a mania for logic who could, occasionally, joke about longstanding "structures" that Frenchmen resisted for a good eighty years. Beneath the naughtiness, beneath the will to shock the bourgeoisie, beneath the exhibitionism, Lacan spoke in a sarcastic manner, which was also self-reflexive:

> I must admit that I am partial to a certain form of humanism, a humanism that comes from an area where, although it is not used with any less cunning than elsewhere, nevertheless has a certain quality of candor about it: "When the miner comes home, his wife rubs him down...." I am left defenseless against such things.

> In a private conversation someone asked me (this was how he put it) whether to speak for the blackboard did not imply belief in an eternal scribe. Such a belief is not necessary, I replied, to him who knows that all discourse has its effect through the unconscious.[36]

In such formulations, theory is good, facts cease (temporarily) to exist, and one can simply enjoy Lacan laughing at his own cleverness, not quite defenseless, reveling in his own textual creation.

Notes

1   Sigmund Freud, "Charcot," *Standard Edition of the Complete Psychological Works of Sigmund Freud* (London,1962), vol. 3, pp. 11-33; J.-B. Pontalis, "Le séjour de Freud à Paris," *Nouvelle Revue de Psychanalyse*, vol. 8, 1973; Léon Chertok, "The Unconscious in France Before Freud: Premises of a Discovery," *The Psychoanalytic Quarterly*, 1978, no. 2, pp. 192-208.

2   Sigmund Freud, *Letters of Sigmund Freud* (New York, 1960), edited by Ernest L. Freud, pp. 171-211.

3   Victor N. Smirnoff, "De Vienne à Paris: Sur les Origines d'une psychoanalyse à la Française,'" *Nouvelle Revue de Psychanalyse*, Autumn, 1979, no. 20, pp. 13-58; see my article, "Sigmund Freud and Romain Rolland: The Terrestrial Animal and his Great Oceanic Friend," *American Imago*, Spring, 1976, no. 1, pp. 1-59, for a discussion of Freud's friendship and debates with an important French literary figure between the wars. Alain de Mijolla, "La psychanalyse en France," in *Histoire de la psychanalyse* (Paris, 1982), edited by Roland Jaccard, pp. 9-105; Elisabeth Roudinesco, *La bataille de cent ans. Histoire de la psychanalyse en France* (Paris, 1982), vol. 1; Roudinesco, *La bataille de cent*

ans. Histoire de la psychanalyse en France, 1925-1985 (Paris, 1986), vol. 2; Jeanine Parisier Plottel, "Jacques Lacan: Psychoanalyst, Surrealist, and Mystic," in *Beyond Freud: A Study of Modern Psychoanalytic Theorists* (Hillsdale, New Jersey, 1985), pp. 333-351, edited by Joseph Reppen; see Marion Michel Oliner, *Cultivating Freud's Garden in France* (Northvale, New Jersey, 1988), pp. 116-130 for a poorly informed dismissal of Lacan's contribution.

4   Sherry Turkle, *Psychoanalytic Politics: Freud's French Revolution* (New York, 1978).

5   Jacques Lacan, "The Mirror Stage as Formative of the Function of the I as Revealed in Psychoanalytic Experience" (1936; 1949), *Ecrits: A Selection* (New York, 1977), translated by Alan Sheridan, pp. 1-7; Anika Lemaire, *Jacques Lacan* (London, 1970), translated by David Macey, pp. 79-81, 176-178; Jean-Baptiste Fages, *Comprendre Jacques Lacan* (Paris, 1971), pp. 13-19; for a technically complex but lucid discussion of the "Mirror Phase (or Stage)," see J. Laplanche and J.-B. Pontalis, *The Language of Psycho-Analysis* (New York, 1976), translated by Donald Nicholson-Smith, pp. 250-252.

6   Jacques Lacan, "The Function and Field of Speech and Language in Psychoanalysis," *Ecrits: A Selection*, pp. 30-113; Lemaire, *Jacques Lacan*, pp. 78-92; Fages, *Comprendre Jacques Lacan*, pp. 19-28; Frederic Jameson, "Imaginary and Symbolic in Lacan: Marxism, Psychoanalytic Culture, and the Problem of the Subject," *Yale French Studies*, 1977, nos. 55-56, pp. 338-395; Anthony Wilden, "Lacan and the Discourse of the Other," *The Language of the Self* (Baltimore, 1968), pp. 159-311.

7   Jacques Lacan, "Seminar on 'The Purloined Letter,'" *Yale French Studies*, 1972, no. 48, pp. 39-72; Lacan, "Desire and the Interpretation of Desire in *Hamlet*," *Yale French Studies*, 1977, nos. 55-56, pp. 11-52.

8   Malcolm Bowie, "Jacques Lacan," in *Structuralism and Since: From Lévi-Strauss to Derrida* (London, 1979), edited by John Sturrock, pp. 116-153; Mark Poster, *Critical Theory of the Family* (New York, 1978), pp. 85-102.

9   Jacques Lacan, "The Agency of the Letter in the Unconscious or Reason Since Freud," *Ecrits: A Selection*, p. 147.

10   Jacques Lacan, "Desire and the Interpretation of Desire in *Hamlet*," *Yale French Studies*, 1977, no. 55-56, pp. 37, 46-48.

11   Sigmund Freud, "The Antithetical Sense of Primal Words" (1910) (New York, 1963), *Character and Culture* (New York, 1963), edited by Philip Rieff.

12   Serge Doubrovsky, "Un parapluie sur le divan," *Le Nouvel Observateur*, no. 807, 28 April 1980, p. 46.

13   Turkle, *Psychoanalytic Politics*, p. 173.

14   See, Maurice Nadeau, *Histoire du surréalisme, suivi de documents surréalistes* (Paris, 1964); Herbert S. Gershman, *The Surrealist Revolution in France* (Ann Arbor, 1974); Walter Benjamin, "Surrealism: The Last Snapshot of the European Intelligentsia," *New Left Review*, no. 108, 1978, pp. 47-56.

15   André Breton, "Second Manifesto of Surrealism" (1930), *Manifestoes of Surrealism* (Ann Arbor, 1974), translated by Richard Seaver and Helen R. Lane, p. 125.

16   Turkle, *Psychoanalytic Politics*, p. 238.

17   André Breton, "Manifesto of Surrealism" (1924), *Manifestoes of Surrealism*, p. 10; Breton,*What is Surrealism? Selected Writings* (New York, 1978), edited by Franklin Rosemont.

18   Jacques Lacan, *The Four Fundamental Concepts of Psychoanalysis* (New York, 1978), translated by Alan Sheridan, pp. 165-166.
19   Jacques Lacan, "Preface," *The Four Fundamental Concepts of Psychoanalysis*, p. vii.
20   Maud Mannoni, "Psychoanalysis and the May Revolution," *Reflections on the Revolution in France: 1968* (Hammondsworth, England, 1970), edited by Charles Posner, p. 215.
21   Jacques Lacan, *The Four Fundamental Concepts of Psychoanalysis*, p. 7.
22   Sherry Turkle, "Lacan: An Exchange," *New York Review of Books*, 1979, no. 9, p. 44.
23   Louis Althusser, "Freud et Lacan," *La Nouvelle Critique*, no. 161-162, December-January 1964; Paul Ricoeur, *De L'Interpretation, essai sur Freud* (Paris, 1965); Lacan also proudly acknowledged his favorable reception by the French philosopher, Jean Wohl, see *Ecrits: A Selection* (New York, 1977), translated by Alan Sheridan, p. 292.
24   Typifying the attack is François George's *L'Effet 'Yau de Poêle, De Lacan et des Lacaniens* (Paris, 1979), in which Lacanian psychoanalysis is viewed as a simpleminded and stupid word play; for a recent hagiography, see Catherine Clément, *Vies et Légendes de Jacques Lacan* (Paris, 1981).
25   "Lacan disperse les siens," *Le Monde*, 11 January 1980, p. 1; Catherine David, "La loi du Seigneur," *Le Nouvel Observateur*, no. 793, 21 January 1980, p. 41; Isi Beller, "L 'École est finie...," *Le Nouvel Observateur*, 28 April 1980, no. 807, pp. 44-45.
26   J.-B. Pontalis, "Le Métier à Tisser," *Nouvelle Revue de Psychanalyse*, Autumn, 1979, no. 21, p. 9, n. 2.
27   Turkle, *Psychoanalytic Politics*, pp. 97-118.
28   Ibid., p. 221.
29   Cited by Turkle, Ibid., p. 121.
30   Ibid., pp. 122-123, 130, 132, 137.
31   Piera Castoriadis-Aulagnier, "Une néo-formation du lacanisme," *Topique: Revue Freudienne*, 1977, no. 18, pp. 3-9.
32   Sigmund Freud, *The Question of Lay Analysis* (1926) (New York, 1950).
33   The Committee's report can be found in *International Journal of Psychoanalysis*, vol. 35, 1954, part 2, pp. 272-278.
34   Mona Ozouf, "Sondage: 65% des Français refuseraient une psychanalyse, même gratuite," *Le Nouvel Observateur*, 28 April 1980, no. 807, pp. 42-43.
35   Stanley A. Leavy, "The Significance of Jacques Lacan," *The Psychoanalytic Quarterly*, 1977, no. 2, pp. 201-219; A. Hesnard, *De Freud à Lacan* (Paris, 1970), pp. 84-110 for a generous assessment of Lacan's teachings by one of the founding fathers of French psychoanalysis.
36   Jacques Lacan, "The Subversion of the Subject and the Dialectic of Desire in the Freudian Unconscious," *Ecrits: A Selection*, p. 324.

2

Sigmund Freud and Romain Rolland:
The Terrestrial Animal and His Great
Oceanic Friend

*I may confess to you that I have rarely experienced that
mysterious attraction of one human being for another as
vividly as I have with you; it is somehow bound up,
perhaps, with the awareness of our being so different.*

—Freud to Rolland,
May 1931

Freud's relationship with Romain Rolland spans the years 1923 to
1939. It began when the two, aged sixty-seven and fifty-seven years
respectively, had reached intellectual maturity. Vast differences
separated them, and their controversies on religious sensation, on
psychoanalysis, and on mysticism sprang partly from divergent
cultural and social formations. Central European and Jewish, Freud
was heir to the nineteenth century's evolutionary and rationalist traditions. While also straddling the two centuries, Rolland was French and
Catholic, a professional historian and musicologist by training, an
artist, novelist, and biographer of epic heroes. Moreover, their personalities contrasted widely.

After the publication of the Freud-Jung correspondence, scholars now agree that Freud's personality decisively stamped itself upon the evolution of psychoanalytic theory and practice.[1] We shall see the ways in which Freud's character played an enigmatic role in his friendship with the French Nobel laureate. Because he was unable to separate men from their ideas,[2] Freud's exchanges with Rolland were at once intimate and marked by personal frictions. In the late 1920s and early 1930s, they reached an impasse on the question of the origins and significance of the "oceanic" sensation. Freud's mixed feelings for Rolland surfaced again in his 1936 paper, "A Disturbance of Memory on the Acropolis," written to celebrate the French writer's seventieth birthday. On the other hand, Rolland opposed various key assumptions of the psychoanalytic method for personal and intuitive reasons. The intellectual paths of Freud and Rolland crisscrossed at a time when a wider European effort was under way to grasp the broader import of a recently ruptured civilization.

The Freud-Rolland relationship began fraternally in February 1923. On the ninth of that month, Freud wrote a short letter to the French scientist and aesthetician, Edouard Monod-Herzen, thanking him for his expression of "human sympathy." This simple gesture had momentarily dispelled the atmosphere of distrust which, according to Freud, permeated postwar Europe. Freud extended Monod-Herzen's expression of fellowship by asking him to convey his greetings to Rolland: "Since you are a friend of Romain Rolland, may I ask you to pass on to him a word of respect from an unknown admirer."[3]

After receiving Freud's greeting from Monod-Herzen, Rolland replied promptly on 22 February 1923 with his first personal letter to Freud. He admitted with pride that he had been one of the first Frenchmen to appreciate Freud's writings, having discovered *The Interpretation of Dreams* some twenty years earlier, long before the world had recognized Freud's genius. He played on Freud's phrase, "unknown admirer," by gently flattering the Viennese physician; he indicated that the Austrian writer and biographer Stefan Zweig and he had often discussed Freud. Rolland used the metaphor of exploration to describe the impact of Freud's discoveries: "You have been the Christopher Columbus of a new continent of the mind." While many artists and philosophers had already discovered the unconscious, they had arrived at their perceptions haphazardly. Freud offered a systematic access to the mind; his "conquests" were advancing not only other branches of psychology and medicine, but were also benefiting those involved in literary activity. Rolland confessed that Freud's "subliminal visions" corresponded to "some of [his] intuitions."

He attributed the melancholy in Freud's letter to Monod-Herzen to the "present miseries" of living in a defeated country. Rolland reassured Freud that belonging to the vanquishing nation was not substantially better. He refused to associate himself with the Pyrrhic triumph of the Allies after the war, preferring to identify with those who had suffered. Victory was always more catastrophic for the conquerors than for the conquered. The contemporary crisis in European life was so severe that he predicted "the political ruin of Western Europe." Notwithstanding the "convulsions" shaking the West and the prospect of further brutality, Rolland was confident that "renewal"—at least on the intellectual or spiritual level—could be the end result. He concluded by expressing his "respect and admiration" for Freud.[4]

Rolland's letter pleased Freud. Soon after receiving it, he wrote his Berlin-based friend and psychoanalytic colleague, Karl Abraham, that the French writer's letter contrasted with the wretchedness of the times: "A charming letter from Romain Rolland arrived here like a breath of fresh air; he mentions incidentally that he was interested in analysis twenty years ago."[5]

On 4 March 1923, Freud replied personally to Rolland in what was to be the first in a series of eleven letters. He associated Rolland with three separate but overlapping activities: humanitarianism, pacifism, and art. For many men of Freud's generation, Rolland was the ideal "European," the man who was committed uncompromisingly to internationalism, Franco-German reconciliation, and genuine cooperation among human beings. Without questioning Rolland's sincerity, Freud viewed his noble goals as illusory and unrealized, the projection on to mankind of Rolland's unfulfilled wishes: "Because for us your name has been associated with the most precious of beautiful illusions, that of love extended to all mankind."[6]

Freud now shared some of the idealism in Rolland's antiwar perspective. He clung to the "hope" that mankind would learn to channel its hostile urges into constructive avenues. If mankind did not "divert" its destructive instincts, the entire species might be annihilated. Either through his friendship with Stefan Zweig, or perhaps through reading some of Rolland's pacifist writings during World War I, Freud had become conscious of the French writer's dissenting position.[7] Characteristically, Freud echoed Rolland's antiwar stances by formulating his hope for peace in terms of science and progress:

> But if this one hope cannot be at least partly realized, if in the course of evolution we don't learn to divert our instincts from destroying our own kind, if we continue to hate one another for minor differences and kill each other for petty gain, if we go on exploiting the great progress made in control of natural resources for our mutual destruction, what kind of future lies in store for us?

Freud clearly appreciated Rolland's creative achievements; he indicated familiarity with some of the French writer's dramatic works as well as with the Noble Prize-winning, epic novel, *Jean-Christophe* (1904-1912). Yet, curiously enough, Freud referred to Rolland's writings ambivalently, mingling his admiration with personal contrast: "My writings cannot be what yours are: comfort and refreshment for the reader."

Earlier in the same letter, Freud had singled out three aspects of his personality which distinguished him from Rolland—his Jewishness, his devotion to science, and his age. He insisted that the burden of hundreds of years of persecution, exacerbated by the presence of anti-Semitism in postwar Central Europe, was not conductive to faith in illusions. Because Freud's scientific method proceeded by tearing away the masks which hid human defenses, anxieties, and desires, his technique often proved to be a painful one, however therapeutic. In undermining human self-deception, he had not spared himself. "A great part of my life's work (I am 10 years older than you) has been spent trying to destroy illusions of my own and those of mankind."

Freud thought that Rolland might be interested in his preliminary efforts to move from an analysis of individual psyches to those of society. Thus, besides sending him a copy of *Group Psychology and Analysis of the Ego* (1921), not a "particularly successful" work, he threw out a daring observation: "It is surely hard enough to preserve the continuation of our species in the conflict between our instinctual nature and the demands made upon us by civilization."

Freud's preoccupation with his old age, his Jewishness, his investment in the psychoanalytic science, and the dilemma of the individual's relationship to his society recurs throughout the Freud-Rolland relationship.

Rolland felt Freud's first letter was written with "much bitterness," primarily because of Freud's dual burden: that of being a "destroyer of illusions" and of bearing the massive weight of being Jewish, "proscribed and humiliated in the Middle Ages and now again made responsible in Austria for the war, in Germany for the disastrous peace." Above all, Rolland found Freud "very pessimistic about the future of humanity."[8]

Soon after receiving Freud's letter, Rolland mailed him a copy of *Liluli* (1919)—a play which ironically deflated contemporary mystifications about modern warfare. Freud was touched by the gift and by Rolland's personal dedication, which has now been retrieved from the archives of the Freud Museum in London. The complete text of Rolland's dedication in *Liluli* reads:

> To the Destroyer of Illusions Prof. Dr. Freud with a token of respect and cordial sympathy.[9]

The tone of Freud's letter of acknowledgement is one of warmth and affection for the French writer and familiarity with his creative works:

> March 12, 1923
>
> Dear Friend
>
> Thank you very much for the small book. I have of course been long familiar with its terrible beauty. I find the subtle irony of your dedication well deserved since I had completely forgotten *Liluli* when I wrote the silly passage in question in my letter, and obviously one ought not to do that.
>
> Across all boundaries and bridges, I would like to press your hand.
>
> Freud[10]

In May 1924 Freud read a newspaper account of Rolland's planned visit to Vienna[11] and asked Zweig to arrange a meeting between Rolland and himself:

> On reading in the paper that Romain Rolland is in Vienna I immediately felt the desire to make the personal acquaintance of the man I have revered from afar. But I did not know how to approach him. I was all the more pleased to hear from you that he wants to visit me, and I hasten to submit to you my suggestions.

Freud expressed enthusiasm about the prospect of meeting Zweig's "great friend," as well as some concern about Rolland's precarious health. (Rolland suffered from insomnia and a chronic bronchial condition.) Still feeling severe discomfort after his first operation for cancer of the jaw in April 1923, Freud urged Zweig to act as interpreter during the meeting. Although he spoke and read the language, Freud's pain from his prosthesis impeded his ability to converse in French.[12] Freud's delight over the opportunity of meeting Rolland appears in a letter written to Lou Andreas-Salomé: "everything else, especially social contact, I keep at bay. (Of course Romain Rolland, who has announced himself for tomorrow, I cannot refuse)"[13]

Rolland met with Freud on Wednesday afternoon, 14 May 1924 at Freud's apartment at Berggasse 19 in Vienna. The conversation lasted probably a little more than one hour. For at least part of the time, Freud's youngest daughter Anna was present. Zweig introduced the two and translated. (Rolland read and understood spoken German, but could not speak it himself.) Despite the presence of a small garden, Rolland characterized the "old Professor's" living quarters as a bit "somber." Because of the decorations and collection of antiquities, the rooms seemed cluttered, in a state of "pandemonium": "filled with small gods, fetishes, amulets, hallucinated projections of the erotic and religious dreams of humanity."

Rolland was struck by Freud's age and sickness, and his capacity to bear gracefully the discomfort from his cancer. He described him as "thin, his head a little simian." Despite his scientific breakthroughs and a considerable international reputation, Freud said fatalistically: "My time is past." Rolland reported that Freud did not have a salaried or professorial title at the University of Vienna, and consequently continued to practice six hours of psychoanalytic sessions, or "lessons" each day. Freud never complained about his misfortunes, but displayed "a beautiful example of heroic energy and vitality."

A professor of "psychoanalytic pedagogy" in her own right, Anna Freud also served as a loyal collaborator and secretary to her father. In praising her "beautiful, tranquil, intelligent eyes," Rolland admitted a powerful magnetic physical and mental attraction to her.

Zweig's relationship to and admiration for Freud dated back several years. His intimacy with Freud and his "literary curiosity" prompted him to ask Freud to make his clinical files public. Freud countered that it was essential to maintain them secretly as privileged information between psychoanalyst and patient; he referred jokingly to Zweig as a "newsmonger!"

Regarding the psychoanalytic technique, Rolland affirmed that their epoch had seen no more "precise" and "formidable" documentation of the human mind than Freud's. Speaking of psychoanalysis, Rolland used Catholic imagery; he saw therapy as a form of "confession" and Freud himself as a "confessor." Gifted with an "infallible memory" and a "lucid" intelligence, Freud had heard "the most dreadful secrets" of hundreds of personalities. Rolland also discovered that Freud read voraciously and that he was familiar with several of his guest's works. Freud told Zweig in the course of the conversation that he thought Rolland's novel, *Annette et Sylvie* (1922), beautifully written. Flattered by this praise, Rolland added that Freud's comments were of "a singular scientific value for [him]." Freud asked Rolland to send him his recently published biography of Gandhi and gave him in exchange a copy of the *Introductory Lectures on Psychoanalysis* (1916-1917).

The Freud-Rolland conversation covered a broad territory: the topics ranged from contemporary violence, the power and authenticity of man's instincts, the force of the "moral lie," to a general exchange on the nineteenth century, which was viewed by Freud as an era of peace and by Rolland as one of fear and hypocrisy. Their literary discussion focused on nineteenth-century French and Russian novelists and on the relationship between creative genius and epilepsy. Here Freud asserted unequivocally that Dostoevsky suffered from hysteria rather than from epilepsy. Likewise, Freud suggested that historical personalities such as Caesar, Alexander, and Napoleon were "pretended epileptics."[14] The conversation concluded with a discussion of Freud's past and present isolation. Rolland felt that the Viennese physician was "touched to know that [Rolland had] read him twenty years ago." During that period his work had remained almost "without echo" in France. Currently, Freud thought that his science was treated with "hostility" in Germany, and although "famous" in America, the Americans, Freud insisted, "understand absolutely nothing about it."[15]

By the middle 1920s, Rolland had emerged as the European popularizer of Gandhism.[16] Within his influential biography of the Indian leader, *Mahatma Gandhi* (1924), he proclaimed his conversion to the doctrine of noncooperation and absolute nonviolence. Soon after his visit with Freud, he sent his friend a copy of the work.

On 15 June 1924, Freud wrote Rolland thanking him for the book and reminiscing about the French writer's recent visit to his home. Rolland's presence had greatly moved Freud:

June 15, 1924

Dearest Friend

Mahatma Gandhi will accompany me on vacation which will begin shortly.

When I am alone in my study, I often think of the hour that you gave me and my daughter here, and I imagine you again in the red chair which we set out for you. I am not well. I would gladly end my life, but I must wait for it to unravel.

My cordial wishes for you and your work.

Yours
Freud[17]

Rolland inscribed sections of Freud's letter in his personal diary, underlining the last sentence of the second paragraph, and singling out the German word *die Abwicklung* (the end) for special attention. In the letter, Freud had alluded to his illness and to thoughts about his own death. It reinforced Rolland's perception of Freud's "stoical pessimism."[18]

Rolland's affectionate feelings for Freud, the man, never interfered with his opposition to the basic foundations of psychoanalysis. Before beginning his correspondence with and his meeting Freud, Rolland had discussed various aspects of depth psychology with the Geneva-based psychiatrist and poet, Charles Baudouin. Arguing from his own theories of child psychology and from personal observations, he disagreed with the Freudian postulation of infantile sexuality, the Oedipus and Electra complex, and the reduction of the complicated network of the human mind to an "inflexible," "monotonous," and at times "extravagant" symbolism. The problem with the theory of childhood eroticism was that it imposed "obscure and subconscious" feelings onto healthy, young organisms; insistence on the theory, Rolland added, might cause disarray and even "ruin" the child's efforts to develop and reach maturity. It was psychoanalysts, not children, who were "haunted." Rolland objected to the universalization by psychoanalysts of the Oedipus complex; it could be detected only in abnormal people and in exceptional situations. He questioned whether normal children experienced either profound attraction to or repulsion from their parents. Psychoanalytic explanations of the various enigmas of the mind were "simplistic." More often than not, men and/or children were put into "pigeonholes," instead of being studied as unique cases with individual dispositions and problems. While conceding that a vast number of psychoanalysts were intelligent, and that psychoanalytic insights were incisive, he observed that most practitioners were "not very normal.... And [they] are fatally, almost unconsciously, attracted toward the exception. That is evident not only in Freud, who has at least a powerful vitality, but also in the Geneva psychologists." Refusing to argue issues on substantive grounds, psychoanalysts self-servingly viewed criticism as a manifestation of their opponent's unanalyzed complex or resistance.

Essentially, Rolland was criticizing the method of studying the abnormal in order to arrive at an understanding of the healthy; the hypothesis that "pathology is the magnification of the normal" remained to be proved. Since health implied a delicate, if not Pythagorean, equilibrium of organic and psychic forces, it required a dangerous inductive leap to draw general conclusions from the evidence that concerned disorders.[19]

Stimulated by his visit to Freud, Rolland sketched his thoughts on psychoanalysis in his posthumously published autobiographical work, *Le Voyage intérieur* (1959). On the one hand, he admired both Freud the man and the historical value of his path-breaking discoveries. On the other hand, Rolland disagreed with the genetic psychoanalytic approach, the emphasis on the Oedipal origins of neuroses and infantile sexuality. While discounting the seminal role of Oedipal feelings in his own life, he stressed generational factors, the barriers which separated young people from their elders. Adolescence played a more formative role than early childhood in the development of mature psyches. From the ages of sixteen to twenty, the young adult experienced self-awareness with a rare intensity; during the process of self-discovery, he learned how to dream, to act, to be passionate, and independent.

> I must very clearly bear witness against the Freudian cosmogony of the childhood Eros of the dreaming child.... I have the greatest respect for Freud, whom I have known, and I honor the fearlessness of the pilot who, equal to his great Phoenician ancestors, first adventured in the circumnavigation of the black Continent of the Mind. What he has observed with his eyes, he has said; and he has also arranged, drawn, and divided the half-true, half-fabulous, mad accounts of caravans of souls spun out of orbit, which have been told to this great confessor.... But I declare with calm certainty: this black continent which he describes is not mine. I am of another people. In the shell of its memory, my race carries across the ages echoes of other voices, barkings of other monsters, and songs of other gods.[20]

Perhaps because of the ambiguous reference to race, Rolland footnoted these comments by clarifying that they were written "in 1924, a little after my visit to Freud and the beginning of my friendly relations with him—ten years before the mass mobilization of the Nazi ideologies against him."[21]

In the appendix of *Le Voyage intérieur*, Rolland revealed that he had first found a copy of *The Interpretation of Dreams* in Zurich, shortly after its second edition appeared in 1909.[22] Rolland drew an analogy between the contributions and reception of the works of Freud and Arnold Schoenberg; these creative geniuses had charted entirely "new roads" in their respective fields. The world erroneously thought that their breakthroughs dated from the postwar period, rather than from the beginning of the century, again proving how far in advance were these courageous "precursors" and "navigators." Rolland had recognized the force of Freud's findings in 1909, having seen Freud as a fellow "pilgrim." Rolland's method of exploring the darker recesses of his own unconscious was through music: "alone, without guide, pushed forward by the demon of music—my master and my self."[23]

With Freud in mind, Rolland speculated on a number of personal conflicts in several brief passages of the same text; he entitled these fragments "Chapter of Principal Psychoanalytic Confessions." He assumed that a psychological equilibrium of the mind's structures was attainable, even though the balance could be tipped easily. In his own psyche, he detected a partially involuntary self-regulating mechanism. Referring to the mechanism as one of "self-defense," or "self-correction," Rolland felt it worked by deflecting and reversing, often violently, opposed functions of the mind. For example, the "monstrous" and "abnormal" excesses of his temperament were restrained by conscious activity, specifically the duties which he imposed by means of work and moral discipline. Inadequacies ("lacks") were similarly compensated for in this manner. Within him the movement toward equilibrium flowed in several directions, not merely from consciousness exercising control over the unconscious. Nonetheless, he understood that the antagonisms which divided man could explode at any moment, that the repressions of instinctual desires might overwhelm the psyche. Equilibrium was at best precarious:

> But the danger is that the violence of these opposite joltings does not demolish the organism—or that self-defense in surpassing its limits, not be a worse danger than that which it attempts to ward off. (This is the case with regard to me, and one of the reasons for my gnawing insomnia.)[24]

Stefan Zweig continued to play the role of intermediary between Rolland and Freud. Besides providing news of their respective activities, Zweig reminded the two of birthdays, and urged that they remain in contact through letters. Devoted to French culture, Zweig helped to translate and disseminate Rolland's works in Central Europe during and after the First World War.[25] To honor Rolland's sixtieth birthday in 1926, Zweig collaborated with the young French novelist, Georges Duhamel, and with the Russian writer Maxim Gorky, on an international *Festschrift*. German contributors such as Hermann Hesse, Albert Einstein, and Freud would pay tribute to Rolland in the collection entitled *Liber Amicorum Romain Rolland*.[26]

Freud's birthday contribution to Rolland consisted of an open letter dated 29 January 1926. He applauded the "unforgettable man" for his highmindedness and creative achievements. Freud asserted that, although he had always supported the idea of "love for mankind," he did so for "sober, economic reasons," for reasons based on sound psychoanalytic premises and "not out of sentimentality or idealism." He reiterated his concern about the inevitable contradictions between individuals and society. At stake in this conflict was the preservation of the human species. To alleviate the tensions generated by his "instinctual drives and the world as it is," man's nondestructive impulses counted as much as scientific and technological advances. Alluding to their meeting in May 1924, Freud expressed his surprise "to find that you appreciate strength and energy so highly, and that you yourself embody so much will-power." The reality of Rolland the man began to clash with Freud's image of the artist as undisciplined, passive, given over to fantasy, and incapable of tenacious struggle. After acknowledging Rolland's years of "hardship and suffering" as the "apostle of love for mankind," Freud wished him another decade of "fulfillment." He signed the birthday remembrance with his name and added "aetat. [aged] 70," obtrusively raising the issue of his old age and, perhaps, his imminent death.[27]

Having recognized that Freud derived enormous satisfaction from his intellectual labor, Rolland's seventieth birthday greeting wished his "friend" long life and good health so that he might continue with his work of enlightenment. "May the light of your mind pierce the night of life for a long time."[28]

Zweig informed Rolland about the events in the "days of celebration"—as Freud dubbed his birthday festivities—in a letter dated 21 May 1926. He mentioned that the official world had "ostentatiously" ignored Freud's seventieth birthday; the University of Vienna, the Ministry of Instruction, the Medical Society, and the world of "high literature" had omitted all reference to his life or work. To console Freud, "who will not live long," Zweig continued to support his candidacy for a Nobel Prize.[29] Freud corroborated Zweig's observations in a letter to Marie Bonaparte earlier in the same month. There, he mentioned Rolland's letter as particularly gratifying: "Among the written congratulations those that pleased me most came from Einstein, Brandes, Romain Rolland, and Yvette Guilbert." However, Freud's general assessment of the celebration was deflating and insightful; what he said pertained to Rolland's qualified appreciation of his discoveries. Freud realized that his theories had won a grudging acceptance, but even those who recognized his writings had rejected the foundations and practice of psychoanalysis: "General impressions: The World has acquired a certain respect for my work. *But so far analysis has been accepted only by analysts.*"[30]

Freud thanked Rolland for his birthday remembrance in a letter addressed to his "Friend" on 13 May 1926. The letter began and ended on a personal note of flattery and tenderness:

Your lines are among the most precious things which these days have brought me. Let me thank you for their contents and your manner of address.

But when men like you whom I have loved from afar express their friendship for me, then a personal ambition of mine is gratified. I enjoy it without questioning whether or not I deserve it; I relish it as a gift. You belong to those who know how to give presents.[31]

Yet, in the body of the letter, Freud raised questions about the intentionality, substance, and reception of Rolland's creations. What was intimated in earlier letters now became expressed, namely Freud's delineation of sharp oppositions between artistic and idealistic activity and the activity of science. He stated that, in contradistinction to Rolland's work, his own had not given people pleasure, consolation, higher wisdom, or easily digested images of themselves. Freud's bitterness about the years of unpopularity of the psychoanalytic movement partially explains the envy and invidiousness of his comparison:

Unlike you I cannot count on the love of many people. I have not pleased, comforted, edified them. Nor was this my intention; I only wanted to explore, solve riddles, uncover a little of the truth. This may have given pain to many, benefitted a few, neither of which I consider my fault or my merit.[32]

Ironically, Freud exaggerated the general expression of "love" for Rolland by "many people." In France particularly, Rolland had been more or less ignored by the French artistic and critical community despite the fact that the public continued to buy and read his writings. Apart from a tiny group of young non-Communist, left-wing intellectuals who clustered around the Parisian review, *Europe*, the majority of the nationalistic population stigmatized him as anti-French; they had not forgiven his "treason" during the war. Zweig drew a parallel between Rolland's isolation in France and the lack of appreciation for Freud in Vienna; he suggested that George Bernard Shaw shared a similar situation in England. Geniuses paid the price for their brilliance by being treated as nonpersons in their homelands.[33]

In late 1926, after receiving a copy of a polemical book against Freud written by the French novelist and physician Jean Bodin,[34] Rolland's attention returned briefly to Freud. To correct Bodin's unjudicious critique of psychoanalysis, Rolland stressed the historical value of Freud's theoretical findings, his intellectual honesty, and his role as a courageous forerunner. Bodin conveniently forgot how Freud's work cut through much of the hypocrisy and mystifications of *fin-de-siècle* Europe. One could criticize his doctrine's distortions and

the rigidification of his ideas into a mechanical system, at the same
time that one recognized the originality and the lasting profundity of
some of his insights:

> While one can object legitimately to Freud (and I do not exclude myself), my
> gratitude to him dates from long ago. It was around 1906 or 7, I think, that I bought
> the *Traumdeutung* in Zurich which had just appeared [in second edition]. It opened
> a monstrous but powerful internal world, wild, hallucinated, a little archaic (like
> that of Hellenic pre-history) that one carried in oneself, that one knew very well,
> but that one dared not look full in the face. Abusive error? Disordered vision?
> Excessive deformation? Yes. But that is worth more than the deliberate and
> imposed lie in which the mentality of this time lived.... We see today of what
> psychiatric cyclones, of what ethnic convulsions he was the precursor.... Every
> system of thought must be replaced in its time.[35]

While on vacation in Vienna in July 1927, Rolland met the French
lay analyst Marie Bonaparte, who happened to be staying at the same
hotel. She and three other disciples of Freud visited him there. His
impressions of the Greek princess were mixed: she was "young,
robust, laughing," yet confused and brusque in her thinking. Rolland
sensed that these young Freudians had not entirely assimilated much
of the master's conceptual apparatus, nor had they learned fully
Freud's clinical professionalism. They enjoyed their access to the
intimate secrets of their patients and played the role of "confessor"
with a flirtatious lightness and a flippant curiosity. Furthermore, he
learned from Marie Bonaparte and her colleagues that Freud was
closed off to music, that he had a "total, irremissible occlusion" to it.
More interesting was that Freud neither understood nor felt anything
for music but that it troubled him. Rolland was baffled by this bit of
information: on the one hand, he wondered why Freud had not
perceived the cathartic possibilities of music; and on the other hand, if
music made Freud uneasy, why did he not analyze the roots of his
resistance to it in order to overcome it? Freud's insensitivity to music
caused Rolland to speculate: "And how could he ever read into the
subconscious of souls, if he does not possess the key to the language
of the subconscious?"[36]

Freud sent Rolland a copy of the first edition of *The Future of an
Illusion*, first published in Vienna in November 1927. This triggered
an intriguing debate on the origins, nature, and significance of
religious sensation.

Though not his first sustained analysis of cultural problems or religion, he used the insights gleaned from his clinical and theoretical findings to polemicize against religious institutions, doctrines, and rituals, specifically the belief in an anthropomorphic God. In the twentieth century, Freud contended, religion represented a retrograde world view; religious believers perpetuated a body of ideas which had originated at a relatively backward stage of mankind's development. Since the psychical origins of religion were illusions that arose from the child's ambivalent feelings for his father, his need for protection and his longing for the father's love, mankind would never advance if it did not jettison its fixation on infantile wish fulfillments. More than illusions, religious beliefs were similar to a "universal obsessional neurosis of humanity"; they implied a repudiation of reality, a refusal to accept adulthood, and a consoling retreat into "blissful hallucinatory confusion."

However, Freud attacked religion because it no longer assisted modern man in reconciling himself to civilization, to the regulations, instinctual renunciations, and coercions demanded of the individual while living in society. Religion would only increase the uncertainty of man's condition. It could not accommodate him to life's compromises, to the obligations of labor, to the sublimations and repressions necessary for survival. Because religion was regressive and reactionary, it provided man with an obfuscating compensation for his misery. Besides distorting the childhood of many people through proscriptive interdictions and the inculcation of guilt, religion interfered with the establishment of a more sensible basis for coping with the demands of civilization and grounding ethical demands. Freud advocated an irreligious "education to reality." The oppressive nature of civilization could be ameliorated if man would apply the legacy of his scientific conquests, his reason, and his experience.

Freud concluded his book with an impassioned defense of science and a plea for science to weaken and eventually overthrow religious faith. Optimistically, he judged that science itself was not an illusion, but rather an impartial instrument, a tool for research, which presupposed accurate observation and reasoning in order to arrive at empirically verifiable and predictable results. These results were commensurate with the laws of external reality. Unlike religion, science was built upon working hypotheses which could be modified or discarded in the light of new knowledge. Just as science was his hope, so too was it mankind's: "The voice of the intellect is a soft one, but it does not rest till it has gained a hearing."[37]

Rolland reacted to the essay in a letter addressed to Freud on 5 December 1927:

> Thank you very much for your kindness in sending me your lucid and valiant little book. With a calm, common sense and a moderate tone, it tears the blindfold from eternal adolescents, all of us, whose amphibious mind floats between the illusion of yesterday and ... the illusion of tomorrow.

> Your analysis of religions is fair. But I would have liked to see you analyze spontaneous *religious feeling* or, more exactly, religious *sensation....*

> I understand by that—quite independently of all dogma, of all Credo, of every Church organization, of every Holy Book, of all hope in a personal survival, etc.— the simple and direct fact of the *sensation of the "eternal"* (which may very well not be eternal, but simply without perceptible limits, and in that way oceanic).

> This sensation is, as a matter of fact, subjective in character. But as it is common to thousands (millions) of men presently living with thousands (millions) of individual nuances, it is possible to submit it to analysis with an approximate exactitude.

> I think that you will classify it among the *Zwangsneurosen* [obsessional neurosis]. But I have had the occasion to establish often its rich and beneficial energy, whether amongst the religious souls of the West, Christian or non-Christian— familiar to me—among whom I count friends. And I am going, in a forthcoming book, to study two almost contemporary personalities (the first is from the end of the 19th century; the second died in the first years of the 20th), who have demonstrated a genius of thought and action powerfully regenerative for their country and for the world.

> I, myself, am familiar with this sensation. Throughout my whole life I have never lacked it; and I have always found it a source of vital renewal. In this sense I can say that I am profoundly "religious"—without this constant state (like an underground bed of water which I feel surfacing under the bark) in any way harming my critical faculties and my freedom to exercise them—even if against the immediacy of this internal experience. Thus I carry on simultaneously, freely and smoothly, a "religious" life (in the sense of this prolonged sensation) and a life of critical reason (which is without illusion)....

> I add that this "oceanic" feeling has nothing to do with my personal aspirations. Personally, I aspire to eternal rest; survival has no attraction for me. But the sensation that I feel is thrust upon me as a fact. It is a *contact*. And since I have recognized it to be identical (with multiple nuances) amongst numerous living souls, it has allowed me to understand that there was the true subterranean source of *religious energy*—which next is tapped, canalized, and *desiccated by the*

Churches: to the point that one could say that it is inside the Churches (wherever they are) that one finds the least of true "religious" feeling.

Eternal confusion of words, the same one which means now *obedience or faith* in a dogma, or a word (or a tradition), now: free vital gushing *[jaillissement vital]*.

Please believe, dear friend, in my affectionate respect.

Romain Rolland[38]

The French writer appreciated the value and courage of Freud's book even to the point of accepting his critique of established religion. What he found lacking in *The Future of an Illusion* was a psychoanalytic inquiry into spontaneous religion sensation. Such a scientific approach might introduce an empirical dimension and a conceptual clarity into the discussion of the "oceanic" feeling. He tentatively defined religious sensation as a prolonged intuitive feeling of contact with the eternal, a feeling of vastness, of living in or with immense forces. Rolland attested to the reality of this subjective communion with the timeless and ineffable but ubiquitous sensation both from his recent research on Hindu mysticism and from firsthand evidence; he confessed that he had experienced the sensation throughout his entire life. Yet he qualified his admission of his religious nature by stating that within him the operation of critical reason and the spontaneous feelings of the "oceanic" were not mutually exclusive. Thus, he too could distinguish reality from unreality, and he was not deceived by illusion. Rolland believed that "oceanic" energies were more or less identical in all religious souls, that they derived from the same "subterranean source," and that they might be an untapped mine of world unity and renewal. Totally unlike the objectifications of religion into institutions, dogmas, rituals, and the false promises of salvation, religious sensation was an experience shared by millions. Because of the extensiveness of the experience, the reality of the "oceanic" had to be acknowledged; then and only then could this "free vital gushing" be comprehended by a disinterested analysis.

Rolland's letter touched a sensitive nerve. In *The Future of an Illusion*, Freud had glossed over rather than analyzed ecstatic states or deep introspective feelings. Tactically, he evaded such a discussion either by asking rhetorical questions or by dismissing these states as rare, specific, and difficult to interpret. Moreover, he justified his dismissal of religious feeling in ad hominem fashion, albeit in the name of science.[39]

Freud delayed his answer to Rolland's letters for nineteen months, a period in which he wrote little and suffered a great deal from his illness. While composing the final draft of *Civilization and Its Discontents* in the summer of 1929, Freud's thoughts returned to his friend's suggestions on religious sensation; he thought of beginning his essay with a preliminary assessment of the "oceanic" feeling. "Beset with doubts" about the propriety of using personal material for his book, he wanted the French writer's permission to quote his "private remarks" before the work was published. These interpretative passages would serve as an addendum to *The Future of Illusion*, as a transition between the two works. They were not related integrally to the central themes of the new book. "My essay could be given another introduction without any loss, perhaps it is altogether not indispensable." Furthermore, Freud stated that Rolland's December 1927 letter had disturbed him, adding the disclaimer: "I always think of you with feelings of most respectful friendship."

> Your letter of December 5, 1927 containing remarks about a feeling you describe as "oceanic" has left me no peace. It happens that in a new work which lies before me still uncompleted I am making a starting point of this remark. I mention this "oceanic" feeling and am trying to interpret it from the point of view of our psychology. The essay moves on to other subjects, deals with happiness, civilization, and the sense of guilt. I don't mention your name but nevertheless drop a hint that points towards you.[40]

Even though he had forgotten the exact text of his letter, Rolland was "honored" to learn that he had urged Freud on to new investigations of religious sensation; he granted him full permission to begin his essay with a discussion of the "oceanic." Just as Freud's letter crystallized the themes of *Civilization and Its Discontents*, Rolland's letter indicated that his forthcoming three volume work, *Essay on Mysticism and Action in Living India*, would summarize several varieties of French, European, and Asian mysticism. That essay would argue that barriers between the Orient and Occident were superficial, that profound and spontaneous spiritual links existed between the two civilizations. "Oceanic" feelings, Rolland contended, provided an essential bridge between cultures. "I have been struck ... that it is not true at all that East and West are two worlds apart from one another—but that both are the arms of the same river of thought. And I have recognized in both the same 'Ocean river.'" On the one hand, his study of Hindu mysticism had corroborated and deepened his knowledge of the wide scale presence of the "oceanic" sensation; and on the other hand, his reading of classical treatises on yoga had provided him with physiological evidence to support his claims. Finally, he promised to send Freud copies of his work soon after it was published—the first volume in late 1929 and the second in January 1930.[41]

Three days later, Freud answered that he could not accept Rolland's permission to use his private discussion of the "oceanic" until he had reread the original 5 December 1927 letter; to expedite matters, Freud forwarded it. He then expressed a confused series of thoughts with respect to his correspondence with the French writer: "I possess so few letters from you that I do not like the idea of renouncing the return of this, your first one. I am not normally a hunter of relics, so please forgive this weakness."[42] Contrary to Freud's statement, Rolland's December 1927 letter had been the fourth in the series sent by the French writer to Freud, the first dated back to 1923. Freud's faulty memory suggests the possible repression of some conflict or unpleasurable feeling. Freud's display of possessiveness, the awkwardness of his prose, followed by an uncharacteristic lapse of memory, suggests defensiveness vis-à-vis Rolland's letter. Something about Rolland or the contents of Rolland's letter had disturbed Freud's memory.[43]

Freud cautioned Rolland not to expect a systematic psychoanalytic interpretation of religious sensation, but rather an approach which would sort out its origins and intensity. "But please don't expect from my small effort any evaluation of the 'oceanic' feeling. I am experimenting only with an analytical diversion of it; I am clearing it out of the way, so to speak."[44]

Freud concluded by expressing his mixed feelings towards Rolland. He felt a distance from, yet an attraction to his friend's various universes. Whenever Freud spoke of his personal limitations, he did so with an edge of ironic self-defense. This is particularly evident when they discussed their antithetical responses to the less tangible aspects of human existence. In switching from "I" to "we," Freud emphasized the characterological as well as the epistemological differences between the music lover, artist, mystic, and the psychoanalyst:

How remote from me are the worlds in which you move! To me mysticism is just as closed a book as music. I cannot imagine reading all the literature which, according to your letter, you have studied. And yet it is easier for you than for us to read the human soul![45]

Almost immediately after receiving the letter, Rolland replied that his position on the "oceanic" had not altered substantially; thus, his "great friend" could begin his new book with a discussion of the concept. He added that "it is difficult for me to think that mysticism and music are foreign to you." This signified disequilibrium in Freud's outlook and mental makeup. It suggested that Freud's suspicion of intuitive cognition sprang from an overvaluation of man's rational faculties. Rolland was aware of living two lives simultaneously: one was of the mind and the other was of the emotions. Unlike Freud, he made no value judgment as to which was more real or superior. While not denying the uniqueness and strength of these competing forces, Rolland asserted that man was capable of reconciling them and of achieving a desirable wholeness. As a corrective to Freud's imbalance, Rolland offered the Heraclitian and musical ideal—the task of striving for the resolution of clashing forces. For him, the "highest joy" consisted in the perfect realization of a psychological harmony. Actualizing this ideal implied neither the subordination of "seeing, believing, and doubting" to the unfettered play of the unconscious, nor did it preclude the role of intuitive and nonrational forces.[46]

Having completed the draft of his book in July 1929, Freud published *Civilization and Its Discontents* late that year, before Rolland's three volume work appeared. His extraordinary esteem for Rolland—his allusions to the French writer as "one of the exceptional few," "the friend whom I so much honor"—complemented his intention to consider critically Rolland's objections to *The Future of an Illusion*. Clearly, Freud had Rolland explicitly in mind when he spoke of the "great men" who were admired by their contemporaries, who did not use "false standards of measurement," and who comprehended "what is of value in life." In a footnote added to the second edition in 1931, Freud ended the secrecy and stated plainly: "I need no longer hide the fact that the friend spoken of in the text is Romain Rolland."[47]

In the first chapter of *Civilization And Its Discontents*, Freud discussed Rolland's assertion that the "oceanic" was the vital source of religious energy. Yet, he began his analysis by identifying Rolland with the expression of magical or wishful thinking. He pointed to *Liluli* (1919) as a poem in which the French author had "once praised the magic of illusion."[48] Here, Freud was mistaken; *Liluli* was a play and not a poem, and although it contained some verse, it was an Aristophanic farce which attacked war in particular as mankind's greatest folly and those mystifications and lies in general which had contributed to mass destruction.[49] Secondly, Freud's discretion about Rolland's identity was unnecessary; there was no reason for him to maintain the confidentiality that Rolland was the man alluded to in the text, for the French writer had twice granted Freud permission to use his remarks in their letters. Thus, the essay opens with a combination of praise and slight blame, and a touch of self-conscious reserve toward Rolland. Evidently, Rolland's position caused Freud "no small difficulty."

As he moved into the interpretative sections, Freud wedged his argument between understatements and qualifications. He admitted honestly that he had never experienced religious sensations, and that they were extremely unsuitable for psychoanalytic evaluation: "I cannot discover this 'oceanic' feeling in myself. It is not easy to deal scientifically with feelings."[50] And again: "Let me admit once more that it is very difficult for me to work with these almost intangible quantities."[51]

After summarizing accurately (without directly quoting Rolland's description of the "oceanic" feeling), Freud focused his discussion not on the physiological characteristics of the sensation, but rather "on the ideational content which is most readily associated with the feeling."[52] He suggested that the "oceanic" feeling consoled man regarding his mortality and the uncertainty of much of his existence. Without denying the existence of the sensation, he questioned whether it was the key source of man's religious needs or the most elementary of man's emotions. "From my own experience I could not convince myself of the primary nature of such a feeling."[53]

The "oceanic" emanated from a stage in the child's development where there were fewer distinctions between the ego and the world, where an "intimate bond" connected the child's self and his immediate surroundings, especially his mother. In adults, it was not contradictory for the feelings of "oneness with the universe" to coexist with those

more developed stages of the ego in which the ego functioned simultaneously to separate the self from the external world and to defend
the self against the "sensations of unpleasure." Since psychoanalysis
posited that no phase of the psyche was ever destroyed, it followed
that Rolland's "oceanic" sensations were preserved residues of primitive feelings which could be differentiated from other more mature
aspects of the mind, specifically its critical capacity. Though there was
no necessary disparity between experiencing the "oceanic" and being
capable of conscious "reality-testing," Freud indicated that pathology
often resulted if the boundary line was blurred between the ego and
the external world.[54]

However, in granting that the "oceanic" was "a purely subjective
fact," Freud contested that it was the fundamental source of religious
energy. While he traced such all-embracing feelings to "an" early
phase of the mind's development, he held that it did not incarnate
man's strongest and most recurring fears and wishes. Thus, he rele-
gated Rolland's "oceanic" feeling into the background as a secondary
manifestation of the ego, and repeated emphatically the main thesis of
The Future of an Illusion with respect to the neurotic origins of
religion:

> The derivation of religious needs from the infant's helplessness and the longing for
> the father aroused by it seem to me *incontrovertible*, especially since the feeling is
> not simply prolonged from childhood days, but is permanently sustained by fear of
> the superior power of Fate. I cannot think of any need in childhood as strong as the
> need for the father's protection.[55]

Hence, it was the Oedipal configuration deriving from infantile
helplessness which furnished the needs and ambivalent energies in
religious believers.

As for as the origins of Rolland's "oceanic" sentiment, Freud tossed
out two speculations, both of which he left in fragmentary form. First,
the "oceanic" might correspond to the narcissistic function of the ego,
maximized to include a feeling of love for the world ("might seek
something like the restoration of limitless narcissism"). Secondly, the
feeling might derive from the ego's efforts to ward off concrete
dangers in the external world by means of a total identification with
the universe. The "oceanic" was consoling because, through the
process of incorporation, the threatening aspects of reality were

neutralized and/or absorbed ("a first attempt at a religious consolation, as though it were another way of disclaiming the danger which the ego recognizes as threatening it from the external world.")[56]

Rolland published his most sustained defense of the "oceanic" sensation in his three-volume *Essay on Mysticism and Action in Living India*. While answering Freud's critique of mysticism in the introduction and appendix of the work, he also challenged traditional postulates of scientific investigation in general and of psychoanalysis in particular. This did not, however, prevent Rolland from pressing for a scientific inquiry into mystical experience.

European scientists and psychoanalysts were obstructing the efforts of civilization interpenetration by waging a battle against religion on two fronts: they condemned the religious consciousness without having experimented with the *fact* of religious experience, and they confused the articulation and ritualization of religious feelings with the intensity, durability, and imaginative possibilities of such "spontaneous eruptions."[57] To correct the superficial treatment of religion by the twentieth century's "extreme rationalists," Rolland made a case for Hindu mysticism. Through the study of two exemplary Indian personalities, Ramakrishna and Vivekananda, and by means of comparisons with European forms of mysticism and music,[58] he provided the details and an historical point of departure for further knowledge about nonrational modes of perception and existence.

The section entitled "Concerning Mystic Introversion and the Scientific Value for Its Knowledge of the Real" presupposed that science and religion were not incompatible. Despite their distinct modes of application, both were roads to freedom, ways of knowing and attaining the truth. The problem with the modern scientific approach to religion was its tendency to analyze external phenomena and its commensurate inability to penetrate to the depths of the religious mind. Nonetheless, the "oceanic" sensation was not comprehensible by known methods of the "intellectual dialectic." Consequently, Rolland urged that scientists study transcendent states of consciousness and deep introversion (mysticism)—he borrowed the term from Carl Gustav Jung—in order to complete their explanations of the mind's total activity.[59]

To study mysticism objectively, the spirit of William James, not of Freud, had to be emulated.[60] Rolland held that scientists should stop dissociating reason from intuition. Scientists should acknowledge the legitimacy of "generative intuitions" in all mental activity, including theory building and interpretation. They should be aware that another reality exists "outside of reason and the senses." The project was to delve into the working of the "oceanic" feeling with the hypothesis that mysticism was another dimension of human experience, not an isolated eccentricity. By exploring this state of consciousness, science could enrich itself, discover internal laws for mystical activity, at the same time that it made available to others nonrational modes of discipline, discourse, and ways of reaching the truth. To handle the difficulties of all inquiries into mystical experience, Rolland called for a radical type of research, a technique which would narrow the gap between the researcher's subjectivity and objective inquiry. He suggested that the observer identify with and experience the sensation of the object observed: "the Plotinian identity of the seer and thing seen."[61]

In proposing a psychoanalytic investigation into the feelings which were the religious sensation, rather than the ideational elements clustered around it, Rolland was anticipating subsequent revisions of classical psychoanalysis as theory and practice. By suggesting the end to the separation between analyst and analysand, he foreshadowed some of the "therapies of commitment" which challenged Freudian hegemony during Freud's lifetime and after his death. His desire to integrate Freud's work on the unconscious with the discoveries of spontaneous religion and creative art paralleled the approach of Jung on a certain level. Rolland's writings also prefigured the synthetic studies of Norman O. Brown and Herbert Marcuse.[62]

Rolland hypothesized that noninstitutional spirituality might be a strong way of mediating between man as he was then and as he could become. One could not afford to ignore the "oceanic" sentiment because it might be the source of universal energies capable of uniting mankind. The task for the future was to create man, to "reawaken God in man."[63]

He defined his concept of religion organically: it was "perpetual birth," constant striving, unrelenting aspiration. If one displayed a courageous attitude in the quest for truth, if one grasped an end which superseded individual life, and if one were prepared for long periods of self-sacrifice, one could be considered religious. Rolland's stance was that of the monist: he assumed that men and societies were unitary wholes with no independent parts. The divine was an idea-force which lived in every man. This "living-unity" connected man's soul to the universe and generated the release of religious energies. Rolland described this divine essence as mythical: it existed beyond the categories of time, space, and causality. He used water imagery to objectify it cyclical and creative qualities:

> I belong to a land of rivers.... Now of all rivers the most sacred is that which gushes out eternally from the depths of the soul and from its rocks and glaciers. Therein lies primeval Force and that is what I call religion. Everything belongs to this river of the Soul, flowing from the dark unplumbed reservoirs of our Being, the conscious, realized, and mastered Being.... From the source to the sea, from the sea to the source, everything consists of the same Energy, of Being without beginning and without End.[64]

Rolland speculated that the "oceanic" feeling might be the generating force, the deep structure, of all religious existence. The self's feeling of oneness with the environment, the end to the distinction between subject and object, might be the agency of the future unification of mankind. Furthermore, the primary gratification of those who experienced the "oceanic" was real and omnipresent.

As a disseminator of Hindu mystical thought, Rolland also tried to destroy the stereotyped misunderstandings about Indian religiosity. He pointed to India's movement for independence in order to illustrate that mysticism need not be socially passive. Gandhi's life and work proved that Hindu spiritual forces could be harnessed into purposeful social and political channels. Rolland disagreed with the commonplace that introversion meant flight, that it was an escape from life's conflicts. The true nature of mystical activity, as practiced by Ramakrishna, and especially Vivekananda, was struggle. Moreover, since mysticism did not have a "sporadic character," as William James had written, but "a daily, methodical quality," Europeans had to realize that mystical enlightenment was another form of self-discovery. Mysticism led to the purification of ideas. The realm of the pure idea was a place where energies collected in compressed but powerful form, and where they were in natural harmony with the universe:

And it would be strange if mental joy were a sign of error. The mistrust shown by some masters of psychoanalysis for the free natural play of the mind, rejoicing in its own possession—the stigma they imprint upon it of "narcissism" and "auto-eroticism"—betrays in them unknowingly a reverse kind of religious asceticism and renunciation.[65]

In turning to his critique of modern psychological theory, Rolland's aim was to show how leading theoreticians placed certain aspects of religious sensation into a preconceived, narrow theoretical framework.[66] He thought that Ribot, Janet, Bleuler, and Freud had erred in extending their analysis of "functional disorganization" to the entire realm of the mind. Freud's use of the concept of "regression" sprang from his own notion of a hierarchy of the mind's activities. Since he accorded science and the exercise of reason the highest place, Freud denigrated religion as a neurotic residue of a primitive and now surpassed stage of development. The term "regression" carried a "pejorative sense." Rather than disparage unconscious functions of the mind with regard to religious sensation, pure speculation, or imaginative activity, Rolland asserted that these activities could be as disinterested as scientific pursuits. Introversion worked by going back into one's unconscious in order to move forward into enlightenment. More significantly, these early, if not primary, operations of the mind were "those which disappear last—they are the foundations of Being."[67]

Despite Freud's "customary energy" in defending established scientific laws, Rolland challenged his uncritical faith in evolutionary theories. What Rolland stressed was the indestructible and universal aspects of man's spiritual nature, not the mind's more recent—and less firmly anchored—acquisitions. He accepted a modified Lamarckian view that the human condition was the product of innate characteristics (heredity) interacting with acquired characteristics (man's adaptation to his environment). Freud's error was that he downgraded man's innate possessions.[68]

Similarly, Rolland rejected Freud's implicit scale of values vis-à-vis the "supreme function of the mind." He excoriated the sharp divisions set up between the reality and pleasure principles, the opposition between action in the external, material world and creative representation in a fantasy or dream world. He advocated the integration of generative intuitions and scientific method:

But if this great effort is rejected with the disdainful gesture of the exclusive rationalists, and particularly of the psychopathologists who throw discredit on "*the criterion of intellectual satisfaction*" or—as the great Freud says with austere scorn—on "*the pleasure principle,*" which is in his eyes that of the "*maladjusted*"—those who reject it are far less the servants of the "*real*" as they imagine themselves to be, than a proud and Puritan faith whose prejudices have become their second nature.[69]

Rolland judged that Freud's conceptual apparatus so devalued intuitive and instinctual functions of the mind that his theory lacked proportion. Consequently, psychoanalysts failed to comprehend how unconscious forms of cognition were legitimate in their own right, and how intuition blended with rational activity. "The irreverent observer is tempted to say, 'Physician, heal thyself!'"[70]

Because of their biases, and because of the limited, however innovative, nature of their conquests, Rolland questioned why psycho- analysts appointed themselves the "standard bearers" for the reality principle. Why did they circumscribe the boundaries and functions of the real? And ultimately were scientists best equipped to make deter- minations about objective and subjective reality?[71]

Once the process of synthesizing science and intuition had begun, man would take a gigantic step toward realizing his whole nature and would move in the direction of an amorous fusion with humanity. "Man was not yet," Rolland concluded with a statement of his pessimistic optimism. But man would become man through education, meditation, and above all, through renunciation and sacrifice.[72]

Rolland mentioned proudly to Stefan Zweig that he had not only "provoked" several themes in *Civilization and Its Discontents*, but also that he was the "unnamed friend" whom Freud had hinted at in the first pages when he discussed the "oceanic feeling." He regretted that Freud's essay had appeared before his three volume work on Hindu mysticism was published; if Freud had only waited he would have found ample "experimental materials" of the "oceanic feeling" to submit to analysis:

And his argumentation would have been more precise and efficacious with these materials. Above all he would have seen that contemporary man is not involved alone, that this issue of soul proceeded without interruption for centuries, and that it be charged with no symptom of weakness. Error or truth, what's the difference? Everything is, perhaps, an illusion. But every lived illusion is a fact.[73]

Fulfilling his promise, Rolland sent Freud his volumes on mysticism immediately after their publication in Paris in 1930. In his letter of thanks for the gift, written on 19 January 1930, Freud replied playfully to some of Rolland's criticism of psychoanalysis:

> Of course I soon discovered the section of the book most interesting to me—the beginning, in which you come to grips with us extreme rationalists. That you call me "grand" here I have taken quite well; I cannot object to your irony when it is mixed with so much amiability.[74]

Freud's old resentment with respect to his break with Jung resurfaced here. He quickly dismissed his former disciple's writings as partially mystical—a denigration that Rolland would surely not appreciate:. "the distinction between 'extrovert' and 'introvert' derives from C. G. Jung, who is a bit of a mystic himself and hasn't belonged to us for years. We don't attach any great importance to the distinction and are well aware that people can be both at the same time and usually are."[75]

Freud contested Rolland's allegation that various psychoanalytic concepts were inherently pejorative; he argued that they were nonnormative descriptive terms. Rolland was simply wrong in imputing a value judgment to Freud's conceptual terminology:

> Our terms such as regression, narcissism, pleasure-principle are of a purely descriptive nature and don't carry within themselves any valuation. The mental processes may change direction or combine forces with each other; for instance even reflecting is a regressive process without losing any of its dignity or importance in being so.[76]

Without elaborating them, Freud then affirmed that psychoanalysis had priorities and a hierarchy of values. Since psychoanalysis was a collateral branch of science, not a *Weltanschauung*, he conceived of its basic function as a therapeutic one. The therapeutic goal was neither to furnish a key to the meaning of life nor to chart a course for mankind's unification. Its objectives were more humble. Above all else, psychoanalysis was designed so that individuals could comprehend their limitations and adjust to their external reality.

> Finally, psychoanalysis also has its scale of values, but its sole aim is to enhance the harmony of the Ego which is expected successfully to mediate between the claims of the instinctual life (the "Id") and those of the external world, thus between inner and outer reality.[77]

Mysticism, Freud added, might provide answers to the various metaphysical puzzles of human existence, as well as an intuitive means of exploring man's unconscious. But the problem with knowledge gained by irrational means was that it did not enhance, and might even weaken, the ego which was continually barraged by hostile forces. The external world remained a threat, and man was obliged to cope with its demands regardless of the profundity of his insights into the "soul's" vicissitudes. Freud's impasse with Rolland on these issues appeared total:

> We seem to diverge rather far in the role we assign to intuition. Your mystics rely on it to teach them how to solve the riddle of the universe; we believe that it cannot reveal to us anything but primitive, instinctual impulses and attitudes—highly valuable for an embryology of the soul when correctly interpreted, but worthless for orientation in the alien, external world.[78]

Freud's critique of Rolland's mysticism, of his use of intuition, and his search for integrated unities, was destined to become the orthodox Freudian reaction to later philosophical and utopian expressions of belief. According to the critique, mystics (and idealists) were immature, retrograde, and escapist. They retreated from external reality out of fear or because of an inability to cope with the compromises and submissions that social life demanded. As such, the solutions they posed were fallacious because they rested on metaphysical foundations and childhood wishes.[79]

Freud concluded his letter on a conciliatory note. He realized that his half-private, half-public controversy with Rolland was deadlocked, that neither was likely to yield to the other's position. Since his feelings for the French writer were "warm," he wanted to end the debate less disputatiously. For this reason, he shifted his point of view in the letter from the personal "I" to the less personal "we" form. Nevertheless, he made one last point about his own epistemological orientation which contrasted implicitly with Rolland's desire for a grand synthesis. Given the limited nature of man's knowledge about the world and himself, Freud affirmed (in the "I" form) that there were certain phenomena which remained inexplicable at the present hour. If he refused to make prophesies about the future, he hoped his idealistic friend would not mistake him for a complete skeptic:

Should our paths cross once more in life, it would be pleasant to discuss all this. From a distance a cordial salutation is better than polemics. Just one more thing: I am not an out-and-out skeptic. Of one thing I am absolutely positive; there are certain things we cannot know now.[80]

The last paragraph of this remarkably condensed letter clarifies the first paragraph of the same letter, which had opened conspicuously with a joke. The joke itself, as Freudian theory instructs us, posed both the outline of the problem dynamically and a sketch of its solution:

I shall now try with your guidance to penetrate into the Indian jungle from which until now an uncertain blending of Hellenic love of proportion, Jewish sobriety, and philistine timidity have kept me away. I really ought to have tackled it earlier, for the plants of this soil shouldn't be alien to me; I have dug to certain depths for their roots.[81]

The joke reveals Freud's feelings of self-denigration, as well as the defensive reassertion of his individuality. As a scientist, a Jew who had mastered pagan cultures, and a cultivated Central European intellectual who passed judgments on artistic creation, Freud was unintimidated by the "alien" realm of Indian religiosity. Besides associating it with the id, perhaps he identified the "Indian jungle" with passivity and femininity.

Thus, the humor plays a defensive role. At this juncture in the Freud-Rolland relationship, temperament, intellectual inclination, artistic appreciation, historical role, and world view all converged and clashed. Freud's feelings were unmistakenly divided: he felt a blend of attraction and repulsion, respect and envy, and, above all, the strange sensation that Rolland and he were utterly different. Rather than spoil the friendship with a serious polemic, and a permanent breach, Freud called a truce. The conflict had entered an insoluble stage, and Freud managed it by letting it drop. As he aptly said: "But it isn't easy to pass beyond the limits of one's nature." Clearly, he was not going to transcend his background, age, personality, or theoretical bent. Rolland could accomplish this no more than he. However, both men's final views on the "oceanic" had yet to be expressed, and Freud's mixed feelings for Rolland would reemerge in another context in 1936.

Rolland mentioned to Charles Baudouin that his work on Indian mysticism had precipitated a controversy with Freud. He explained that the old master had rejected the categories of "introversion" and "extroversion," associating them with Jung's mystical inclinations. "I have exchanged several letters with Freud concerning my work. He defended himself about condemning any one of the two forces of the mind—centripetal, centrifugal; and he flung back the error to Jung." Though there is no evidence that Rolland knew of the Freud-Jung split of 1913, he recopied Freud's sentence in German ("who is a bit of a mystic himself and hasn't belonged to us for years"), and he added parenthetically: "that smells of excommunication."[82]

Freud sent Rolland a copy of the second edition (1931) of *Civilization and Its Discontents* with an amusing dedication inscribed on the first page: "The Terrestrial Animal to his great oceanic Friend." (*Seinem grossen, ozeanischen Freund, das Landtier,* 18.3.1931) This confirmed that Rolland had been the "unconscious inspiration" of the first pages of Freud's book. The dedication from Freud impressed him as being "ironic and affectionate."[83]

Freud's dedication is crucial because the terrestrial animal-oceanic dichotomy links the intellectual and personal relationships of Freud and Rolland. In their conflict over religious sensation, the disputants had not met on the same footing. Consequently, no decision could be reached. Yet, there had been dialogue and an affective bond was established between the two. Rolland was everything that Freud was not; thus Freud, the scientific psychologist, identified himself with the material world, with the concrete, with intellectual life which had broken through to the preconscious or conscious stage. For Freud, Rolland swam in the boundless waters of eternity and universal love— his mind held back at the stage of the undifferentiated unconscious. Freud's fraternal sentiments were mixed with feelings of infatuation for the French writer. Rolland was a gentile, a practicing mystic, a music lover, a philosophical idealist, and a humanitarian writer who uplifted and consoled mankind. It is quite possible that Freud saw in Rolland various facets of his own personality, elements that he had long suppressed, such as his susceptibility to mystical ideas, his own creative aspirations, and his desire to serve mankind.

Using Freud's seventy-fifth birthday as an occasion, Rolland pursued the theme of reconciliation in the personal tone and the content of his letter. He felt a moral bond with Freud because of the psychoanalyst's fearless and disinterested search for truth. What was "psychologically curious" about Rolland's own mind was the balancing of three facets of his personality: feeling, knowing, and desiring. In him, feeling corresponded to the "oceanic," knowing corresponded to "nothing—to total, boundless effacement." Thus, Freud's juxtaposition of his own earthbound nature and Rolland's "oceanic" impulses, the concrete and the abstract, the material and the metaphysical, were forced and unnecessarily antagonistic oppositions. To see without illusions was not incompatible with feeling a connection with past and present humanity.

He reiterated that the "oceanic" sensation was an innate feature of the human personality, that it existed objectively in men of all historical periods and classes regardless of ethnological or geopolitical boundaries. Since he had published his volumes on Indian mysticism, echoes had reached him from many sources, including Austrian ones, which corroborated the wide-scale presence of such "invisible forces." The form and substance of this "vital feature" of man's existence remained to be studied; the contours of the "truth" of the "oceanic" remained a task for men of the future to determine. Arguing from a Jamesian pragmatic point of view, he opposed the analysis of intuitive sensations with preconceived categories. Philosophers and activists would be foolish to neglect the impalpable but highly explosive nature of "oceanic" forces. Rolland proclaimed that he lived by the motto "be what you must be"/ "do what you must do" not simply out of infantile rebellion or delight in his own uniqueness, but rather as a necessary point of departure in his quest for human abundance and serenity.[84]

Freud, deeply moved by Rolland's intimate tone and struck by the tenacity of his defense of intuitive forces, replied:

> You answered my pleasantry with the most precious information about your own person. My profound thanks for it.
>
> Approaching life's inevitable end, reminded of it by yet another operation and aware that I am unlikely to see you again, I may confess to you that I have rarely experienced that mysterious attraction of one human for another as vividly as I have with you; it is somehow bound up, perhaps, with the awareness of our being so different.
>
> Farewell![85]

Distance, age and illness would prevent a cordial resolution of their debate and a fresh restoration of their friendship. Most crucially, Freud admitted his own ambivalence about Rolland: his feeling of "mysterious attraction" and yet of "our being so different." The unusual force of the letter derived partially from Freud's sense of guilt about his mixed feelings toward his friend. The alternation between closeness and distance was accentuated by the ever-present consciousness of his impending death.

Rolland reacted to Freud's May 1931 letter in an exchange with Zweig in early June of that year. "Exchange of interesting letters with Professor Freud. The last received from him had an affectionate accent which touched me. It hinted at the feeling that death was near." He claimed that Freud's postulation of Eros and the death instinct paralleled his own intuitions concerning this metapsychological opposition: "The enlargement of his theory (to this double element, life and death) corresponds curiously to the self-confession that I made to him."[86] Rolland might have added that Freud had compressed these twin concepts into powerful emotions when expressing his secret feelings about Rolland.

A contemporary historian has argued that the origins of psychoanalysis were "counterpolitical."[87] After summarizing Freud's positions in the debate on the "oceanic," this conceptual frame can be broadened by adding that the consequences of psychoanalytic theory were counter-religious, countermystical, and more or less suspicious of all intuitive forms of cognition. Despite his sensitivity to literary, plastic, and representational forms of artistic expression, Freud was disturbed by and distrustful of artistic creations which had their origin in the realm of the id. While his theory neutralized politics by positing the primacy of instincts and sexuality, it attacked religion and irrational doctrines as culturally repressive. Mystics and believers acted immaturely because they resolved falsely the perennial tensions between individuals and their social and cultural milieus. A great opponent of fully integrated world views, Freud saw the world as permanently atomized; one could not wish away the myriad levels of the individual's estrangement in society. Man was by definition sick, divided, and incapable of escaping from the submissions required for his daily existence. Those who postulated syntheses or liberation on an abstract plane were misleading men, soothing them with promises of individual transformation, happiness, and perfection when only information and compromise were really possible. From the Freudian viewpoint, the best that could be expected was the therapeutic goal: accommodation to the external world as it was, amelioration of man's painful internal conflicts, and fortification of the ego against internal and external assaults on it.[88]

On the other hand, Rolland's point of reference was idealistic, prophetic, and synthetic. His view of human nature presupposed that man could be radically transformed. Rolland rejected Freud's determinism as pessimistic and reductive, and he believed that man was neither good nor evil, sick nor healthy, but rather capable of achieving a symphonic balance of his mental and organic processes. To fulfill this equilibrium and to maintain it was man's task. Rolland was far more preoccupied with character building and the release of man's latent ethical capacities than was Freud. Though the French writer was aware of the dangers of the excessive constraints of conscience, Freud perceived the hazards of guilt and repression far more incisively than did Rolland. In opposition to Freud's dualism, Rolland contested the inevitable antagonisms between material reality and the "oceanic" reality, the pleasure principle and reality principle, induction and deduction, the life and death instincts. To be whole for him meant attaining a psychological balance; it did not mean becoming ego-syntonic. The ego was part of the balance, but had to coexist with, not ward off or replace, the unconscious and the superego.

What Rolland expected from Freud, but did not receive, was an empirical psychoanalytic exploration of the various dimensions of the "oceanic" sensation.[89] Influenced by the contributions of Bergson, Le Roy, and James, Rolland defended religious sensation as a practicing mystic. Yet he also assumed that religion could be anti-institutional, nondeistic, and even actively subversive of established attitudes and norms. Mysticism for Rolland was not a pathological state. His concept of religion did not correspond to either of Freud's two prototypes: the Catholic Church and the Jewish religion. Although he was unclear about the ultimate truth and significance of the "oceanic," he was certain that the sensation could be felt without impairing the exercise of one's critical faculties. Rolland's belief in the "oceanic" was nonauthoritarian; it was a faith built on insights which grew out of experience, and it was historically verifiable.[90]

Just as he opposed Freud's overvaluation of critical reason, Rolland opposed the methodological foundations and some of the major conclusions of Freudian theory. In the same manner that he had challenged the orthodox theory and practice of Marxism-Leninism in the 1920s for its prescriptive laws and rigidity,[91] he combatted efforts to systematize Freud's findings in the social and cultural realm. He thought that much of Freudian terminology was emotionally charged, and that Freudian concepts were often connotative as well as denotative. As a contemporary critic who was not a member of the international psychoanalytic movement, Rolland recognized a religious component in the institutionalization of Freudian psychoanalysis. Perhaps because of his own Catholic childhood, he saw Freud's discoveries developing into a new church which included masters and disciples, dogma, confessions and secrets, strict requirements for membership, and excommunications of dissident members.

On one level, Rolland's reaction to Freudianism reflected the eclectic, heretical, and nonanalytic aspects of his own intelligence. On another level, it mirrored the slowness and difficulties with which Freud's ideas were being accepted in France, even by someone who was acquainted with seminal texts as early as 1909.[92] One cannot explain Rolland's cavalier dismissal of the Oedipal configuration and of infantile sexuality as merely a residue of the nineteenth century's romanticization of children and the family. It is quite possible that Rolland was disturbed personally by Freudian theory. His resistance to some of the revolutionary implications of psychoanalysis paralleled Freud's inhibitions regarding mysticism and music.

It is difficult to ascertain how well Freud understood Rolland the man or his ideas. The converse is equally difficult to judge. More likely than not, there was partial comprehension on both sides. Rolland liked and respected Freud as a person. What he found compelling about Freud was his piercing intelligence, his stoicism, his tireless activity, his vigorous allegiance to science and to theory building and, as shown by their letters, his candor about the nearness of death. Freud had been defensive, intolerant, and disputatious with Rolland; yet he had also revealed his vulnerability, warmth, and an intense affection for his French friend. Because he could not distinguish between Rolland the man and Rolland's ideas, Freud's feelings toward him were always double-edged, full of reversals. It is this ambivalence, the oscillation between attraction and aversion, that creates the mysterious and dynamic element in their relationship and debates.

After 1930 the impact of the world depression and the fearful spreading of international fascism forced Rolland into an agonizing reassessment of his positions vis-à-vis contemporary affairs. As he became more engaged in social and political struggles in Europe, his commitments to Hindu mysticism and Gandhian nonviolence waned. In the spring and summer of 1932, Rolland collaborated with the Communist intellectual, Henri Barbusse, to create a united front movement on the left. What became designated the Amsterdam-Pleyel Movement was inaugurated at a large international congress in August 1932. To publicize the congress, Barbusse appealed to the European medical profession both to attend and support the Amsterdam meeting. Ernest Jones reports that Freud signed the appeal.[93] Thus, Rolland's political activity indirectly touched his relationship to Freud.

From 1933 to 1939, Rolland emerged as one of the political and symbolic heads of the international antifascist movement. Within the framework of antifascist resistance, he critically endorsed Popular Front governments, and he was particularly enthusiastic about the Republican campaign in Spain. Fascism jolted him out of his immersion in mysticism and religious questions. Opposition to fascism was the crucial factor which mediated between his support of Gandhian methods and Soviet Communism.[94] It would play a role in his last contacts with Freud.

Though burdened by illness and age, taxed by the heightened level of anti-Jewish sentiment in Vienna, and faced with the prospect of emigration, Freud was aware of Rolland's political engagement. When asked by Victor Wittkowski, a German writer, to help celebrate Rolland's seventieth birthday, Freud replied that he would not be able to contribute a new piece of writing for his "revered Friend Romain Rolland" because his creative energies were exhausted. He alluded to Part I of the then unpublished *Moses and Monotheism* which he thought might "have been of special interest to R. R., but it suffered from one defect which prevented it from being published and since then my ability to produce has dried up." Nonetheless, Freud was irritated by Wittkowski's qualification that political topics be excluded from all birthday contributions. In the highly politicized ambience of Europe, and especially in the light of Rolland's committed stance, such a request was debilitating:

If there is something that makes this refusal easier for me, it is that "all references to politics" has to be excluded. Under this paralyzing restriction—not being allowed to follow my urge to praise his courage of conviction, his love of truth, and his tolerance—I couldn't do anything, even if I were in my prime.

Instead of offering a contribution, Freud would personalize his birthday greeting to Rolland: "On January 29 I shall tell him in a few lines that I am thinking of him with affection."[95]

Wittkowski fared no better with Rolland than he had with Freud in this period. Rolland was irked by Wittkowski's insensitivity to his antifascist engagement. The German writer erred in trying to compartmentalize Rolland's multifaceted existence and in depoliticizing his social and intellectual activities:

I do not ... separate my artistic work from my social activity.... One day you will understand that the social struggle in which I am participating is also the greatest combat for the defense of Culture which is threatened by the international fascist barbarism and by the breath of death of everything which clings to the past.[96]

Princess Marie Bonaparte solicited Rolland's aid in trying to secure a Nobel Prize for Freud. Because of the grace and lucidity of Freud's style, she believed he would have a better chance for the literary award than the Nobel Prize for Medicine. Rolland was delighted to submit Freud's name to the Swedish Academy; however, his expectations for success were low primarily because the contents of Freud's writings aroused fear and anxiety in his readers. Freud probed too deeply; his conclusions were unsettling. Furthermore, many great writers had been ignored by this celebrated world organization:

You know my affectionate admiration for S. Freud. It would be a pleasure and an honor for me to nominate him to the Swedish Academy for the Nobel Prize of Literature.

But I greatly fear that the proposal has little chance. The example of Bergson that you invoke is explained by the magic of his style and by his reassuring idealism. S. Freud is hardly reassuring! I do not forget with deep bitterness that the greatest of the English writers of our times, Thomas Hardy, never received the prize.... [97]

On 29 January 1936, Freud telegraphed Rolland a greeting in honor of his seventieth birthday. It read: "Best wishes your faithful, Sigmund Freud."[98]

Despite his gloomy forecast, Freud mustered the strength to

produce more than a mere telegram to celebrate Rolland's seventieth birthday. The intimate yet elusive paper, "A Disturbance of Memory on the Acropolis: An Open Letter to Romain Rolland on the Occasion of his Seventieth Birthday," (dated January 1936), demonstrated, on a surface level, Freud's extraordinary fondness for his French friend. Taken at face value, Freud's opening paragraph was eulogistic:

> I have made long efforts to find something that might in any way be worthy of you and might give expression to my admiration for your love of truth, for your courage in your beliefs, and your affection and good will towards humanity; or again, something that might bear witness to my gratitude to you as a writer who has afforded me so many moments of exaltation and pleasure.[99]

What Freud gave, however, was not a eulogy, but the "gift of an impoverished creature." A close analysis of the text may provide a significant clue to the recurring tension in Freud's attitude toward Rolland—the psychical source of Freud's ambivalent feelings for his "revered friend."

The paper appeared to have nothing whatsoever to do with Rolland, nor was it clear why the French writer might be interested in its subject matter. In it, Freud recounted the details of an incident which had occurred in late August 1904. While on vacation in Trieste, Freud and his younger brother Alexander changed their plans to visit Athens. Although the idea of visiting Greece left them both "discontented," they travelled there for some inexplicable reason. Once in Athens, Freud experienced a strange feeling of disbelief; his thoughts were expressed in the exclamation: "So all this really *does* exist, just as we learnt in school!"[100] Freud focused the remainder of the paper on an analytical evaluation of this thought, including an explanation of his brother's astonishment at his expression of disbelief, an elucidation of the concept of "derealization," and an interpretative solution to the riddle of the incident—why it recurred in his memory.

To interpret the underlying causes of his memory disturbance and the accompanying distortion of history, Freud argued that his incredulity at seeing the Acropolis arose from a childhood doubt that he would ever see Athens; he had not doubted the existence of Athens itself. His skepticism about his ability to "travel so far" was related to his lifelong love of travelling, which in turn derived from a wish to escape certain burdens of his youth and family life. The disturbing quality about going "such a long way" was that it involved surpassing his father, both in term of the grandeur of the wish and in terms of the prohibition against fulfilling the impulse. The guilt Freud felt on his arrival at the Acropolis, like the depression experienced at Trieste, was the unconscious guilt felt by a son about his superiority over his father. Thus, an ostensibly pleasurable moment had precipitated Freud's implied father criticism for having accomplished something beyond the realm of his father's capacities; this led to uneasiness on Freud's part. And so Freud concluded: "Thus what interfered with our enjoyment of the journey to Athens was a feeling of *filial piety*."[101]

Though Freud's self-analysis of the recurring nature of this incident is plausible, other explanations are possible. Scholars have viewed Freud's letter to Rolland as a "small masterpiece," a "literary gem," a "work of art," and as proof of Freud's "great admiration for him [Rolland]."[102]

Slochower accounts for the unanalyzed voyeuristic aspects of the paper and for Freud's sensation of having once seen the Acropolis (of having been there before) by emphasizing the dominant role of mother figures. Freud's memory was disturbed, Slochower speculates, because he associated the Acropolis with a menacing image of his mother. The memory disturbance arose because of the conflict between seeing the symbolic image of the mother's genitalia and Freud's fear of doing so; this conflict explains Freud's guilt and his desire to conceal the episode. Slochower traces the classic fear of castration in Freud to a repressed memory of having seen his mother nude as a four year old child. Historically, the episode might have been triggered by Freud's uneasiness about his "Oedipal relationship" to Wilhelm Fliess; the friendship with Fliess had taken a bad turn in 1904, Fliess claiming that Freud had plagiarized his discovery of bisexuality.[103]

Kanzer approaches the paper as a "self-analytic session." He uncovers three instances of Freud's ambivalence and/or hostility toward Rolland: first, the paper is not celebratory in content, the giver ungraciously admitting his "difficulties" in writing the Open Letter; second, Freud's insistence on his own loss of power implies that Rolland's creative energies will likewise diminish as he ages; third, Freud's veiled comparison with Rolland's mode of serving humanity, the oblique reference to the consolations of religion and art is opposed to the demystifying insights of psychoanalysis and science.[104]

Furthermore, Kanzer observes that Freud reverses his identity with Rolland on several occasions within the body of the paper. As Freud becomes the patient in the self-analytic session, the French writer becomes the analyst, hence Fliess' successor. With Rolland addressed, but silent, Freud replaces him as a writer. Because of the "transference" phenomena in Freud's chain of associations, Rolland's role in the paper becomes displaced onto the sibling substitute, Alexander Freud. And finally, while fantasizing himself in Napoleon's place at the moment of coronation at Notre Dame in Paris, Freud usurps both Rolland's religious faith and nationality.[105]

Kanzer concludes that Freud's rigorous and imaginative self-analysis not only eliminates Freud's rival father and brother, but also by inference eliminates the rival Rolland; Freud's analysis has allayed his guilt without having eradicated the unhappiness of an old man with bitter memories. Yet for Kanzer, Freud's confrontation with old age is ultimately "realistic," that is, insightful without being either neurotic or consolatory; his self-analysis has led to the "harmonious resolution of the conflicting force."[106]

In contrast to the definitiveness of this assessment, I see the paper more problematically; I hold that Freud's analysis has not resolved the various ambiguities in the paper. This is particularly apparent with regard to its conclusion when Freud reasserts his uneasiness, his anxiety about old age and declining power, and when he pleads for restraint and patience from Rolland.

The following line of argument is suggested. The text has a contrapuntal structure which centers around Freud's projection of extreme strength and weakness onto himself. It is written by a man who had "seen better days," yet by the same man whose scientific discoveries could be applied "by a bold extension, to the human race as a whole." In the same paragraph in which he discusses his relative dissatisfaction and powerlessness as an adolescent, he speaks of his zest for travel in epic terms: "one feels oneself like a hero who has performed deeds of improbable greatness."[107] Freud evokes another grandiose image of himself in comparing a make-believe conversation he might have had with Alexander as a child to a remark allegedly made by Napoleon to his brother at the moment of the Corsican's "coronation as Emperor." Finally, there is Freud's sense of a loss of productive powers, his desire to create something worthy of Rolland, expressed at the beginning of the paper, and a concluding—almost pathetic—plea for Rolland's "forbearance" because of age and an inability to travel. Moreover, Freud's rhetoric about his humility and impotence was contradicted by the reality of his ability to pose brilliant theoretical solutions to problems—in this instance to explicate the meaning of the memory disturbance.

Alongside of his own personal hesitations, Freud's attitudes toward Alexander had been marred by "interference" at the time of the incident. They both had felt gloomy about the prospect of going to Greece while in Trieste. However, once they had reached the Acropolis, and after Freud had experienced his sensation of amazement, he did not ask his brother how he felt: "A certain amount of reserve surrounded the whole episode."[108] The specific "interference" between them, Freud asserted, had been his brother's astonishment at his expression of disbelief. "What he had been expecting was rather some expression of delight or admiration." Furthermore, it is explicitly stated in the paper, as well as repeated in a letter to Arnold Zweig during the same month,[109] that Freud associated Rolland with his brother; they were the same age: "My brother is ten years younger than I am, so he is the same age as you—a coincidence which has only occurred to me."[110] What associates Rolland and Alexander further was the expectation on both their parts that they would receive expressions of pleasure from Freud on two happy occasions; neither Rolland on his seventieth birthday nor Alexander on first seeing the Acropolis were presented with the anticipated response. When Freud makes the transition from the descriptive to the analytical section of the paper, he switches his narrative from the first person singular to the first person plural. The logical implication is that Alexander shared Freud's guilt toward his father. What Freud is doing here is projecting unconsciously his own criticism of his father onto his brother.

Most crucially, Freud's associations in the paper lead him from an analysis of the brothers' impressions to the idea of joint guilt with reference to their father. In the process, he draws an unflattering characterization of his long-deceased father: "Our father had been in business, he had no secondary education, and Athens could not have meant much to him."[111] Yet Freud's explanation of his memory disturbance, that his sentiments of filial piety arose from reverence for and faithfulness to his parents, particularly his father, is incomplete. One could argue that the unanalyzed incongruities in the paper, in addition to Freud's personal fluctuations, derive from basic conflicts in Freud's psyche. Thus, the memory disturbance, the depression, the emergence of interference and incredulity between Freud and his brother give rise to unavowed but disturbed feelings from Freud toward Rolland. Freud's interference with Alexander spills over to Rolland. Furthermore, the unconscious discrepancy between Freud's feelings of heroism and powerlessness point to guilt as the key causal agency in the episode.

Guilt explains why the incident was only partially explained in the paper. This guilt itself derived from Freud's ambivalent attitude toward his father. His internal conflict manifested itself through patricide as well as through superego identification ("filial piety") with his father. The classical love-hate feeling, the impulse to outstrip his father which clashed with his awareness of the forbidden nature of that wish, converged to produce Freud's defensiveness and guilt. In psychoanalytic terms, Freud's anxiety over his desire to kill his father, matched by his longing for his father's love and protection, provide the censoring agency and dynamics for this specific episode. Metapsychologically, Freud's unresolved Oedipal feelings for his father became the motor force in the inevitable tension caused by Freud's urge to love (the instinct of Eros) and to hate (the instinct of destruction).

Freud connected age with the loss of intellectual power ("I am ten years older than you and my powers of production are at an end.") His neurosis about his age went hand in hand with his paternalistic feelings toward the younger Rolland. The Freud-Rolland relationship, in Freud's mind, reenacted the father-son pattern in terms of an elder brother's feelings for a cherished younger sibling. In the paper, Freud had compared two varieties of disbelief, the sensations of derealization and of "too good to be true."[112] Freud's sensation of incredulity in Athens in 1904 was not unlike one which he described in a 1926 letter to Rolland: there, he implied Rolland's friendship surpassed his expectations and fulfilled a specific ambition.[113] Freud's guilt about his father was exacerbated by having presented Rolland with a birthday present with such emotionally charged contents. We know that Freud disliked "exaggerated" expressions of sympathy, especially for celebrations like birthdays.[114] In his revolt against this "convention," he offered a gift which not only recorded his own divided psyche, but which also questioned whether he "deserved" Rolland's friendship—a man who "knew how to give presents."

If we assume that Freud's ambivalence toward his father was displaced onto Rolland, it is probable that Freud's laudatory remarks, one might say his effusive flattery of the French writer in the first paragraph of the open letter, were intended to compensate Rolland. Freud disguised his dual feelings for Rolland by exaggerating the positive nature of his friendship; perhaps he also wished to make amends to his friend for the wounding psychological truths about himself, and the feelings about his father, expressed in the main body of the paper. Due to their prior, unresolved debate on the "oceanic" sensation, and because Freud's feelings of ambivalence had surfaced in his May 1931 letter, Freud's memory of Rolland involved mixed emotions. It is probable that Freud harbored a grievance against Rolland, and that no details of the "oceanic" incident were forgotten. The Acropolis episode reawakened his feelings of attraction for and separation from Rolland, the unbridgeable differences between the great oceanic friend and the terrestrial animal. Having felt unworthy because of criminal feelings for his father, Freud asked for "forbearance," hoping that Rolland (like his father) would exercise patience and restraint with regard to the more aggressive side of his ambivalence, that side which pictured him as unheroic, a rival, or a failure.

In short, Freud had hit upon a deep truth when he made the confession: "the person who gave expression to the remark was divided, far more sharply than was usually noticeable."[115] Without entirely realizing it himself, Freud's chronic ambivalence for his father was extended to his feelings toward Rolland.

It is likely that Rolland was informed about but did not read Freud's analysis of the memory disturbance. After thanking Freud for his birthday telegram, he spoke of his feelings of respect and affection for the Viennese physician. In the letter which would be the last direct communication from Rolland to Freud, the French writer seemed unaware of Freud's ambivalent feelings for him. With controlled emotion, he mentioned both the birth of their friendship, his eternal gratitude to Zweig for having introduced them, and his sense of the mutuality of their relationship. "You know what profound respect I have for the man whose fearless glance has penetrated to the bottom of the internal abyss. I have admired him for a long time. I am happy and proud of his sympathy.[116]

Zweig continued as intermediary between Freud and Rolland in Freud's last years. On 17 February 1936, he requested Rolland's signature for an international committee honoring Freud's eightieth birthday.[117] Freud thanked Rolland for participating in the birthday celebration in a two part note. The printed part read: "I thank you cordially for the part you played in the celebration of my eightieth birthday. Yours Freud." The personally inscribed section read:

> I cannot tell you how glad I was to receive your autographed note. I am far from being as insensitive to praise and blame as I would like to appear through natural self-defense.[118]

The last direct contact between Rolland and Freud occurred in early 1937. Rolland's second wife, Marie Romain Rolland, had written Freud asking for several copies of signed manuscripts which would be sold at an auction to raise money for the Spanish Republicans. Freud complied and added ironically:

> Dear Madame
>
> Herewith two samples of my handwritten production. Do you truly believe that people would give money for that?
>
> My cordial regards to you and Romain Rolland.
>
> > Your devoted
> > Freud[119]

Enthusiastic after seeing Freud in Vienna in February 1937, Zweig wrote that only the "old" continued to struggle intellectually in the modern world.[120] Late in 1937, Zweig revisited his master in Vienna; he found Freud "admirable, clear in mind, full of unshakable convictions and new kindness in his old age."[121]

The Nazi invasion of Austria on 12 March 1938 made life insupportable for Freud. He left Vienna with his family for London on 4 June 1938. Zweig mentioned his "joyful" reunion with Freud in England in a letter dated 21 June 1938. Although the fascists had stripped him of his material resources and tried to destroy his books, Freud's mind remained "independent and combative." Because of his ill health, Zweig again requested Rolland's support in obtaining a Nobel Prize for Freud.[122]

Rolland had followed the news of Freud's harassment by the Nazis and his forced expatriation. Hitler's entrance into Vienna and the harsh treatment of Freud by the fascist invaders stimulated Rolland to declaim angrily about those "bestially brutalized" men who suffered under the fascist yoke:

> The world has lost its sense of honor.... The energetic intervention of the Ambassador of the United States was necessary to save old Professor Freud, octogenarian and sick, from insults and death, and the works of his whole life.... When one evoked the ruins of the ancient world under the rush of the Barbarians, one would have believed that an indestructible dike had been constructed around civilization. But, all the same, the barbarians are amid civilization.... [123]

Never blind to heroic behavior, Rolland commented on Freud's traumatic, poignant last journey in a letter written to Zweig in London. "Send Freud greetings on my behalf. Present him with my affectionate respect. I have never doubted his bravery for an instant. His entire life has been the example of it.[124]

That Rolland was fond of Freud and recognized the value of his theoretical contribution can be documented by a letter he wrote to Alfred O. Mandel during this period. Mandel, the American editor of Pyramid books, was compiling a series of introductory essays on the world's great thinkers. Having reappraised his mixed feelings for her, Rolland suggested that Marie Bonaparte be given the commission to write on Freud in the collection: "Besides, she is Freud's best student and his Antigone on the earth of exile." Notwithstanding other "remarkable" personalities in the Freudian school, Rolland supported the choice of Princess Bonaparte. To associate their names together, he added, would be a "magnificent demonstration"—a tribute to Freud's powerful influence in all realms of intellectual life.[125]

While expressing his genuine sympathy for Freud the man, his work, and his plight, Rolland never allowed personal sentiments to blunt his critical opposition to basic Freudian theory. In a letter to Monod-Herzen, the man whose letter had first begun the Freud-Rolland relationship, he expressed his "revulsion" at the current wave of psychoanalytic explanations by scientists, psychologists, and historians, including some of his own friends. Still resisting some of the universal postulates of the psychoanalytic movement, Rolland confessed that he "never had trouble in harmonizing within himself the father and the mother." The central problem with the contemporary "morbid, maniacal utilization" of Freudian constructs was the reductionism which accompanied it: "I believe life to be more rich and more complex. The Freudian hypothesis seems to me to falsify it, in simplifying life to the extreme—and I add not in the most natural and healthy sense.[126]

Rolland recorded somberly the news of Freud's death on 22 September 1939 in his private journal: "Death in London of Dr. Sigmund Freud, who escaped from the Nazis of Austria thanks to aid from America. He was 83 years old."[127]

With Freud's death and with Europe on the eve of a second world war, some of the vast issues which the two had discussed and disagreed over no longer seemed so vitally important. Praise and blame, ambivalence and resistance, analysis and synthesis, irony and affection, all receded into the background as Europe's "discontented" civilization appeared to be giving way to barbarism. It was in the mood of fellowship and of sensitivity to the suffering of others that Rolland wrote a letter of bereavement to Zweig dated 27 September 1939. "I have seen through the accounts of Freud's interment that you were at the side of the old master whom you loved."[128]

Notes

1   William McGuire, ed., *The Correspondence Between Sigmund Freud and C. G. Jung* (Princeton, 1974), translated by Ralph Mannheim and R. F. C. Hull. Also consult Lionel Trilling, "The Freud/Jung Letters," *The New York Times Book Review*, 21 April 1974, pp. 1, 32, 33; Frank Cioffi, "A Special Relationship," *The Guardian*, 27 April 1974, p. 20; Charles Rycroft, "Folie à deux," *The New York Review of Books*, 18 April 1974, pp. 6, 8.

2   Philip Rieff, *The Triumph of the Therapeutic: Uses of Faith After Freud* (New York, 1960), p. 80.

3   Letter, Freud to Edouard Monod-Herzen, 9 February 1923, in Ernst L. Freud, ed., *Letters of Sigmund Freud 1873-1939* (London, 1970), translated by Tania and James Stern, p. 346. (Hereafter cited as *Freud Letters*.)

4   Letter, Rolland to Freud, 22 February 1923, Archives Romain Rolland. (Hereafter cited as A. R. R.) I would like to express my deep gratitude to Madame Marie Romain Rolland for allowing me to see the rich collection of

unpublished documents in the Fonds Romain Rolland in Paris; this collection is now housed in the Bibliothèque Nationale in Paris.

5   Letter, Freud to Karl Abraham, 4 March 1923, in Hilda C. Abraham and Ernst L. Freud, eds., *A Psycho-analytic Dialogue: The Letters of Sigmund Freud and Karl Abraham 1907-1926* (London, 1965), translated by Bernard Marsh and Hilda C. Abraham, p. 334. Freud reiterated his esteem for Rolland in a letter to his youngest son Ernst dated 14 March 1923: "A delightful letter and exchange of books with Romain Rolland. One is always amazed that not everyone is rabble."

6   Letter, Freud to Rolland, 4 March 1923, *Freud Letters*, p. 346.

7   In late 1918, at the moment of the convening of the Versailles Peace Conference, Rolland and Freud, along with 100 other European intellectuals, signed a "Petition" circulated by the Dutch Committee of the Peoples' Federation. See, Romain Rolland, *Journal des années de guerre 1914-1919* (Paris, 1952), p. 1670. Both Rolland and Freud knew and corresponded with Frederik van Eeden, who might have played an intermediary role between them during the war. Rolland's antiwar essays have been collected under the title *L'Esprit libre* (Geneva, 1971). "Au-dessus de la mêlée," the most influential of his articles, was first published in September 1914.

8   Romain Rolland, *Journal intime*, extract written between 4 March 1923 and 31 December 1923, A. R. R.

9   Romain Rolland, "Dedication," *Liluli*, March 1923. I owe this reference to Michael Molnar, Researcher at the Freud Museum.

10   Letter, Freud to Rolland, 12 March 1923, A. R. R. I would like to thank Sigmund Freud Copyrights Ltd. for authorization to publish this and the four other unpublished letters from Freud to Rolland. Four of these letters were first cited by Colette Cornubert, *Freud et Romain Rolland. Essai sur la découverte de la pensée psychoanalytique par quelques écrivains français*, Faculty of Medicine, Paris, 1966. Cornubert was apparently not aware of the letter of 12 March 1923. She cites Freud's letter in French; the translations may be Rolland's.

11   For details about Rolland's two week sojourn, the main object of which was to participate in the Richard Strauss Festival, see Romain Rolland, *Richard Strauss et Romain Rolland. Correspondance, Fragments de Journal* (Paris, 1951), pp. 39, 90, 106; letter, Rolland to Stefan Zweig, 28 April 1924, in Henry G. Alsberg, ed., *Stefan and Friderike Zweig: Their Correspondence 1912-1942* (New York, 1954), p. 171.

12   Letter, Freud to Stefan Zweig, 11 May 1924, *Freud Letters*, p. 353.

13   Letter, Freud to Lou Andreas-Salomé, 13 May 1924, *Freud Letters*, p. 354.

14   Sigmund Freud, "Dostoevsky and Parricide" (1928), *The Standard Edition of the Complete Psychological Works of Sigmund Freud, Vol. 21*, pp. 177-194, edited by James Strachey. There are many parallels between the Freud-Rolland conversation and Freud's paper on Dostoevsky. In both, Dostoevsky's neurosis is classified as "hysteroepilepsy" and not epilepsy; in terms of the relationship between epilepsy and intellectual impairment, Freud considered the case of Helmholtz the exception to the rule. (See, pp. 179, 181, 184.)

15   The best account of the Freud-Rolland visit is in Rolland's *Journal intime*, 1 January-6 December 1924, pp. 85-87; other details of the conversation can be found in letters, Rolland to Jean-Richard Bloch, 15 June 1924, Rolland to

74   Cultural Theory and Psychoanalytic Tradition

Marcel Martinet, 19 June 1924, A. R. R.

16   Romain Rolland, *Mahatma Gandhi* (Paris, 1966); for a more detailed discussion, see David James Fisher, "Romain Rolland and the Popularization of Gandhi 1923 to 1925," *Gandhi Marg* (Journal of the Gandhi Peace Foundation), vol. 18, July 1974, no. 3, pp. 145-180; David James Fisher, *Romain Rolland and The Politics of Intellectual Engagement* (Berkeley, California, 1988), pp. 112-144.

17   Letter, Freud to Rolland, 15 June 1924, A. R. R. By permission of Sigmund Freud copyrights.

18   Romain Rolland, *Journal intime*, 1 January-6 December 1924, p. 122, A. R. R.

19   Letter, Rolland to Charles Baudouin, 19 January 1922, A.R.R.

20   Romain Rolland, *Le Voyage intérieur, Songe d'une vie* (Paris, 1959), p. 112.

21   Ibid., p. 112, n. 1.

22   Rolland's language here mirrors Freud's in the second "Preface" to *The Interpretation of Dreams, The Standard Edition*, vol. 4, p. xxv.

23   Rolland, *Le Voyage intérieur*, p. 314

24   Ibid., pp. 318, 319.

25   See Dragan Nedeljkovic, *Romain Rolland et Stefan Zweig* (Paris, 1970) and Robert Dumont, *Stefan Zweig et la France* (Paris, 1967), pp. 121-242. Also consult, Romain Rolland, "Préface," in Stefan Zweig, *Amok ou Le Malaisie* (Paris, 1927), pp. 5-12; Rolland mentions Freud's friendship with Zweig on page 8.

26   Letter, Stefan Zweig to Rolland, 12 October 1925, A. R. R. In his letter to Rolland of 30 December 1925, Zweig discussed his efforts to obtain the Nobel Prize for Freud. Freud's seventieth birthday was mentioned in letter, Zweig to Rolland, 25 April 1926 and in letter, Rolland to Zweig, 27 April 1926, A. R. R.

27   Letter, Freud to Rolland, 29 January 1926, *Freud Letters*, p. 365; this was first published in *Liber Amicorum Romain Rolland* (Zurich, 1926) eds., Maxim Gorky, Georges Duhamel, Stefan Zweig, p. 152.

28   Letter, Rolland to Freud, 6 May 1926, A. R. R.

29   Letter, Stefan Zweig to Rolland, 21 May 1926, A. R. R.

30   Letter, Freud to Marie Bonaparte, 10 May 1926, *Freud Letters,* pp. 369-370.

31   Letter, Freud to Rolland, 13 May 1926, Ibid., p. 371.

32   Ibid.

33   Letter, Stefan Zweig to Rolland, 1 August 1926, A. R. R.

34   Jean Bodin, *La Sibylle. Critique de toute psychologie de l'inconscient*, Thesis, University of Paris, Faculty of Medicine, Paris, 1926.

35   Letter, Rolland to Jean Bodin, 10 December 1926, in Jean Bodin, ed., *Jean-Christophe et Armel. Correspondance entre Romain Rolland et Jean Bodin* (Lyon, 1955), pp. 144-145.

36   Romain Rolland, *Journal intime*, October 1926-July 1927, pp. 111-112, A. R. R.

37   Sigmund Freud, *The Future of an Illusion* (1927), *The Standard Edition*, vol. 21; also consult, *Psycho-Analysis and Faith: The Letters of Sigmund Freud & Oskar Pfister* (London, 1963), translated by Eric Mosbacher, pp. 109-131.

38   Letter, Rolland to Freud, 5 December 1927, in *Un Beau Visage A Tous Sens: Choix de letters de Romain Rolland (1886-1944)* (Paris, 1967), *Cahiers Romain Rolland*, no. 17, pp. 264-266.

39   Freud, *The Future of an Illusion*, pp. 28, 31-32

40   Letter, Freud to Rolland, 14 July 1929, *Freud Letters*, p. 388

41   Letter, Rolland to Freud, 17 July 1929, A. R. R.
42   Letter, Freud to Rolland, 20 July 1929, *Freud Letters*, p. 388.
43   Sigmund Freud, *The Psychopathology of Everyday Life* (1901), *The Standard Edition*, vol. 6, pp. 4-7, 146-147, 239-240, 267-268.
44   Letter, Freud to Rolland, 20 July 1929, *Freud Letters, p. 389.*
45   Ibid.
46   Letter, Rolland to Freud, 19 July 1929, A. R. R.
47   Sigmund Freud, *Civilization and Its Discontents* (1930), *The Standard Edition*, vol. 21, p. 65, n. 1.
48   Ibid., p. 65.
49   Romain Rolland, *Liluli* (Paris, 1919); for Rolland's explanation of his intention in *Liluli*, consult letter from Rolland to Istar de Thionville, 13 May 1920 in *Un Beau Visage A Tous Sens*, pp. 164, 165.
50   *Civilization and Its Discontents*, p. 65.
51   Ibid. p. 72.
52   Ibid., p. 65. Rather than evaluate the physiological basis of mysticism, or discuss the link between mysticism and trances, Freud dropped the issues by quoting a text from Schiller. Possibly, the unnamed "another friend of mine" is an allusion to Rolland. (pp. 72-72.)
53   Ibid., p. 65.
54   Ibid., p. 66.
55   Ibid., p. 72 (my italics).
56   Ibid., p. 72.
57   Romain Rolland, *The Life of Ramakrishna* (Calcutta, 1970), translated by E. F. Malcolm-Smith, pp. 4-5. This was first published as *Essai sur la mystique et l'action de l'Inde vivante: La Vie de Ramakrishna* (Paris, 1929).
58   At the same time that Rolland was writing on Hindu mysticism, he was working on the early volumes of his massive study of Beethoven; see, Romain Rolland, *Beethoven. Les Grandes epoques créatrices de l'Héroique à l'Appasionata* (Paris, 1928) and Romain Rolland, *Goethe et Beethoven* (Paris, 1930). For a provocative study of Rolland's religiosity and the role of Beethoven in his faith, consult Paul Claudel, "La Pensée religieuse de Romain Rolland," in *Accompagnements* (Paris, 1949), pp. 62-88.
59   Romain Rolland, *The Life of Vivekananda and the Universal Gospel* (Calcutta, 1970), translated by E. F. Malcolm-Smith, pp. 333, 334. This was first published as *Essai sur la mystique et l'action de l'Inde vivante: La Vie de Vivekananda et L'Evangile Universel*, 2 volumes (Paris, 1930).
60   Ibid., p. 346 n. 1. Rolland thought very highly of William James, *L'Expérience religieuse: Essai de psychologie descriptive* (Paris, 1906), translated from English to French by Frank Abauzit.
61   Rolland, *The Life of Vivekananda*, p. 312.
62   Norman O. Brown, *Love's Body* (New York 1966), pp. 82, 88, 89, 141, 211. There are real differences between Rolland's position and Brown's; most important, Brown's emphasis on bodily liberation and polymorphous perversion as opposed to Rolland's stress on renunciation. Also consult, Herbert Marcuse, "Art as Form of Reality," *New Left Review*, no. 74, July-August 1974, pp. 51-58.
63   Rolland, *The Life of Vivekananda*, p. 315.
64   Rolland, *The Life of Ramakrishna*, pp. 6-7.

65   Rolland, *The Life of Vivekananda*, pp. 343-344.
66   Rolland, *The Life of Ramakrishna*, p. 5; *The Life of Vivekananda*, pp. 334, 339-340.
67   Rolland, *The Life of Vivekananda*, p. 336.
68   Ibid., pp. 334-337.
69   Ibid. p. 343.
70   Ibid., p. 336.
71   Ibid., pp. 335, 340-341, 344. Rolland did not write the chapter on mystic introversion as a dilettante. He cited specialized works in the Bergsonian tradition, in contemporary psychology, aesthetics, educational psychology, and scientific methodology. See respectively, Ferdinand Morel, *Essai sur L'Introversion mystique: étude psychologique de Pseudo-Denys L'Aréopagite et de quelques autres cas de mysticisme* (Geneva, 1918); Charles Baudouin, "La Régression et les phénomènes de recul en psychologie," *Journal de Psychologie*, 15 November-15 December 1928, pp. 795-823; Edouard Monod-Herzen, *Science et Esthétique: Principles de morphologie générale* (Paris, 1927), 2 volumes; Edouard Le Roy, "La Discipline de L'Intuition," *Vers L'Unité*, no. 35-36, August-September 1925, pp. 23-26; Adophe Ferrière, *Le Progrès spirituel* (Geneva, 1927); and Jean Perrin, *Les Atomes* (Paris, 1912).
72   *The Life of Vivekananda*, p. 254.
73   Letter, Rolland to Stefan Zweig, 30 December 1929, A. R. R.
74   Letter, Freud to Rolland, 19 January 1930, *Freud Letters*, p. 392.
75   Ibid.
76   Ibid.
77   Ibid.
78   Ibid., pp. 392-393.
79   Philip Rieff, *The Triumph of the Therapeutic*, pp. 232-262; Rieff, *Freud: The Mind of the Moralist*, pp. 281-360; Paul Ricoeur, *De L'Interprétation. Essai Sur Freud* (Paris, 1965), p. 523; Michel Dansereau, *Freud et l'athéisme* (Paris, 1971), pp. 121-122.
80   Letter, Freud to Rolland, 19 January 1930, *Freud Letters*, p. 393.
81   Ibid., p. 392.
82   Letter, Rolland to Charles Baudouin, 13 March 1930, A. R. R. In an letter to Baudouin dated 16 April 1929, Rolland stated that most "masters of pathological psychology" were better suited to be observed as case histories than to serve as "model observers." Their incapacity to grasp religious sensations revealed a loss of "contact with a living, full, and healthy reality." A. R. R.
83   Romain Rolland, *Journal intime*, November 1930-December 1931, p. 56. A. R. R.
84   Letter, Rolland to Freud, 3 May 1931, A. R. R.
85   Letter, Freud to Rolland, May 1931, *Freud Letters*, p. 405.
86   Letter, Rolland to Stefan Zweig, 6 June 1931, A. R. R.
87   Carl E. Schorske, "Politics and Patricide in Freud's Interpretation of Dreams," *American Historical Review*, vol. 78, no. 2, April 1973, pp. 328-347.
88   Philip Rieff, *The Triumph of the Therapeutic*, pp. 29-107; Rieff, *Freud: The Mind of the Moralist*, pp. 361-392; Erich Fromm, *Psychoanalysis and Religion* (New Haven, 1972), pp. 1-20.
89   For a contemporary comparison of the similarities between psychoanalysis and

mysticism, consult Herbert Fingarette, "The Ego and Mystic Selflessness," in *Identity and Anxiety: Survival of the Person in Mass Society*, edited by Maurice R. Stern, Arthur J. Vidish, David M. White (New York, 1960), pp. 552-583.

90   Rieff, *The Triumph of the Therapeutic*, pp. 179, 179 n. 50; Rieff, *Freud: The Mind of the Moralist*, pp. 291-292.

91   For a complete discussion of Rolland's reaction to Marxism and the Russian Revolution in the early 1920s, see David James Fisher, "The Rolland-Barbusse Debate," *Survey*, Spring-Summer, 1974, vol. 20, no. 2-3, pp. 121-159; Fisher, *Romain Rolland and The Politics of Intellectual Engagement*, pp. 79-111.

92   Edith Hesnard-Félix, "Les débuts de la psychanalyse en France," *Europe*, no. 539, March 1974, pp. 69-87; Colette Cornubert, *Freud et Romain Rolland. Essai sur la découverte de la pensée psychoanalytique par quelques écrivains français*, Faculty of Medicine, Paris, 1966. op. cit.

93   Ernest Jones, *Sigmund Freud: Life and Work, The Last Phase 1919-1939* (London, 1957), vol. 3, p. 182. Curiously enough, Jung also signed the appeal. For the text of this petition, see "L'Appel des médecins," in Wladimir Martel, *Vers la guerre où la révolution* (Alençon, 1933), pp. 61-62.

94   For a detailed account of Rolland's political evolution from Gandhism to fellow traveler of Communism, see David James Fisher, *Romain Rolland and the Politics of Intellectual Engagement*, pp. 147-291.

95   Letter, Freud to Victor Wittkowski, 6 January 1936, *Freud Letters*, p. 427.

96   Letter, Rolland to Victor Wittkowski, 19 May 1936, A. R. R.

97   Letter, Rolland to Marie Bonaparte, 20 January 1936, also see, *Journal intime*, 1 October 1935-July 1936, p. 60, A. R. R.

98   Telegram, Freud to Rolland, 29 January 1936, A. R. R. By permission of Sigmund Freud Copyrights.

99   Sigmund Freud, "A Disturbance of Memory on the Acropolis: An Open Letter to Romain Rolland on the Occasion of his Seventieth Birthday" (1936), *The Standard Edition*, vol. 22, pp. 239-248.

100   Ibid., p. 241.

101   Ibid., pp. 247-248.

102   See respectively, Marthe Robert, *D'Oedipe A Moise. Freud et la conscience juive* (Paris, 1974), pp. 43-44; Harry Slochower, "Freud's 'Déjà Vu' on the Acropolis: A Symbolic Relic of 'Mater Nuda,'" *The Psychoanalytic Quarterly*, vol. 39, no. 1, 1970, p. 90; Mark Kanzer, "Sigmund and Alexander Freud on the Acropolis," *American Imago*, vol. 26, no. 4, Winter, 1969, p. 353; Anna Freud and James Strachey, eds. *The Standard Edition*, vol. 22, p. 238. For other assessments of this paper, consult John Abbot, "Freud's Repressed Feelings about Athena on the Acropolis," *American Imago*, vol. 26. no. 4, Winter, 1969, pp. 353-363; Irving B. Harrison, "A Reconsideration of Freud's 'A Disturbance of Memory on the Acropolis' in Relation to Identity Disturbance," *Journal of the American Psychoanalytic Association*, 14, 1966, pp. 518-527; Max Schur, "The Background of Freud's Disturbance on the Acropolis," *American Imago*, vol. 26, no. 4, Winter 1969; and Julian L. Stamm, "Freud's 'Disturbance of Memory on the Acropolis' and the Problem of Depersonalization in Freud's 'Disturbance on the Acropolis,'" *American Imago*, vol. 26, no. 4, Winter 1969, pp. 364,372.

103   Slochower, "Freud's 'Déjà Vu' on the Acropolis: A Symbolic Relic of 'Mater Nuda,'" pp. 92, 99, 101.

104   Kanzer, "Sigmund and Alexander Freud on the Acropolis," pp. 324, 325, 342.
105   Ibid., pp. 325, 326, 343.
106   Ibid., 337, 339, 343.
107   With unrelenting Freudian logic, Kanzer interprets Freud's ambition to visit the Acropolis as the fulfillment of a powerful Oedipal desire: "the experience of the journey as worthy of a hero's reward—an incestuous reunion with the mother in this incomparable setting." Ibid., p. 334.
108   Freud, "A Disturbance of Memory on the Acropolis," p. 243.
109   Letter, Freud to Arnold Zweig, 20 January 1936, in *Sigmund Freud-Arnold Zweig Briefwechsel* (Frankfurt Am Main, 1968), Ernst L. Freud, ed., p. 130.
110   Freud, "A Disturbance of Memory on the Acropolis," p. 240.
111   Ibid., p. 247.
112   Ibid., pp. 242-243.
113   Letter, Freud to Rolland, 13 May 1926, *Freud Letters*, p. 371; Freud said: "It seems to me a surprising accident that apart from my doctrines my person should attract any attention at all. But when men like you whom I have loved from afar express their friendship for me, then a particular ambition of mine is gratified. I enjoy it without *questioning* whether or not I *deserve* it, I relish it as a gift." (My italics.)
114   *The Psychopathology of Everyday Life, The Standard Edition*, vol. 6, pp. 154-155.
115   Freud, "A Disturbance of Memory on the Acropolis," p. 241.
116   Letter, Rolland to Freud, 8 February 1936, A. R. R.
117   Letter, Stefan Zweig to Rolland, 17 February 1936, A. R. R.
118   Letter, Freud to Rolland, May 1936, A. R. R. By permission of Sigmund Freud Copyrights.
119   Letter, Freud to Marie Romain Rolland, 22 January 1937, A. R. R. By permission of Sigmund Freud Copyrights.
120   Letter, Zweig to Rolland, 18 February 1937, A. R. R.
121   Letter, Zweig to Rolland, 7 December 1937, A. R. R.
122   Letter, Zweig to Rolland, 21 June 1938, A. R. R.
123   Romain Rolland, *Journal intime*, January 1938-January. 1939, p. 29, A. R. R.
124   Letter, Rolland to Stefan Zweig, 25 August 1938, A. R. R.
125   Letter, Rolland to Alfred O. Mandel, 23 September 1938, A. R. R.
126   Letter, Rolland to Edouard Monod-Herzen, 6 March 1939, A. R. R.
127   Romain Rolland *Journal intime*, 22 September 1939, A. R. R.
128   Letter, Rolland to Stefan Zweig, 27 September 1939, A. R. R.

3

The Analytic Triangle: Freud, Jung, and Sabina Spielrein

We are and remain Jews. The others will only exploit us
and will never understand or appreciate us.

—Freud to Spielrein,
29 September 1913

For the historian of psychoanalysis archival discoveries excite, perplex, and create multiple difficulties. He must immediately consider the issue of disclosure and confidentiality. Should the sources be concealed, censored, stashed away, published partially, or published fully but with editorial annotations and scholarly paraphernalia? Contemporary writers are astonishingly eager to expose the secrets and to exhume the corpses of famous psychoanalysts. Audiences are curious to devour these texts, especially if the content proves to be scandalous or salacious. All too often, gifted pioneers of psychoanalysis are treated tactlessly and exhibitionistically, without the slightest regard for their struggles, their relationship with their times, and their lasting contribution. Time and distance usually permit one to scrutinize a life dispassionately, even with nuance, thereby allowing the public access to the salient facts, encouraging them to draw their own conclusions. Recent studies in psychoanalytic scholarship, biography most egregiously, have trivialized the genre. Frequently, untrained authors present us with wild speculations and distorted autopsies of the mind. The studies have tended to be debunking and reductionistic, often gratuitously so. With their undue emphasis on the sensational, the irrelevant, the gossipy, and the polemical, these works have undermined attempts to appraise judiciously the life and significance of a given psychoanalyst or psychoanalytic school.

Documents, of course, do not speak for themselves. They often disguise their meanings. They must be situated, placed in an intellectual and historical context, and understood in terms of the life history of the individual. Above all, the archival sources must be interpreted.

Aldo Carotenuto, a Jungian analyst and professor of Psychology at the University of Rome faced these choices in 1977, when he was presented with a fascinating cache of unpublished material discovered in Geneva at the Institute of Psychology. Carotenuto examined documents left behind by Sabina Spielrein, a forgotten and rather remarkable personality in the psychoanalytic movement. The Spielrein collection included as its center piece a forty-one page diary written from 1909 to 1912; framing the diary were triangular exchanges between Spielrein, Jung, and Freud; specifically, there were forty-six letters from Jung to Spielrein (which the Jung estate refused authorization to publish); twelve letters from Spielrein to Jung; twenty letters from Freud to Spielrein; and two letters (or drafts) from Spielrein to Freud.

In *A Secret Symmetry*,[1] Carotenuto presents the documents in superb translations and then narrates Spielrein's life and times. His strategy is to discuss her theoretical writings with a linear account of her psychoanalytic and cultural milieu. Carotenuto writes from the perspective of analytic psychology. While much of his exposition is valuable, I found his interpretative passages unconvincing, tendentious, and regrettably off target. When his language is not plainly presumptuous, it is apologetic for Jung and his transparently indecent behavior. For me, the primary documents are more compelling than the accompanying essay.

The great discovery in this text is Spielrein herself. And what a magnificent person she was! On first encounter I was struck by her versatility and ecumenical interests, her probing doubt and poignant self-doubt. I was impressed by her self-consciousness and self-reflexiveness, her capacity for continuous emotional and intellectual growth. This sensitive soul, with slightly mystical and neo-romantic tendencies, reflected on and transcended her own deep-seated, psychological disturbances in an imaginative, synthetic fashion. She was a vibrant personality who possessed a rare blend of artistic intuition, scientific rigor, and theoretical originality. Spielrein belongs to that generation of brilliant and willful women who were committed to psychoanalysis because psychoanalytic theory and practice sprang from the depths of their beings. Psychoanalysis became her life, her calling, her bridge to the past and to the future. Her analytic work complemented her scholarly investigations of folklore, mythology, the psychology of religion, music, art history, and that frontier region where language and psychoanalysis intersect. Her inventiveness, intellectual audacity, visceral devotion to research, psychological perspicaciousness, her capacity to survive a tumultuous ordeal and to generate fertile ideas, all seem so exceptional that she appears larger than life.

But she was not a character in a novel.[2] Spielrein was born in 1885 in Rostov-on-Don, the eldest child and only surviving daughter in a family with four siblings. She came from the cultivated Russian-Jewish bourgeoisie, a bourgeoisie which was educationally conscious and oriented toward Europe. Her grandfather and great-grandfather had been rabbis. Spielrein's early childhood was marked by painful, extended episodes of feces retention, often lasting two weeks. She recurrently fantasized about defecating on her father. In addition, she feared soiling herself. (Curiously, her name translates as "clean-play" in German). Spielrein masturbated compulsively and expressed confused, ambivalent feelings for the people in her life. She was periodically depressed; her suicidal thoughts alternated with uncontrollable bouts of laughing, weeping, and screaming. In 1904, at age twenty, her parents brought her to the Burghölzli mental hospital in Zurich, Switzerland, an institution renowned for its treatment of severe psychic disorders—psychopathology that we would classify today as borderline or psychotic. Her physician was Jung. Jung apparently treated her according to Freud's methods. He diagnosed her illness as severe hysteria, or as he put it to Freud, "psychotic hysteria." Bruno Bettelheim argues that she was schizoid and probably experienced one or more schizophrenic episodes.[3] In 1905, Spielrein had recovered enough to enter the University of Zurich to study medicine. In 1911 she graduated as a doctor in medicine, with a specialty in psychiatry, after writing her thesis on "The Psychological Content of a Case of Schizophrenia."[4]

In 1912, Spielrein published a seminal paper entitled "Destruction as a Cause of Coming into Being."[5] Written in German, it appeared in the *Yearbook for Psychoanalysis and Psychopathological Research*; the paper was a daring inquiry into the death instinct, anticipating by eight years Freud's discussion of the same subject in *Beyond the Pleasure Principle*.[6] Several of Spielrein's insights prefigure the findings of existential psychoanalysis in the 1930s and 1940s. She spent the period of October 1911 to November 1912 in Vienna, where she became closely associated with Freud's circle and the Vienna Psychoanalytic Society. She also lived in Berlin for a time. In 1913, Spielrein wed Dr. Paul Scheftel; while little is recorded about the marriage, we do know that her daughter, Renate, was born in September 1913.

From 1914 until 1923, Spielrein became the proverbial wandering Jew, practicing psychoanalysis in Swiss cities such as Lausanne, Chateau d'Oex, and Geneva. For eight months in 1921, she analyzed the great cognitive psychologist, Jean Piaget, in Geneva. Possibly under Piaget's influence, she published a 1922 paper called "Consideration of Various Stages of Linguistic Development: The Origins of the Childish Words Papa and Mama."[7] Here she attempted to integrate semantic and perceptual approaches to the mind within a psychoanalytic conceptual frame. Passages from her papers reveal her incisive grasp of issues—the symbolic importance of the breast and the baby's activity of sucking at the mother's breast; the centrality of language in the psychoanalytic dialogue and the role of otherness in the unconscious—which Melanie Klein and Jacques Lacan would subsequently highlight in their theoretical projects. Spielrein was a forerunner, a powerful germinal thinker.

In 1923 and clearly out of sympathy with the social experiment under way in the Soviet Union (in 1923 Lenin was still alive, though gravely ill; Stalin had not yet emerged as his successor, nor consolidated his power), Spielrein returned home to Rostov-on-Don. She did so with Freud's blessing. She became involved in the Russian psychoanalytic movement, participating in a research endeavor on psychoanalytic pedagogy. She helped to design a special home for infants and children combining psychoanalytic views of sexual education and early childhood development with a socialist environmentalism and a commitment to humanize the community. Her last paper, dated 1931, focused on children's drawings, comparing those executed with eyes open and those with eyes closed;[8] the metaphor of seeing and nonseeing may indicate her frustration with the practical attempt to synthesize the ideas of Marx and Freud. In 1936 the Communist Party outlawed psychoanalysis in the Soviet Union.[9] Spielrein herself probably perished in Stalin's purges in 1937. She left behind some thirty papers.[10]

So much for the contours of her life.

Spielrein's diary and letters, however, reveal that the Jung-Spielrein connection exceeded the boundary and propriety of the patient-physician relationship. All the available evidence suggests a passionate love affair between the two, almost certainly one that was consummated sexually. Jung was Spielrein's first love. He came to represent not only that indispensable person who had "cured" her, but also her "savior," "rescuer," her personal charismatic hero. She collaborated with Jung in his early papers on association. They shared a vast spectrum of interests, intellectual and emotional pursuits. Jung confided to her his own dreams during her therapeutic sessions; he requested that she read his intimate journal, and invited her to meet his wife and children in the Jung family circle. Since Jung's letters remain unpublished, we can only guess at the motives of his heirs. Cover-up seems likely. We may never know. The love affair with Spielrein clearly threatened Jung's professional career. It decisively shifted Freud's perception of him.

While it is impossible to date the precise beginnings of the affair, we know that it became public knowledge in 1909. In all probability Emma Jung, Jung's wife, wrote to Spielrein's mother in Russia bringing the salient facts out in the open. Soon after Spielrein wrote Freud informing him of the matter, requesting his advice and intercession. Jung then wrote a self-serving and malicious letter to Spielrein's mother, rationalizing his betrayal on the grounds that he was not paid a fee for his services. Payment, according to Jung's self-serving logic, and not some other moral or professional code, is what guaranteed an analyst's integrity, restraint, and respect for his patient. Instead of taking responsibility for his breach of clinical ethics, Jung claimed that money was the real issue and not his dubious behavior; and he urged Spielrein's mother to compensate him for his services. After reading this letter, and hearing Jung's corroboration of Spielrein's version, Freud revised his earlier opinions of both Spielrein and Jung, the latter his chosen successor. Freud stated that he had been "wrong" in automatically siding with Jung, "wrong" in misconstruing the facts to Spielrein's disadvantage, and pleased with Spielrein's maturity in resolving the disturbing intimacy with Jung.

Yet, Spielrein resolved her conflict with Jung in her own peculiar fashion. She stepped "between" Jung and Freud; that is, she became the self-appointed intermediary, attempting to conciliate the two systems, and promoting a rapprochement between the estranged thinkers after their split in 1913.

If words can describe Jung's behavior toward Spielrein, they are adjectives not verbs. The epithets shabby, disrespectful, inexcusable, and dishonest fit. Jung himself admitted being a scoundrel and a knave. Spielrein called Jung a "No-good." She felt used and abused by him, desiring to "forgive him or murder him." On one occasion she slapped Jung in the face, while threatening him with a knife. Carotenuto labels Jung's behavior a betrayal. He intimates that Jung may have been incapable of loving, that he had marked paranoid tendencies, and that he was opportunistically concerned with his professional reputation. Technically, he explains Jung's amorous involvement with his patient in terms of "psychotic countertransference," alleging that the analyst's emotional reaction to Spielrein triggered some "psychotic nuclei" in the Zurich psychiatrist.

In other passages, nonetheless, Carotenuto attributes Jung's errors to youth, inexperience, bad taste, exuberance, even his intuitive faculties. The account of Jung's irresistibility to women is circular: women found him "seductive" because of Jung's supposed "feminine" nature. By implication, Carotenuto manipulates us to forgive Jung, to remain conscious of fifty years of solid and creative contributions, and to recall Freud's immature blindspots; Carotenuto repeatedly compares the Spielrein affair with Freud's infatuation with cocaine.[11] Comparisons are always invidious. Carotenuto's analogies, however, are not persuasive; they work against holding Jung accountable for his actions.

To vilify Jung with accusations of bad faith is one thing, to offer a critical analysis is quite another. The documents reveal that the Spielrein matter came to light at a crucial historical conjuncture when relations between Freud and Jung began to deteriorate. Without rehashing the complex reasons for the Freud-Jung split,[12] we need to be aware that personal and theoretical differences converged to produce the rupture.

We know that Freud's Jewishness, the so-called "Jewish question," always operated in Freud's relations with Jung. Jung appeared an excellent choice to succeed Freud because he was a respectable Gentile; that is, Freud felt that this son of a Protestant Swiss pastor would help bring psychoanalysis a measure of legitimacy in the Christian world and visibility in the psychiatric universe. Under Jung's guidance, Freud hoped, psychoanalysis would exit from its ghetto-like seclusion, overcome the public's perception of its Jewishness, and hence become more widely diffused and accepted in medical and scientific circles. In short, resistance to the theory would not center around racial prejudice, specifically the Jewishness of the theory's founder and its chief practitioners.

After the rupture with Freud, Jung characterized psychoanalysis as a "Jewish psychology."[13] There is abundant, and I think irrefutable, evidence that Jung made anti-Jewish and pro-Nazi statements during the era of the Third Reich, asserting, for example, that the Jewish unconscious lacked the vitality, universalism, rootedness, and creative depths of the Germanic people. From 1934 to 1940, Jung served as editor of the National Socialist controlled *Zentralblatt fur Psychotherapie*, writing inflammatory letters against the "corrosive" nature of the Jewish point of view in psychology and castigating Freud for his "soulless materialism."[14]

The Spielrein documents illustrate that Jung's anti-Semitism played a critical and dissolving role in the Freud-Jung relationship, long before Hitler entered the historical stage.

As a "non-Jewish Jew"[15] who came into consciousness in anti-Semitic Vienna, Freud's Jewishness was an integral part of his subjective and professional identity. While not observing Jewish rites or believing in the religious theology, Freud never denied his Jewishness, never opted for strategies of assimilation, and never embraced any form of Jewish nationalism. Nor did he accept the anti-Semitic stereotypes of Jews that pervaded many strata of Viennese society and culture, including the university. For him, Jewishness was a metaphor for pride, for thinking rigorously and independently. In brief, being Jewish allowed Freud to think against himself and to risk thinking against the scientific and moral biases of his contemporaries. He also associated Jewishness with a vague kind of "ethical" consciousness, a commitment to honesty in human relations, to candor in the practice of the psychoanalytic dialogue. Jewishness, lastly, provided Freud with a limited sense of community and fraternity; despite his protestations about his unpopularity and isolation, certain Jewish colleagues made him feel understood and at home.[16]

During her liaison with Jung, Spielrein had a recurring fantasy of bearing Jung a son. She named the boy child Siegfried, picturing him to be some kind of Wagnerian hero, an Aryan conqueror. Siegfried would be the visible sign of the Jung-Spielrein union, the living symbol unifying the Aryan and Jewish souls. Siegfried also entered into the latent content of Spielrein's dreams.[17] From a Jungian slant, the dream could be interpreted synthetically, that is, that the great Aryan-Semitic hero might effectuate a lasting bond between Jung's typologies, his interests in parapsychology, and the occult with Freud's libido theory and his more clinically grounded psychological science.

Carotenuto quotes a fragment of a letter from Jung to Spielrein, dated September 1911, in which Jung stiffly and didactically advises his pupil how to court Freud in order to win his favor. I find the advice mocking and contemptuous of Freud: "Approach him as a great master and rabbi, and all will be well."[18] Spielrein took issue with several of Jung's anti-Jewish accusations in January 1918. As a Russian Jew with a rabbinical heritage, she was aware of the rich Jewish mystical and messianic tradition. Jung ought to know that Jewish spiritual life had existed for centuries and that it had a contemporary vibrancy; she also replied to Jung's reproach, so prototypically anti-Semitic, that the Jews were historically responsible for the murder of Christ. In defense of Freud, she asserted that he did not reduce all of man's activity to primitive instinctual wishes; nor did Freud's theories denigrate man's higher spiritual or artistic accomplishments, simply because he understood the roots of culture in the repression and sublimation of primitive urges.[19]

To be sure, Freud reacted more negatively to the Siegfried fantasy than did Jung. He instructed Spielrein to break her dependency on Jung by coming to Vienna and by entering into analysis with him. Even after her marriage, Spielrein remained pathologically attached to Jung, Freud thought, still victimized by her unanalyzed negative transferences to her former Swiss physician. This suggested self-hatred on her part, an unconscious masochistic identification with her anti-Semitic aggressor. When feeling threatened or enraged, Freud, too, proved unable to resist the vocabulary of the chosen people: "My wish is for you to be cured completely. I must confess, after the event, that your fantasies about the birth of the Savior to a mixed union did not appeal to me at all. The Lord, in that anti-Semitic period, had him born from the superior Jewish race. But I know these are my prejudices."[20] Freud repeatedly referred to Jung, nastily, in the letters to Spielrein as her "Germanic hero." Part of his hatred for Jung was associated with Jung's Aryan posturings and his racial arrogance; he unsubtly invited Spielrein to make the same choice as he had made: "I imagine that you love Dr. J. so deeply still because you have not brought to light the hatred he merits."[21]

Despite Freud's words, Spielrein clung to her poetic fantasy about generating a Siegfried. Upon learning of Spielrein's pregnancy, Freud attempted to shatter her Wagnerian notions with irony: "I am, as you know, cured of the last shred of my predilection for the Aryan cause, and would like to take it that if the child turns out to be a boy he will develop into a stalwart Zionist."[22] Only a fanatical Jewish nationalist, by implication, could combat a mythically hostile anti-Semite. As a psychoanalyst and as a Jew, Freud was convinced that one had to recognize and ultimately to sever ties with one's anti-Jewish enemies. He located Jung in the latter camp, asserting that Jung belonged there characterologically; nor should one engage the anti-Semites in scientific or logical dialogue. No wishful fantasy about a blond hero could re-recruit Jung to the psychoanalytic cause. Mixing nonrecognition, bitter resignation, reverse racism, and penetrating realism, Freud did not mince his words to Spielrein: "We are and remain Jews. The others will only exploit us and will never understand or appreciate us."[23]

After the birth of Spielrein's daughter, Freud's letter of congratulation mingled joy with anger: "Now we can think again about the blond

Siegfried and perhaps smash the idol before his time comes."[24] It is possible to read in Freud's last letter to Spielrein, dated 9 February 1923, supporting her move to Russia—"Lastly, you will be on home ground"[25]—a tacit approval of her return to her Jewish origins. Just as returning to Russia may have represented her way of liberating herself from her idealization of Jung, so it may have been her subjective way of accepting her Eastern European Jewish roots, culture, environment, and sense of self.

The Spielrein correspondence is not the only place where Freud denounced Jung's anti-Semitism. He once accused Jung of "lies, brutality, and anti-Semitic condescension towards me."[26] It may seem a bit excessive to accord so much importance to Jung's anti-Jewish opinions in his break with Freud. Spielrein, however, felt the issue to be quite central. Her stance "between" Freud and Jung, between "two stools," as Freud dubbed it, meant straddling different methods of theory, research, and clinical practice, but above all, divergent mental, political, and moral orientations.

Regarding splits, Freud took the position that in most instances reconciliations were unproductive. Adversaries had to be so designated, diluters had to be opposed, crude misinterpreters had to be jettisoned, or at least labeled vulgarizers. Freud's originality as a thinker, his strength as the founder of an international movement, partially consisted in his ability to name things that stare us in the face. Once he assigned names that made these things visible, their meaning could then be deciphered. He was against mediators if they significantly altered what was unique, especially if they made dissimilar things the same.

Spielrein's creativity was as such a mediator. She attempted to fuse opposites, to discount specificity, and to obscure difference, in order to achieve a union of psychological theories and techniques of analysis. Spielrein's strivings for integration may have derived from her inability to accept endings, her incapacity to tolerate permanent loss and separation. Equally important, however, was her need for affirmation. To counter the destructiveness she encountered in life, to offset Jung's personal sadism toward her, to balance the cruel sexual attraction of the anti-Semitic Jung for the beautiful and brilliant Jewess, to reverse the violation of their clinical and professional relationship, she created mythical linkages, an ecumenical vision, which nullified contradictions. Instead of succumbing to her own destructive wishes, instead of floundering in the morass of Jung's deceit, she became fascinated by the symmetries between Jung and Freud, disregarded the asymmetries, inventing in the process a language of harmony and unity. Who knows if, in the long run, Spielrein's thrust toward wholeness may have born fruit?

Notes

1   Aldo Carotenuto, ed., *A Secret Symmetry: Sabina Spielrein Between Jung and Freud* (New York, 1982), translated by Arno Pomerans, John Shepley, and Krishna Wisston.

2   D.M. Thomas, *The White Hotel* (New York, 1981); Thomas published a review of *A Secret Symmetry* in *The New York Review of Books*, 13 May 1981, p. 3 commenting on the similarities between his fictional character Lisa Erdman and Sabina Spielrein.

3   Bruno Bettelheim, "Commentary," in Aldo Carotenuto, ed., *A Secret Symmetry* (New York, 1984), paperback edition, pp. xv-xxxix. This was first published in *The New York Review of Books* in 1983.

4   Sabina Spielrein, "Uben den psychologischen Inholt eines Falles von Schizophrenie (Dementia Praecox)," *Jahrbuch für psychoanalytische und psychopathologische Forschugen*, 3 (1911), pp. 329-400.

5   Sabina Spielrein, "Die Destruktion als Ursache des Werdens, ibid., 4 (1912), pp. 465-503.

6   Sigmund Freud, *Beyond the Pleasure Principle* (1920), in *The Standard Edition of the Complete Psychological Works of Sigmund Freud*, vol. 18; see the essay by John Kerr, "Beyond the Pleasure Principle and Back Again: Freud, Jung, and Sabina Spielrein," in Paul E. Stepansky, ed., *Freud: Appraisals and Reappraisals* (Hillsdale, New Jersey, 1988), vol. 3, pp. 3-79 for an attempt to sort out the personal and theoretical entanglements around the origins of the concept of the death instinct.

7   Sabina Spielrein, "Die Entstehung der kindlichen Worte Papa und Mama," *Imago*, 8 (1922), pp. 345-367.

8   Sabina Spielrein, "Kinderzeichnungen bei offenen und geschlossenen Augen," *Imago*, 16 (1931), pp. 259-291.

9   For material on the history of the psychoanalytic movement in the Soviet Union, see Jean-Michel Palmier, "La Psychanalyse en Union Soviétique," in Roland Jaccard, ed., *Histoire de la psychanalyse* (Paris, 1982), pp. 187-235.

10   For a complete list of her known publications, see "Writings of Sabina Spielrein," in Carotenuto, *A Secret Symmetry*, pp. 238-239.

11   Aldo Carotenuto, "The Story of Sabina Spielrein," ibid., pp. 154, 159-161, 167-169, 171, 174-175, 213-214.

12   Peter Gay, *Freud: A Life for Our Time* (New York, 1988), pp. 225-243; Linda Dorn, *Freud and Jung: Years of Friendship, Years of Loss* (New York, 1988), pp. 8, 15, 22-23, 73-74, 87-88, 122, 174.

13   Letter, Carl Gustav Jung to C.E. Berda, 19 June 1934, cited in Ronald W. Clark,

Freud: The Man and The Cause (New York, 1980), p. 494.

14   Geoffrey Cocks, *Psychotherapy in the Third Reich: The Goring Institute* (New York, 1985), pp. 127-135.

15   Isaac Deutscher, "The Non-Jewish Jew" (1958), in Deutscher, *The Non Jewish Jew and Other Essays* (London, 1968), pp. 25-41.

16   See Freud's letter to the Members of the B'nai B'rith Lodge, 6 May 1926, in Ernst L. Freud, ed., *The Letters of Sigmund Freud* (New York, 1960), translated by Tania and James Stern, pp. 366-367.

17   See "The Diary of Sabina Spielrein," in Carotenuto, *A Secret Symmetry*, pp. 21-24.

18   Letter, Jung to Spielrein, 21-22 September 1911, cited in ibid., p. 182.

19   Letter, Spielrein to Jung, 27-28 January 1918, ibid., pp. 82-86.

20   Letter, Freud to Spielrein, 20 August 1912, ibid., pp. 116-117.

21   Letter, Freud to Spielrein, 8 May 1913, ibid., p. 120.

22   Letter, Freud to Spielrein, 28 August 1913, ibid., p. 120.

23   Ibid., p. 121.

24   Letter, Freud to Spielrein, 29 September 1913, ibid., p. 121.

25   Letter, Freud to Spielrein, 9 February 1923, ibid., p. 127.

26   Letter, Freud to James Jackson Putnam, 8 July 1915, in *James Jackson Putnam and Psychoanalysis* (Cambridge, 1971), edited by Nathan G. Hale, Jr., p. 189.

4

Psychoanalysis and Engagement: Otto
Fenichel and the Political Freudians

In psychoanalysis nothing is true except the exaggerations.
—Theodor W. Adorno

Russell Jacoby's exceptionally well-written essay, *The Repression of Psychoanalysis—Otto Fenichel and the Political Freudians* (1983), is a study of psychoanalysis and political engagement. His research centers on Otto Fenichel (1897-1946) and a circle of friends who first clustered around him in Berlin, who were then dispersed by the rise of fascism and the coming of the Second World War. Several in the circle emigrated to America. These seven colleagues (Annie Reich, Edith Jacobson, Kate Friedländer, George Gero, Barbara Lantos, Edith Gyömröi, and possibly Berta Bornstein) shared a number of things in common besides being born around 1900; these cohorts represented the second generation of European psychoanalysis. As young men and women, they were marked by the Great War and came into consciousness during a period of postwar social revolution and repression, economic dislocation, and the clash of mass movements on the left and the right. Their early years were decisively colored by radical youth movements, leftwing politics, the early inspiration of the

Russian Revolution, a serious immersion in Marxist culture, a commitment to either Socialist or Communist parties, and a desire to integrate classical psychoanalysis into a broader framework of Marxist social theorizing.

Jacoby undermines the conventional picture of Fenichel as simply an outstanding and prolific contributor to "mainline" psychoanalysis. He forces us to reconsider the legacy of the mainline. The "big" Fenichel, *The Psychoanalytic Theory of Neurosis* (1945), served as an encyclopedic and reliable compendium to analysts for twenty to twenty-five years after its publication.[1] The "little" Fenichel, *Problems of Psychoanalytic Technique* (1941), set forth guiding principles for a theory of psychoanalytic therapy;[2] it surpasses anything that Freud ever ventured to do, namely, to collect all of his thoughts about technique into a single unified text. Both of Fenichel's books are balanced and sensible; both refuse either a biological or cultural reductionism; both cling to instinctual drive theory and indicate Fenichel's deep attachment to Freud and to his early training at the Vienna Psychoanalytic Society. However, Fenichel's *engagé* past, his radical politics, and his devotion to a vast project of psychoanalytic social theorizing have been forgotten, or dimly remembered. Jacoby not only rehabilitates Fenichel, but also retrieves a lost chapter in psychoanalytic history. The extinction of a political psychoanalysis within a Marxist epistemological framework, he claims, has led to a decline of American psychoanalysis, resulting in a loss of health for the psychoanalytic enterprise.

Jacoby has mastered a sophisticated version of the Frankfurt School's method of social analysis.[3] He blends a classical Freudian psychoanalysis with a nondogmatic, Hegelian version of Marxism. Jacoby's main preoccupation is with memory, with the social repercussions of forgetting. Just as he has no mercy for conformist forms of nonpsychoanalytic psychology, so, too, does his Marxism contain a denunciation of mindless leftist posturing, an impatience with the banalities of Leninism, and a polemical contempt for the pieties and infantile aspects of vulgar Marxism. *The Repression of Psychoanalysis*, like his earlier books, *Social Amnesia* (1975)[4] and *The Dialectic of Defeat* (1981),[5] demonstrate Jacoby's proficiency in critical theory. His books are exercises in the power of the negative dialectic. To read Jacoby is to confront the revolutionary, even the dangerous, aspects of reason. He has a dissolving approach to fixed ideas. He demystifies received forms of knowledge, especially those officially sanctioned by internationalists or by academics. Jacoby offers a view of the totality which unites apparently separate fields of human activity and which intersects different universes of discourse. As a social critic deliberately addressing a wide literate audience, Jacoby's prose sparkles. He wastes no words. As a stylist, he surpasses his German born mentors, Herbert Marcuse, Karl Korsch, and Theodor W. Adorno, in his mastery of English prose and in his deft, frequently felicitous, handling of abstract ideas. He is a Hegelian with a sense of humor. That alone would make him a wonderful read; his humor is dry, deadpan, ironic. If his style is corrosive, his manner of addressing his public is polemical, which will not be to everyone's taste.

Jacoby is impassioned about his subject and he wages war for the sake of ideas and their consequences. His foray into the history of the psychoanalytic movement is done in order to extrapolate the revolutionary spirit and content of those who lived this history. He writes about psychoanalytic commitment from a committed vantage point. But his revolutionary enthusiasms work neither to idealize nor sentimentalize the past. Compared to the inoffensive judiciousness and party-line perspective of official narratives, Jacoby's essay is a refreshing contrast. His impassioned history also vividly contrasts with the widespread apathy in and around psychoanalytic institutes in contemporary America, an indifference best exemplified by a loss of serious interest in their own history, in their political and philosophical foundations, and by a demonstrable inability to criticize themselves constructively. Jacoby, incidentally, also joins a group of first-rate researchers denied access to the Freud Archives by Kurt Eissler.

In tracing Fenichel's itinerary, Jacoby brings alive a nearly forgotten generation of European psychoanalysts who were also radical humanists and nonconformists; they were deeply influenced by a Central European Marxist tradition of social theorizing. Psychoanalytic culture in the period between the wars was inseparable from an intellectual and political milieu saturated by leftwing social movements and ideologies. To be a psychoanalyst in this era was to be a progressive, a freethinker, a maverick, and a renegade. Moreover, Fenichel and his circle were not dismissed as alienated outsiders, peripheral to any significant movement. They were insiders, well trained and respected within the classical psychoanalytic community. Fenichel presented his first paper before the Vienna Psychoanalytic Society in the early 1920s. Members of his circle were esteemed as teachers and supervisors; they were clinically astute; figures like Edith Jacobson and Annie Reich conducted research and made important contributions to psychoanalytic literature. Jacoby depicts his protagonist as a well-educated, highly cultivated Central European intellectual. Psychoanalysis appealed to Fenichel and his circle because it challenged received scientific and philosophic ideas; psychoanalytic theory and methodology oriented them to an increasingly disoriented world. Moreover, psychoanalysis was irreverent. It was critical. They came to psychoanalysis as dissenters, hoping to preserve and revitalize a leftwing political tradition within classical psychoanalytic parameters.

Jacoby's sketch of Fenichel catches the exuberance and obsessional qualities of the man; the portrait is all too brief, one wishes he could have extended it into a full intellectual biography. Fenichel's mania for lists and remembering went with a spontaneous zest for living, traveling, joking, and communicating with others. He was an omnivorous reader. He was both a brilliant lecturer and a good listener. If he loved compiling the works of others, he also had a taste for poetry and an admiration for Rilke. Another typical product of *fin-de-siècle* Vienna,[6] Fenichel's identification with high German culture did not mean an antidemocratic contempt for the masses and for the economically and culturally deprived; nor did it result in a rejection of his Jewish cultural heritage or a sense of himself as a Jew. With his prodigious capacity to work, his impressive memory, his love of many branches of learning, his introspective discipline, Fenichel's clinical work was careful and empathic. Not an original or innovative thinker, he was more gifted in synthesizing the work of others than in staking out new directions of his own.

He refused to separate Freudian individual psychology from an understanding of history and social structure. Knowing and changing oneself, he insisted, had to occur alongside of revolutionizing society. Marx and Freud had to complement one another; Marx provided a methodological key to understanding social relations and Freud to the dimensions of subjectivity and the inner world. Fenichel's devotion to a social psychoanalysis sprang from a youthful rebelliousness, an interest in the subversive aspects of sexuality and the unconscious, which was never quite extinguished prior to his exile. Nor was he a reclusive scholarly type; Jacoby describes his character style as active, quite the opposite of deferential or ivory tower. He spoke up often, identified himself with unpopular causes, such as defending the theories of Wilhelm Reich. He was not one to bow to official authority out of reverence for hierarchy, age, or expediency.

Jacoby dramatically tracks Fenichel's move from Vienna to Berlin in 1922; his exile to Oslo in 1933; then on to Prague in 1935 and to Los Angeles his final destination in 1938. His great archival discovery is the *Rundbriefe*, 119 circular letters, written during Fenichel's exile for eleven and one-half years from 1934 to 1945. They averaged fifteen to twenty-five typewritten pages; the last was composed on Bastille Day, 1945. These letters were simultaneously mailed to at least six other analysts who constituted a secret opposition to the apolitical or conservative psychoanalytic establishment.

The Fenichel circle was decisively influenced by the educational climate and exuberance of the Berlin Psychoanalytic Institute in the 1920s, in addition to the explosive political and cultural ambience of Weimar Germany. With Karl Abraham dead in 1926, the Berlin Psychoanalytic Institute lacked a master thinker on a par with Freud. Freud's fatherly presence in Vienna led to more internal cohesiveness and apparently more conservatism, permitting creative departures in the fields of child and adolescent analysis and theoretical developments in ego psychology, all of which occurred in the Viennese group without necessitating a split or acrimonious quarrels. In contrast, Weimar Berlin was marked by social and cultural openness, by deep political conflicts, and by the rapid polarization of communist and fascist mass movements; within psychoanalysis there was experimentation in education, a clear civic spirit, and a desire to develop forms of psychoanalytic therapy for the economically disadvantaged. Lay analysis was encouraged, even promoted. Subsequent psychoanalytic "heresies" originated in Berlin; one has only to mention the names of Karen Horney, Melanie Klein, and Franz Alexander to sense the diversity of the Berlin group. Ernst Simmel, a subsequent founder of the Los Angeles Psychoanalytic Society, was a Berlin Socialist physician who established the first psychoanalytic sanatorium, the Schloss Tegel, occasionally visited by Freud. The recipients of Fenichel's circular letters originally formed a study group outside of formal seminars at the Berlin Psychoanalytic Institute, calling themselves, perhaps ironically, the Children's Seminar. In rejecting the formality, authoritarianism, and pyramidal structure of the Institute, they constituted themselves as a left-leaning, informal, democratic, antifascist, and rebellious group, generating a good deal of camaraderie toward one another.

Fenichel gravitated toward German communism, as did his colleague Wilhelm Reich. He had clear sympathies for the Russian Revolution until 1932, visited the USSR several times, and publicly lectured on the relationship between psychoanalysis and socialism. According to Jacoby, Fenichel was well versed in a conventional or ordinary, political Marxism characteristic of the 1930s.[7] What appealed to Fenichel about Marxism was its scientific rigor and rational method; its sociology provided a critical theory of society and history that was absent in psychoanalytic theory. If psychoanalytic therapy could help isolated individuals to lead less unhappy lives, the psychoanalytic practitioner was powerless to effect radical social change.

Fenichel and his circle were both personally and intellectually stimulated by Wilhelm Reich, particularly his contributions to psychoanalytic theory and technique in the late 1920s and early 1930s, that is, the period of Reich's greatest creativity. Jacoby's handling of the Fenichel-Reich encounter is sensitive and informed but not uncritical. He avoids almost all of the inevitable cliches in any discussion of Reich. Fenichel, the documents reveal, largely agreed with Reich's Marxism, and defended him both openly and behind the scenes. The circle agreed with the core of Reich's work and his development of a systematic approach to psychoanalytic interpretations and the analysis of resistances, as outlined in the first edition of *Character Analysis* (1933).[8] By 1933, effective dialogue with Reich proved impossible (Annie Reich's marriage with him ended sometime in 1933, and she remained within Fenichel's circle).

Reich demanded that one agree with him even to the point of exclusion from the International Psychoanalytic Association (Reich was expelled from both the Communist Party and the International Psychoanalytic Association in 1934).[9] If they appreciated Reich's originality and potency as a theorist, they refused to accept his personal dogmatism and his mental instability. They welcomed his major contributions, especially the brilliant *Mass Psychology of Fascism* (1933),[10] while distancing themselves from Reich's sexual reductionism and oversimplifications. Technically, Fenichel opposed Reich's demand to shatter the patient's defensive armor as overly aggressive. He disagreed with Reich's tendency to precipitate false crises in the analytic situation by his histrionic interventions, often resulting in nontherapeutic "eruptions."[11]

Fascism and exile shattered the lives and commitments of the political Freudians. Reich's destiny also haunted them. Fenichel and his circle, Jacoby argues, never recovered from their expulsion from Central Europe. They refused to risk censorship or exclusion by the International Psychoanalytic Association. As the European world of their youth crumbled, their subsequent arrival in America resulted not only in a conceptual retreat and conservatism, but also in a turning inward, that is, a "repression" and even a "self-repression" of their pasts and leftwing identities. In fitting in, in achieving personal successes as immigrants, in reestablishing their psychoanalytic careers, they remained a secret opposition until Fenichel's death. Many made brilliant careers in America and England. However, they generated no students, transmitting little of their left-Freudian history or legacy. The Americanization of the Fenichel circle was nothing less than a "cultural defeat," that is, a retreat from public issues and from the public forum. It necessitated burying their own past. As psychoanalytic culture divorced itself from a progressive or Marxist underpinning, it suffered a theoretical retreat, becoming vaporized and prettified. In America, the Fenichel circle defended a classical version of psychoanalysis, while surrendering a political psychoanalysis.

Once in America, Fenichel discovered a political culture and a psychoanalytic setting utterly different from Europe. If fascism ruptured the political continuum in their lives, exile further estranged them from their efforts to synthesize Marx and Freud. As insecure immigrant analysts, triply tainted for being psychoanalysts, Marxists, and Jews, they opted for caution. Here Jacoby shifts gears, abandons his intellectual portrait of Fenichel, and analyzes the impact of America and of American psychoanalysis on his generation of political Freudians.

Jacoby focuses on four features of American life which contributed to the cautiousness, silence, and ultimately the collusion of the Fenichel circle in "repressing" their own European version of a political psychoanalysis: medicalization, Americanization, neo-Freudianism, and anti-Marxism.

By 1938, the American Psychoanalytic Association banned the further training of nonmedical, or lay analysts. Psychoanalysis in America, contrary to Freud's unequivocal position on the matter, became a medical specialty.[12] With the triumph of medicalization, Jacoby argues, there came an accompanying theoretical banalization. Clinical concerns and the vicissitudes of carrying on a successful private practice took precedence over research and a commitment to the subversive aspects of psychoanalytic forms of thinking. Not only did the therapy overwhelm the science, but admissions into analytic training became restricted and bureaucratized. Official American psychoanalysis became a private club with a snobbish and elitist mentality; it provided only limited entry to women, humanists, dissenters, and freethinkers. Jacoby holds that professionalization was inextricably tied to regulation and containment; by preselecting the available pool of candidates to be physicians, the future of American psychoanalysis promised to be dominated by "conventional and conservative" doctors. The medical-psychiatric underpinning also penetrated into the main body of psychoanalytic literature. A heavy, jargon ridden, technical prose replaced the accessible, personal, imaginative, and metaphoric aspects of Freud's writings. Moreover, the straining for "scientific" legitimacy did not generate a respected body of scientific knowledge and replicable research. Instead, it produced an affluent subclass of unimaginative and mediocre specialists who smugly treated an increasingly affluent clientele.

By Americanization, Jacoby is referring to a cultural process by which psychoanalysis became absorbed into peculiarly American institutions and patterns of thinking. For him, Americanization is tantamount to trivialization. Once refracted through American culture, psychoanalytic theory and practice lost its rebellious edge, its orientation toward questioning, its function as a general theory of civilization. What replaced it was a pragmatic, deeply anti-intellectual, impoverished and conformist psychoanalysis—a psychoanalysis which was ultimately narrow, conventional, and conservative, compared to its European predecessor.

The neo-Freudians raised and subsequently dashed the hopes of the Fenichel circle. Erich Fromm, Karen Horney, and Clara Thompson did not mask their social and cultural radicalism nor their opposition to biological reductionism. Fenichel was unable to join the ranks of the neo-Freudians because of their abandonment of instinctual drive theory. Against the neo-Freudians, Fenichel held that psychoanalysis as a critical theory could not surrender its grasp of sexuality and of unconscious process. (Fenichel appeared to reject the late Freud's postulation of a death instinct as "a complete biologization of neuroses.")[13] Freudian orthodoxy in matters of psychoanalytic technique remained more radical, he thought, than those attempting to introduce modifications and reforms in clinical practice; he opposed, for example, Ferenczi's advocacy of more affection and less abstinence and neutrality on the part of the analyst in the analytic situation. Fenichel urged a balance of empathy and insight. The analyst's emotional closeness to the analysand required some distance to maximize the interpretative process. Either/or thinking was anathema to him. Psychoanalytic investigation had to situate itself on an interface where individual subjective experience and early childhood development converged with a specific family and social framework; it could not be oblivious to reality considerations. In America, Fenichel found himself in the paradoxical position of siding with the psychoanalytic conservatives against the neo-Freudians, while disagreeing with the classical psychoanalytic closemindedness about Marxist critical theory. Fenichel himself was claimed by neither faction and never felt at home among the neo-Freudians or the orthodox.

That America in the later 1930s and early 1940s was anti-Marxist does not require further discussion. Communists or fellow travelers were depreciated as "premature antifascists." Fenichel and his circle effectively covered up their radical pasts in such an ambience. The counterpolitical context of America, the absence of a viable Socialist Party or mass movement on the left, led inevitably to a deculturing of classical European psychoanalysis where such movements existed and often provided the cultural context and intellectual vitality of psychoanalytic work. In order to survive in America, Fenichel and his circle censored their own legacy and remained silent about their Marxist commitments. Silence, contends Jacoby, guaranteed that the opposition would remain secret, but more injuriously, that it would generate no students, produce no tradition, and transmit no existing body of literature to posterity. Jacoby implies that the Fenichel group was self-serving; they opportunistically veiled their radical pasts while making successful careers in America. In promoting psychoanalysis as an isolated technical, clinical discipline, they inadvertently contributed to a domestication of American psychoanalysis.

Ernst Simmel had preceded Fenichel to California in 1934. A Psychoanalytic Study Group was founded, largely under his direction. A crucial feature of the Study Group, formalized in 1946 into the Los Angeles Psychoanalytic Society, was the favorable reception offered to lay analysts. In point of fact Simmel and Fenichel, despite having earned their medical degrees in Europe, were designated nonmedical because of a California law on the licensing of medical practitioners. Out of loyalty to Freud and out of profound conviction, Fenichel and his circle openly advocated and sponsored lay analysis. The key figures in the early years of psychoanalysis in Los Angeles were nonmedical analysts, many of whom were trained in Europe, a number of whom were analyzed by Freud and his leading disciples. People like David Brunswick (who translated Fenichel's technique book), Frances Deri, and Hanna Fenichel, Fenichel's wife, were regarded as the leading theoretical minds and clinicians in the early history of the Los Angeles Psychoanalytic Institute. Moreover, the primacy of a medical and psychiatric orientation for psychoanalysis became the pivotal issue in the 1950 split in Los Angeles; the new group reconstituted itself as the Society for Psychoanalytic Medicine of Southern California, accentuating the importance of its "medical" identity and thereby indicating its rupture with the European version of classical psychoanalysis.

Jacoby writes as a professional critic of professionalization; he is an American critic of Americanization with a European bias. In unmasking the embourgeoisement of American psychoanalysis, he points to the loss of its rebelliousness, its creativity, and its extinction of original thinking. It is not my intention to dispute his perception of the acculturation of psychoanalysis in America. There are a number of issues, however, which I would like to dispute, and which call for further research and critical exploration.

Jacoby's analysis of Americanization, while trendy, lacks an explanatory edge to it. For him (and other writers in the lineage of the Frankfurt School), America is the land of the conventional, the consensus mentality, the antitheoretical, the vulgarly pragmatic. America, in short, is considered a second-rate culture and an inferior ideological climate. Hence Americanization always represents a leveling down. (Freud, incidentally, might have agreed with these disdainful sentiments.[14]) The strength of such a view is problematic, given its tautological structure and simple-mindedness.

Likewise, Fenichel's revolutionary activity remains cloudy; he was a revolutionary intellectual, a reflective and scholarly man, not someone who had the time, energy, or inclination to be a party militant, or to participate in demonstrations and forms of leftwing political activism or agitation. Jacoby never nails down the specific limits of Fenichel's political practice, even in the openly Marxist phase of life.

It is unhistorical and probably erroneous to suggest that an indigenous radicalism did not exist within the framework of American psychiatry or American psychoanalysis in the late 1930s and 1940s. To be sure, these radicals represented a minority; except for the isolated Communists, their theoretical leanings owed less to Marx than to nonconformist, romantic, and antiauthoritarian forms of thinking. There were Freudo-Marxists clustered around the psychoanalytic journal, *American Imago*, unmentioned by Jacoby, and certainly deserving of some detailed research (as is the life and work of its editor, Harry Slochower).[15] Similarly, there were East Coast analysts who read, were influenced by, and contributed to The *Partisan Review* in its heyday.[16] Fenichel and his circle most probably revised their commitments to Marxism in the light of Stalin's excesses; their shift in America may reflect a disillusionment with and a reassessment of authoritarian socialism in the Soviet Union as a result of the Moscow Purge Trials of 1936-37 and the Nazi-Soviet Pact of 1939. Jacoby overlooks the possibility that the ideological and utopian aspects of Marxism in the 1920s and 1930s may no longer have made sense in the Stalinist period, nor fit into an American political and cultural context, where struggle revolved more on a conservative versus liberal axis. It remains unclear how much this circle retained of Marxism as a critical method of inquiry.

In documenting and evaluating Fenichel's "repression," Jacoby's thesis is inaccurate; his title unnecessarily impugns the integrity of this generation of European psychoanalysts. Their motives for not disclosing their personal and political histories were complex. To suggest that they consciously suppressed their history is to argue that they were cowards, that they acted in bad faith. This is a resurrection of the "sellout" notion, current in the discourse of cultural criticism in the 1960s. It lacks foundation.

The harsh and insensitive notion of self-repression by the political Freudians overlooks a number of crucial factors about Fenichel and his lifelong commitments. Jacoby misses the obvious continuities in Fenichel's life. Psychoanalysis for him was the very air he breathed. It was simultaneously a practice and a theory, not an immersion in theoretical activity for the sake of theory building. His self-esteem and identity, both in Europe and in America, turned on a concept of himself as a practitioner and theoretician of psychoanalysis. His creativity demanded that he remained tied to Freud, that he not break with the International Psychoanalytic Association, and that he achieve some measure of recognition from the American branch of psychoanalysis. The comparison with Reich here is glaring. Jacoby's high estimation of European theory building glosses over, debunks, practical considerations. Fenichel attempted to integrate the tradition of European psychoanalytic abstraction and speculation into clinical practice and into teaching and transmitting the discipline. Jacoby's criticism moves in the direction of restoring the split, of maintaining the divorce, of theoretical work from clinical application, which was antithetical to Fenichel's assumptions. Because his orientation is philosophical, Jacoby overlooks the fact that Fenichel practiced psychoanalysis to help real people understand and change specifically painful situations in their lives.

Fenichel's position on the relationship between psychoanalysis and politics remained closer to the classical psychoanalytic ethic than to the Marxist one. For this generation, the liberal, individualistic, humanistic foundations of psychoanalysis served as an ideological frame, limiting certain forms of commitment, even if one's sympathies were for revolutionary groups and activities. That ethic precluded the intrusion of politics into clinical work, as well as into supervision, teaching, and theory building. The political tastes and concerns of a given psychoanalyst had to be separated from his practical activity, but certainly they could find expression in public forums as a responsible citizen. Fenichel remained less interested in the politicization of psychoanalysis than Jacoby would have liked. He focused on theoretical and practical solutions to clinical dilemmas rather than on issues of intellectual hegemony, succession of power in local psychoanalytic institutes, the jockeying for control of a given group, or establishing a group's domination over competing groups (such as the neo-Freudians.) Fenichel may have discovered that the politicization of psychoanalysis (such as in local splits or in conflicts with the American Psychoanalytic Association), was exhausting and deflecting; it almost always revived petty conflicts which have little clinical or theoretical importance.

In conclusion, Jacoby might have remembered that psychoanalysis itself is engagement. This engagement is far more subtle than the possibilities entailed in understanding and changing modern society, root and branch. Psychoanalytic engagement is nevertheless a form of thinking and acting along deep structural levels, despite being conducted in a highly private domain of exploration. If there is nothing in the psychoanalytic ethic to prevent the clinician from having political opinions and from maintaining visibility on the public scene, there is always a question about the degree and relativity of the analyst's concrete political practice. Fenichel and his circle understood, perhaps agonized over, the necessity to remain neutral, impartial, and enigmatic personalities in their analytic stance, in order to gain deeper access to the patient's unconscious. The politicization of the analytic situation, or the highly public visibility of the analyst, inhibits the patient's freedom and possibilities for liberation, if they need to think of their analyst as either an identifiable figure on the left or the right. Jacoby is critically astute in seeing the current embourgeoisement of American psychoanalysis as a cultural malaise, which is also inevitably a political malaise. He does not grasp that Fenichel and his circle also appreciated this malaise, struggled against it, while fitting into an American milieu not entirely of their making, and remaining psychoanalytically engaged in their own fashion.

Notes

1   Otto Fenichel, *The Psychoanalytic Theory of Neurosis* (New York, 1945).
2   Otto Fenichel, *Problems of Psychoanalytic Technique* (Albany, New York,

1941), translated by David Burnswick. See also Fenichel, "Concerning the Theory of Psychoanalytic Technique" (1935), in *The Evolution of Psychoanalytic Technique*, M. Bergmann and F. Hartman, eds. (New York, 1976), pp. 448-465.

3 The best introduction to the Frankfurt School is Martin Jay's *The Dialectical Imagination: A History of the Frankfurt School and the Institute of Social Research 1923-1950* (Boston, 1973), especially pp. 86-112.

4 Russell Jacoby, *Social Amnesia: A Critique of Psychology from Adler to Laing* (Boston, 1975).

5 Russell Jacoby, *Dialectic of Defeat: Contours of Western Marxism* (New York, 1981).

6 See Carl E. Schorske, *Fin-de-Siècle Vienna: Politics and Culture* (New York, 1980).

7 For the distinction between ordinary and intellectual Marxism, see Daniel Lindenberg, *Le marxisme introuvable* (Paris, 1975).

8 Wilhelm Reich, *Character Analysis* (1933), 3rd ed. (New York, 1972); for a collection of Reich's early papers attempting to synthesize Marx and Freud, see *Sex-Pol Essays, 1929-1934*, Lee Baxandall, editor (New York, 1972), translated by Anna Bostock, Tom DuBose and Lee Baxandall.

9 On Reich's exclusions from the two internationals, see Myron Sharaf, *Fury on Earth: A Biography of Wilhelm Reich* (New York, 1983), pp. 166-203.

10 Wilhelm Reich, *Mass Psychology of Fascism* (1933), New York, 1970, translated by Vincent R. Carfagno.

11 Fenichel, *Problems of Psychoanalytic Technique*, p. 105.

12 On the Americanization of psychoanalysis, see Nathan G. Hale, *Freud and the Americans* (New York, 1971); Hale, "From Berggasse XIX to Central Park West: The Americanization of Psychoanalysis, 1919-1940," *Journal of the History of Behavioral Sciences*, 14, 1978.

13 Fenichel, "A Critique of the Death Instinct," *Collected Papers* (New York, 1953), pp. 370-371.

14 Sigmund Freud, *Civilization and Its Discontents* (1930), *The Standard Edition of the Complete Psychological Works of Sigmund Freud*, vol. 21 (London, 1961), p. 116.

15 Harry Slochower, *No Voice is Really Lost* (New York, 1945), reissued as *Literature and Philosophy Between Two World Wars* (New York, 1964), particularly pp. 309-318, also see, "The Publications of Harry Slochower," in *Myth, Creativity, Psychoanalysis: Essays in Honor of Harry Slochower* (Detroit, 1978), Maynard Solomon, editor, pp. 215-220.

16 A good place to begin would be the anthology edited by Edith Kurzweil and William Phillips, *Literature and Psychoanalysis* (New York, 1983).

Part II

Psychoanalytic Culture Criticism

5

Reading Freud's *Civilization and Its Discontents*

Your letter of December 5, 1927 containing your remarks about a feeling you describe as "oceanic" has left me no peace.

—Freud to Romain Rolland,
14 July 1929

I can at least listen without indignation to the critic who is of the opinion that when one surveys the aims of cultural endeavor and the means it employs, one is bound to come to the conclusion that the whole effort is not worth the trouble, and that the outcome of it can only be a state of affairs which the individual will be unable to tolerate. My impartiality is made all the easier to me by my knowing very little about all these things.

—Freud, *Civilization and Its Discontents*

Civilization and Its Discontents can be viewed as a starting point for the student of modern Western cultural and intellectual history. This relaxed, imaginative, and discursive essay combines tightly reasoned passages with lyrical flights, speculative leaps with qualifying statements, literary with nonliterary forms of writing. The text also contains some dead ends, some nonsense, and some anachronistic and problematic assertions, which can be jettisoned or radically revised without damaging the richness of the essay. The art of reading Freud is not to take every word as revealed truth; let us follow his insistence on analytic interpretation and on desacralization by viewing his own works in a critical spirit.

Foucault has asserted that Freud began the modern medical and psychological dialogue with unreason; he accomplished this linguistic breakthrough by systematically investigating the physician-patient relationship.[1] Freud was also an "initiator of discourse"[2] on society and culture, employing psychoanalytic perspectives to diagnose the psychological roots of cultural trends, to unearth archaic patterns in "civilized" behavior, and to illuminate the relationship of the individual to society.

In *Civilization and Its Discontents*, we confront an author who writes without precautions, sometimes without apparent transitions, who leaves things out, and who does not always explain his premises.[3] His narrative structure is not linear or focused around one central theme.[4] This places a burden on the reader. To comprehend these absences, these nonlogical juxtapositions, the mixed nature of the style, to grasp the multiple meanings of the text, the reader is well advised to be familiar with psychoanalytic theory, to have a knowledge of Freud's revolutionary works, including the seminal books on dreams, infantile sexuality, jokes, the psychopathology of everyday life, and the case studies, in addition to his social, anthropological, and religious writings. Knowledge of Freud's correspondence, his biography, and the political and cultural history of his era help to situate him and this text in its historical framework.

Psychoanalysis focuses on intrapsychic conflict. Freud conceptualized the mind in dualisms, in binary opposites. I have used the method of deciphering contradictory forces or themes to understand the structure and hidden components of *Civilization and Its Discontents*. Unraveling these oppositions enables the reader to see invisible connections in the text, thus assisting him in making mediations and filling in the gaps between manifest and latent relationships that Freud only hints at.

In this paper I shall discuss the various strategies Freud employs in coming to grips with Romain Rolland's postulation of the "oceanic sensation." I will map out and explain Freud's appeal to his audience and his rhetorical maneuvers in chapter 1 of *Civilization and Its Discontents*; his alternation between a polemical, defensive, and disputatious voice, and one that indicates his warmth, vulnerability, modesty, erudition, and creative audacity. I will examine his mixed feelings; his theoretical and speculative passages that link the oceanic feeling to narcissism; his use of jokes, irony, literary devices, quotations, and humor to evade the issue; and his imaginative but abortive attempt to set up explanatory analogies from other disciplines. The creative ambiguity of Freud's thought will be accounted for in terms of his tolerance for his own theoretical inconsistencies and gaps in knowledge or method; that is, his own certainties coexisted with undecidability and plurality of meaning.

Freud's introduction of Romain Rolland, particularly in chapter 1 but also throughout the text, allows him to scrutinize culture from a highly subjective point of view, in addition to one which appears disinterested. I will indicate how Rolland figures in Freud's analysis of the Judeo-Christian commandment "Love thy neighbor," how one can extend psychoanalytic cultural criticism to see the oceanic sensation as a reaction-formation, a benign desire for unity disguising the sadistic wish for the total annihilation of mankind. I will show the way Freud's ambivalence toward Rolland takes the form of bipolar oppositions in the text: Freud sees Rolland's world view as prophetic and saintly but poses psychoanalysis as a therapeutic tool and an instrument to desacralize religious and mystical modes of thinking. Rolland is present throughout the text as Freud's Double and Other, an object of irresistible attraction and aversion, someone with whom Freud is deeply identified and from whom he felt unalterably different. Rolland simultaneously represents the achievements of Western civilization and the dangers of excessive sublimation. In short, Freud condenses his ambivalent feelings for the French writer into his meditations on civilization as a whole. I view the addition of three footnotes and a one-sentence conclusion to the 1931 second edition as a continuation of the oceanic sensation controversy, a displacement of Freud's mixed feelings toward Rolland onto a parallel text, and Freud's last word on the significance of this intellectual encounter.

After the appearance of the second edition, Freud sent Rolland a personally inscribed copy with a dedication: "From the Terrestrial Animal to his Great Oceanic Friend."[5] This ironic dedication goes to the heart of the debate that the two carried on and gives us a view of Freud's method of thinking and his style of intellectual life. Foucault has specified that, in analyzing discourse, knowledge of the speaker's identity and of his situation is often as important as the text itself or omissions in the text. The terrestrial animal-oceanic friend dichotomy condenses the mixed feelings and the almost unbridgeable divergences of Freud and Rolland. It also suggests that their controversy, which flows into the entire fabric of *Civilization and Its Discontents*, into their letters, into Rolland's three-volume study of Indian mysticism,[6] and Freud's 1936 paper on the Acropolis,[7] was not conducted in the same conceptual context. The debate ended in an impasse, each participant holding to his original position.

Freud, the terrestrial animal, saw himself—possibly too rigidly—as a scientific psychologist, identified himself with the material world, with the biological and earthly realm of instinctual drives, with concrete and observable data. He attempted to speak the language of the reality principle, and evolved a method of inquiry which worked by making unconscious process conscious. Freud's methodology relied on the application of logic to seemingly illogical phenomena. His intelligence was comfortable in the analytic register, and his skepticism moved toward critical inquiry, not toward resignation or despair. Furthermore, his characteristic mode of thinking is analytic. He was authentically self-critical, extending his radical doubt toward himself and toward his own theoretical perspective. The terrestrial animal took seriously Charcot's ironic injunction to combine theory-building with close observation of reality; it was a protective measure against his own speculative inclinations. Nor did Freud ever propose that his writings were definitive on any subject. His humility was closely related to his method of problem-solving. The derogation of his own work was not merely ceremonial, not just a disarming mode of speech, but an essential part of the quest for truth, accuracy, and perpetuation of the process of understanding. Here is Freud's ironic comment upon the completion of *Civilization and Its Discontents;* it reads almost as a paradigm of self-deprecation:

Anna has already told you that I am working on something, and today I have written the last sentence, which—so far as is possible without a library—finished the work. It deals with civilization, sense of guilt, happiness and similar lofty topics, and strikes me, no doubt rightly, as very superfluous—in contrast to earlier works, which always sprang from some inner necessity. But what else can I do? One can't smoke and play cards all day, I am no longer much good at walking, and most of what there is to read doesn't interest me any more. So I wrote, and in that way the time passed quite pleasantly. In writing this work I have discovered afresh the most banal truths.[8]

Rolland, the oceanic friend, swam in the boundless waters of eternity and universal love—his mind retained access to primitive emotions; he valued the images, symbols, affects, and subjective experiences that were derivatives of the undifferentiated primary process. He was a mystic and a religious believer, and his imagination worked intuitively, introspectively, and synthetically; he emphasized similarities, not differences, between people, groups, nations, past and present forms of religious and cultural life. Moreover, his need for transcendence was linked to a search for totality, the goal of which was for the individual to achieve a symphonic balance of competing psychic and social forces.

In his controversy with Rolland, Freud had moved from an analysis of the common person's religion to a theoretical evaluation of the foundations of humanistic mysticism—to what Rolland alleged was the deepest and most universal source of the religious impulse. Rolland had touched a sensitive nerve in pointing out that Freud had not analyzed ecstatic states or deep introspective feelings in *The Future of an Illusion* (1927). Rolland subsequently described and coined the term "oceanic sensation" in an eight-paragraph letter written to Freud in December 1927, in which he pressed Freud for such a scientific evaluation.[9]

Spontaneous religious sensation, he told Freud, was a prolonged intuitive feeling of contact with the eternal, a direct feeling of vastness, of living in or among immense forces. Rolland insisted that the oceanic feeling be researched and understood as an energy which surpassed traditional categories of time, space, and causality. It had nothing to do with organized or institutionalized religion or promises of personal salvation. This "free vital gushing" (*jaillissement vital*) promised to be a spontaneous source of action and thought that might have regenerative powers for the undeveloped nations of the world and for decadent Europe. Because he was an accomplished critical realist, Rolland could not be dismissed as a mindless or crackpot mystic. In his writings he never opposed reason or scholarly and scientific investigations. He asserted, on the contrary, that the oceanic sensation could exist side by side with one's critical faculties, that the oceanic did not give rise to a world of illusions.

Rolland proposed that the oceanic feeling was a sensation of the individual's identity with his surroundings, of sublime connection to objects, to one's entire self, and to the universe as an indivisible whole. It ended the separation of the self from the outside world and from others and promised the individual participation in higher spiritual realms. It resisted traditional Western scientific and empirical explanations, and Rolland attributed the sensation to a primeval force in all people. The oceanic was nothing less than the divine inner core of existence; it had the quality of perpetual birth. The oceanic feeling was an idea-force, a benign form of energy, which could mediate between man as he was now and man as he could become. Since the sensation fostered relatedness among individuals, it could potentially break down the barriers of class, ethnicity, nationality, sexuality, culture, and generation, and could possibly lead to universal fraternity in the distant future. For Rolland the oceanic sensation represented an indestructible moral aspect of man's spiritual nature. It was nothing less than the basis of religious experience: spontaneous, innate, omnipresent, the force responsible for the individual's amorous bonds with other humans and the environment.

The French writer also felt that the oceanic contained enormous imaginative possibilities; that it provided the artist with reservoirs of inspiration, instinctive sources of creativity. It was the force that unified the works of literature, music, and humanistic mysticism. It was a centering and harmonizing emotion. Exploration of the oceanic feeling could lead to new forms of self-discovery and self-mastery, to the purification of ideas, and to insights about the nonrational foundations of being. Not simply a soothing fantasy, Rolland legitimized mysticism as a form of knowledge and cognition that operated through the emotions. If it were practiced on a daily, methodical basis, as in meditation or in yoga, the mystic could expand the oceanic sensation into another mode of discourse, a new spiritual discipline, another way of reaching profound truths.

Freud's treatment of the oceanic sensation in chapter 1 of *Civilization and Its Discontents* deserves careful scrutiny. Freud was obviously not exaggerating when he wrote to Rolland that "your letter of December 5, 1927 containing your remarks about a feeling you describe as "oceanic" has left me no peace."[10] There is a combination of praise and slight blame in this chapter, a touch of self-conscious reserve toward Rolland, and a complex repertoire of rhetorical and analytical strategies.[11] In fact, throughout this chapter Freud is unusually evasive and tentative.

He disarms the reader with his humility, his modesty, his candor, and his admission of personal limitations. He opens by mentioning the difficulties in treating a reputedly universal feeling that is absent in himself: "I cannot discover this "oceanic" feeling in myself" (p. 65).[12] With irony and understatement, the father of psychoanalysis admits how problematic it is to understand human emotions: "It is not easy to deal scientifically with feelings" (p. 65). He states the inadequacies of his insights and his method: "I have nothing to suggest that would have a decisive influence on the solution of this problem" (p. 65). Before beginning to set up linguistic resemblances, he warns the reader to beware of his comparisons: "This analogy may be too remote" (p. 65). He refers to the absence of research and reliable knowledge on the issue: "The subject has hardly been studied as yet" (p. 69).

He briefly takes on Rolland's role, becomes the imaginative writer, the lyricist, the man who gives expression to the fantastic, the unthinkable, and the dreamlike: "There is clearly no point in spinning our phantasy any further, for it leads to things that are unimaginable and even absurd" (p. 70). As his writing becomes dialogic, he anticipates the reader's criticism and attempts to counter the expected rebuttal: "Our attempt seems to be an idle game," "We bow to this objection," and "Perhaps we are going too far in this" (p. 71). He signals the reader to beware of spurious arguments: "To me this claim does not seem compelling" (p. 72); and he refuses to speculate on the unknown and perhaps the unknowable: "There may be something further behind that, but for the moment it is wrapped in obscurity" (p. 72). And he states his inability to analyze diffuse emotional constellations: "Let me admit once more that it is very difficult for me to work with these almost intangible quantities" (p. 72).

It is meaningful that in *Civilization and Its Discontents*, Freud's discourse on culture begins and ends with himself. The first-person point of view—"I," "me," "my,"—is used sixteen times in the second and third paragraphs of the text. Conspicuously, he concludes the essay with thirteen first-person references in the last paragraph of chapter 8. By opening and closing on a personal note, the author indicates his subjective involvement with the questions. In such studies, pseudo-scientific aloofness or value-free detachment is inappropriate.

In the text, disclaimers, qualifications, understatements, and use of the personal idiom run counter to Freud's sweeping generalizations, his universal interpretations, and his *ad hominem* arguments. Within the first chapter, Freud reiterates, but does not prove or demonstrate, the main thesis of *The Future of an Illusion*. "The derivation of religious needs from the infant's helplessness and the longing for the father aroused by it seem to me incontrovertible" (p. 72). A skillful rhetorician, Freud knew how to use adjectives for emphasis. Yet emphatic statements are not substitutes for sustained argument, well-documented evidence, and convincing proof. A nonjudgmental reader, working without a priori limitations on what he is permitted to discover, is not persuaded that the oceanic feeling is by necessity a secondary manifestation of the mind.

Let me mention other evasions and rhetorical strategies in this chapter. Freud deals with the ideational content of the oceanic sensation rather than with the feeling itself or with its physiological signs (p.65). (Rolland had asked for an empirical inquiry into the feeling, and had described the physiological transformations resulting from yoga.) Freud paraphrases but does not quote Rolland's letter on the oceanic, compressing eight paragraphs into one, even after Rolland had twice granted his permission to use the material from their private discussion. Freud's summary, while accurate, does not precisely convey the tone or the substance of the original text. The scientific language Freud uses is different from the metaphorical and imagistic language of Rolland's letter; Freud's version corresponds to a free-floating transcription, an adaptation of vitalistic ideas into a psychoanalytic vocabulary and conceptual framework. Freud's refusal to name Rolland as the friend in the first chapter (of the first edition of *Civilization and Its Discontents*) also suggests some feeling of hostility toward Rolland's view or possibly toward Rolland himself. The emphasis on Rolland's humaneness and on Freud's friendship for him may mask unfriendly feelings. Philip Rieff has observed that Freud was unable to separate men from their ideas;[13] something about Rolland's critique of psychoanalysis and his tenacious defense of mysticism left Freud unsettled.

Moreover, Freud does not always use irony to deflate pretentious ideas or to disrupt the reader's received notions. In this essay irony camouflages his personal limitations, becomes a form of self-defense, and occasionally a technique to mock opposing philosophical or methodological orientations. The irony often works against the spirit of critical inquiry, against the authentic search for a solution to the problem. I suggest that Rolland's account of the oceanic sensation caused Freud to take refuge in a variety of verbal subterfuges—jokes, self-laceration, cynicism, and finally a graceful form of literary dismissal.

In letters debating the oceanic sensation, Freud joked about Rolland's defense of Indian mysticism: "I shall now try with your guidance to penetrate into the Indian jungle from which until now an uncertain blending of Hellenic love of proportion, Jewish sobriety, and philistine timidity have kept me away."[14] The joke acknowledges Freud's consciousness of his differences from Rolland; Freud employed self-mockery to reassert his individuality, his own wide cultural erudition, and his serious commitment to use psychoanalysis to understand nonclinical materials. The ethnocentric labels (Indian, Hellenic, Jewish, philistine) incongruously placed side by side, the clever name-calling ostensibly aimed at himself, all suggest defensiveness on Freud's part. Freud was unwilling to make his way through his friend's Indian jungle; perhaps he feared it would be too primeval, too amorphous to yield to analytical interpretation. His collision with Rolland in their correspondence reminded him of his own personal limitations and blind spots. This made him reiterate the fact that psychoanalytic methods had not illuminated all realms of knowledge and that the science had not achieved an integrated world vision.

One way of dealing with the debate over mysticism was to state candidly, as Freud did, "that it is not easy to pass beyond the limits of one's nature."[15] "Nature" implies his ethnic background, intellectual formation, age, character structure, and theoretical bent. Freud, good tactician that he was, knew when to call a truce in a polemic, also when to retreat. He gracefully ended his discussions of the oceanic feeling in *Civilization and Its Discontents* not by moving into a detailed analysis of parapsychology, trances, and ecstasies but by citing some lines from Schiller: "Let him rejoice who breathes up here in the roseate light!" (p.73). By implication, Freud breathed better on other terrains, felt uncomfortable "above," more at ease in lower, or "Infernal Regions."[16]

Employing maneuvers of classical rhetoric to disarm the reader, admitting that his subject was intangible and puzzling, and warning the reader to beware of analogies, metaphors, and lyricism, Freud used all the devices that he warned against. Before publishing his interpretation, he wrote to Rolland with customary self-deprecation: "But please don't expect from my small effort any evaluation of the 'oceanic' feeling. I am experimenting only with an analytical diversion of it; I am clearing it out of the way, so to speak."[17]

Freud was nonetheless able to develop a compelling analysis of the oceanic sensation. He denied Rolland's hypothesis that the oceanic feeling was at the root of religious beliefs. In illustrating the genetic fallacy, Freud showed that he was nonreductionist in wielding his own theory. Nodal points in psychological development do not automatically derive from the earliest stages of infancy; and the oceanic, while remote, is not primary in the individual's psychosexual development; nor is it the foundation of his religious faith.

For Freud, the oceanic sensation is related to a pre-oedipal period of ego development. The sublime feeling of fusion with the universe reflects sensations of early childhood when the infant distinguishes imperfectly between the self and the external world. With the ego's boundaries with the universe blurred or incorrectly drawn, the infant experiences an indissoluble bond with his surroundings. This feeling of the ego's omnipotence corresponded to the child's merger with the mother, or more specifically with the mother's breast. Freud conjectures that the infant experiences unpleasurable sensations as outside the self. Eventually, through experience the child is forced to distinguish the internal from the external, the self or ego from that which is outside the self. "Our present ego-feeling is, therefore, only a shrunken residue of a much more inclusive—indeed, an all-embracing—feeling which corresponded to a more intimate bond between the ego and the world about it" (p.68).

The oceanic refers to a symbiotic fusion between mother and infant; it is the feeling of being harmoniously unified with the mother, or perhaps the memory of this experience, reinforced by the child's longing for warmth, closeness, protection, and security. The oceanic sensation recaptures the soothing feeling of being enveloped by a benevolent maternal guardian, of being caressed, fed, warmed, nurtured, rocked, and loved. The infant's nondifferentiation from his mother includes all of her parts and attributes, from her voice, gestures, and clothing to her gaze and her language. The infant's lack of separation from the outside world is related to his feeling of being afloat in his surroundings, of swimming in the waters of pleasurable stimuli.[18]

Freud suggested that the oceanic sensation recurred in adult life as a wishful fantasy, reassuring the individual about such disagreeable features of existence as mortality, the harshness of everyday life, and the compromises and accommodations necessary for survival. Thus oceanic feelings were powerful forms of consolation for the precariousness of human existence.[19] Freud also connected the oceanic to the process of introjection, the ability to incorporate dangerous or fearful aspects of psychic reality, which was likewise comforting because absorption countered the given menace. In *Civilization and Its Discontents*, Freud associates the oceanic feeling with masochistic urges, more specifically with the defense against self-destructive rage or self-mutilating impulses. Narcissistic rage and self-devaluation can frequently take the form of suicidal feelings. As if to balance Rolland's cosmic propensities, his urge toward flight and transcendence, Freud cites a literary source, Christian Dietrich Grabbe, to remind his readers that escape from conflict in suicide is not a viable option: "We cannot fall out of this world" (p.65).

In the final analysis Freud viewed the oceanic sensation as largely a regression to a childlike state in which the individual had no conception of himself as differentiated from objects or from the environment, and in which he experienced an ecstatic feeling of well-being. It was related to the narcissistic function of the ego whereby the self could be extended to embrace all of the world and humanity; thus it was, as Freud put it, the self enlarged to "limitless narcissism" (p.72).

Ultimately, he rejected mystical and idealist positions, seeing them as irrational but soothing retreats from external reality; they might endanger the ego's capacity to respond to internal assaults from unconscious impulses and to threats and obstacles encountered by the individual in social life. From the point of view of Freud's psychology and his value system, mysticism was a mystification. He wrote to Rolland:

> We seem to diverge rather far in the role we assign to intuition. Your mystics rely on it to teach them how to solve the riddle of the universe; we believe that it cannot reveal to us anything but primitive, instinctual impulses and attitudes—highly valuable for an embryology of the soul when correctly interpreted, but worthless for orientation in the alien, external world.[20]

Notwithstanding this dialectically complex analysis of the oceanic, Freud, in the first chapter of *Civilization and Its Discontents*, deploys his repertoire of rhetorical and critical skills to elude the oceanic sensation. Just as he is speculative and open-ended in his theorizing, so, too, is he mobile and inclusive in his suggestions for further research. Emphatically stated and firmly grounded psychoanalytic ideas coexist with more fragmentary and problematic interpretations. The result is multiple significances attached to the oceanic, not one definitive solution.

These fragmentary interpretations, in the form of wandering associations, ironic and pictorial juxtapositions, inversions and role reversals, and a dissemination of analogies, show us Freud's mind at work on a particularly baffling issue. Freud blends theoretical speculation and other rhetorical maneuvers in *Civilization and Its Discontents*; I attribute this blend partially to the speed with which the work was written. Freud completed the first draft of it in one month without having access to a library; at seventy-three, he wrote easily, fluently, densely, and with remarkable versatility. His competence as a problem solver was intact.[21] The very speed of the composition underscores his adherence to the psychoanalytic rule: the writer, like the patient, is willing to say without censorship and restriction whatever comes to mind. In short, I see this work as deeply autobiographical, and as one in which Freud constantly employs the device of free association.

To illustrate how the mind is structured and to show how past memories are preserved in mental life, Freud ingeniously borrowed an analogy from another field, archaeology. The psychoanalytic approach to culture is akin to the excavation of ancient sites where layers of buried material and ruins are often preserved next to more modern and restored parts of a city. It is not accidental that Freud selects Rome as his exemplary ancient city. Rolland's first name was Romain, which is French for Roman. To follow the internal logic of Freud's associations to Rolland, we should remember that *roman* is the French word for novel, romance, fiction, and romanesque; moreover Rolland had written two *romans-fleuves (Jean-Christophe* and *L'Ame enchantée)*, which in French is a novel saga, a novel constructed like a river, which flows into the sea. Freud may have been reminded of the Eternal City by the putative eternal quality of the oceanic feeling. He may also have known that Rolland spent a "Roman Spring" in the Eternal City from 1889 to 1891,[22] doing work in the Vatican Archives for his doctoral dissertation on the history of the opera.[23]

Freud's Rome analogy has a tripartite structure: it begins as a historical discourse, glides into archaeology, and concludes with a biological comparison. All three analogies are fragmentary, tentative, and discontinuous; the transitions are not readily apparent or logical. They are linked to Rolland by Freud's chain of associations, and by his assuming the public and professional roles of the French writer.

First, Freud reveals his competence and charm as a historian, mixing vignettes with bits of erudition about ancient and contemporary Rome. Rolland had been trained as a historian at the University of Paris. Here Freud temporarily displaces him as an archaeological historian. The positive pole of Freud's ambivalence toward Rolland corresponded to his exceptional fondness for Rome.[24] The verbs "admire," "grace," and "bequeathed" reveal Freud's affection for the city (pp. 69-71).

Second, Freud shows how identified he is with Rolland's pursuits by usurping Rolland's vocation as a writer. The Rome analogy is written in exquisite and lyrical prose. We should remember that Freud's literary and stylistic genius was recognized in his lifetime; he was awarded the Goethe Prize for Literature in 1930. On two occasions in chapter 1 of *Civilization and Its Discontents*, he interrupts his scientific narrative with these artistic digressions: "Now let us, by a flight of imagination, suppose that Rome is not a human habitation, but a physical entity" (p.70). And, "There is clearly no point in spinning out our phantasy any further" (p.70).

After anthropomorphizing ancient Rome, Freud suddenly abandons his historical and archaeological analogies as inappropriate and introduces an embryological one. His point is to show that the different stages of mental development are preserved, absorbed, or effaced in mature mental structures; or, put more cautiously, are "not *necessarily* destroyed" (p.71), despite the exigencies of the life cycle and the processes of amnesia. Yet, here too, Freud is frustrated. He knows that his analogy is weak and imprecise. Once again he stops trying to conceptualize the mind in spatial or pictorial terms.

Why did Freud try out and then relinquish the biological analogy? One reason may be his association of Rolland with pictorial or naturalistic forms of representation. Rolland had written several books on painters, including a well-known biographical study of Michelangelo. Many of Michelangelo's most sublime creations are, of course, housed in Rome. Freud admired Michelangelo's work and wrote an essay on his Moses.[25] In their letters, Freud once referred to Rolland's mystical knowledge as "highly valuable for an embryology of the soul when correctly interpreted."[26] His own approach to embryology tended to be traditionally scientific, empirical, and ontogenetic. Yet Freud was also quite conscious of the finite parameters of pictorial forms of representation. The psychoanalyst, in short, conceives of the mind with a knowledge of the limitations both of writing and of visual forms of representation.

The first chapter of *Civilization and Its Discontents* effectively shows how inclusive analogies are, even the most ingenious. Rolland's oceanic sensation triggered Roman associations that in Freud gave rise to three abortive analogies and assorted discontinuous attempts to represent his concepts historically, archaeologically, imaginatively, and pictorially. All partially failed. Moreover, the back and forth movement, the offering and relinquishing of the analogies, disrupts the narrative and theoretical flow of Freud's own discourse, muting the definitive impact of the oceanic discussion.

Freud both recognized and gave expression to the difficulties involved in conveying psychoanalytic insights about the layers of the mind. This problem was particularly acute in describing overlapping layers of the mental apparatus where old and new cohabit, where fragment, condensations, and displacements often become the only evidence of earlier content and structures. Freud's own language here is remarkably mobile and shifting. His form of expression seems to reflect the form and content of his material, which is fluctuating, overdetermined, erratic, and cannot be pinned down with one comprehensive picture or one overarching theoretical model.

Various disguised allusions to the question of the oceanic sensation pervade the text. In chapter 8, Freud rejected the Judeo-Christian commandment "Love thy neighbor as thyself," as an unrealistic injunction, which is not only nearly impossible to fulfill, but once fulfilled, caused more injury and anxiety than the aggressiveness against which it is a defense. Freud perceived Rolland to be an advocate of universal love: "Because for us your name has been associated with the most precious of beautiful illusions, that of love extended to all mankind."[27] We also know that Freud read Rolland's biography of Gandhi, in which the French writer updated and popularized the Tolstoyan (and Kantian and Christian) notion of neighborly love, in addition to linking it to the political philosophy of nonviolent resistance. "Mahatma Gandhi," Freud wrote to his friend in 1924, "will accompany me on my vacation which will begin shortly."[28]

In debunking the imperative to love one's neighbor uncritically, Freud is directly replying to Rolland's world vision. The commandment, in his view, contains both a self-absorbed and a self-serving component, for its only practical value is to reinforce the ethical person's sense of self-righteousness. "'Natural' ethics, as it is called, has nothing to offer here except the narcissistic satisfaction of being able to think oneself better than others" (p.143). Psychodynamically, the good conscience of the Christian stems from bad faith. The precept of universal love presupposes a neglect, or a glossing over, of distinctions between the ego and the real world (p.102). It presupposes that one's neighbor is the mirror of one's self, or an idealized image of oneself.

From a psychoanalytic view, Freud objected to the notion of universal love on practical as well as on theoretical grounds. Nondiscriminating love offered to humanity is egalitarian and nonreflective, disregarding differences in the behavior of human beings. Love extended to humanity in general tends to devalue the love directed toward the particular individual. This is an obvious injustice to the one who is loved (p.102). Freud also held that most people were unworthy of love, that it was foolish to love those who were power-hungry or ambitious for success, or who sought material wealth with no authentic desire to serve others. Love and friendship ought to be reserved for the deserving, for those who can reciprocate, and not wasted on the multitudes of people who are hostile, malicious, and impotent, and who crave domination over others. It is in this context that Freud asserts that people are wolves, not gentle creatures; most people, he observes, are unlovely and unlovable (pp.102, 109-111). Furthermore, Freud posits that the idea of universal love is rooted in narcissism— that people are thus motivated to seek out and love idealized aspects of themselves in others, that sharing common values, common interests, and a common cultural orientation also can be traced back in part to a deep need to love a mirror of oneself (pp. 84, 118).

In chapter 5 of *Civilization and Its Discontents* Freud shows that the Judeo-Christian (and Rollandist) precept "Love thy neighbor" is an extension of the feeling of oneness with the universe, of the nondiscerning feeling connected with an amorphous love of humanity. The oceanic sensation and Christian moral injunctions ultimately stem from the same psychical source. To deflate these absolutist moralistic ideals, Freud used unusual, debunking images:

> But if I am to love him (with this universal love) merely because he, too, is an inhabitant of this earth, like an insect, an earth-worm or a grass-snake, then I fear that only a small modicum of my love will fall to his share—not by any possibility as much as, by the judgment of my reason, I am entitled to retain for myself. What is the point of a precept enunciated with so much solemnity if its fulfillment cannot be recommended as reasonable? (P.110)

He states rhetorically that realization of the precept is palpably absurd, and he jokes about the commandment to drain away its pretentiousness. Finally, he cites a hilarious tale by Heinrich Heine about accepting or loving one's neighbors only after they have been murdered: "One must, it is true, forgive one's neighbors—but not before they have been hanged" (p.110 n. 1). Freud is casting Heine's modernistic, ironic parable against Rolland's idealism. He is also illustrating how literary performance can give expression to, can legitimize with humor, forbidden aggressive wishes.

As a diagnostician of civilizational malaise, Freud searched for hidden phenomena in cultural and ideological modes of expression. He pointed out how manifestations of love and forbearance often disguised feelings of deep intolerance. He recalled, for instance, how the love preached by organized Christianity was often offset by the disastrous history of Christian persecutions, massacres, and hostility toward non-Christians (p.114).

I would like to extend the Freudian interpretation of the oceanic sensation by arguing that the feeling which is described as the deep source of religion and of human relatedness on a grand scale is actually a reaction-formation. That is to say, the limitless narcissism of the oceanic conceals or counters a feeling of universal hatred for humanity.

It is arguable that individuals who proclaim love for humanity secretly have powerful feelings of aggression and contempt for humanity, that feelings of eternity actively spring from unbounded feelings of repressed rage, of unsatisfied oral cravings. Rolland's oceanicism conceals a strong sadistic impulse, a monumental fury against humanity, a drive to destroy civilization. The openly proclaimed affection for and overidealization of humanity hides a devaluation of it. The oceanic sensation comforted Rolland by wiping out his recurring feelings of despair and loss of direction; monumental feelings of connection opposed his feelings of unconnectedness. The reactions took the form of feelings of omnipotence, grandiosity, optimism, and the pattern of attaching himself to strong, admired father figures to reestablish his self-esteem. The philosophical idealist may incorporate grandiose objects as a defense against infantile feelings of anxiety, shame, guilt, and lack of self-worth. The person who feels universal love may paradoxically be the one with the harshest and most primitive superego. To defend himself against his own self-punishing conscience, Rolland emerged as a public man of virtue, self-sacrifice, and penance. Thus the narcissism associated with the oceanic sensations does not fundamentally spring from self-love or self-admiration; it may embody an elaborate defense against aggressive impulses.

For Rolland then, and by implication for all humanistic mystics, total love of humanity may be unconsciously fused with the impulse to annihilate humanity totally. This fusion of opposites generated powerful tensions in his art, his cultural criticism, and his engagement with contemporary society. Psychoanalysis can lay bare the psychical roots of metaphorical and idealist modes of expression, such as oceanic feelings. It shows how these apparently benign attitudes become constituted as reactions to these impulses. Under the cloak of universal pity, compassion, virtue, and humane contact, the oceanic sensation may function to counter hostile and immoral impulses, wishes that are incompatible with conscious and civilized outlooks.

> In consequence of this primary mutual hostility of human beings, civilized society is perpetually threatened with disintegration. The interest of work in common would not hold it together; instinctual passions are stronger than reasonable interests. Civilization has to use its utmost efforts in order to set limits to man's aggressive instincts and to hold the manifestations of them in check by psychical reaction-formations ... hence too the ideal commandment to love one's neighbor— a commandment which is really justified by the fact that nothing else runs so strongly counter to the original nature of man. In spite of every effort, these endeavors of civilization have not so far achieved very much. (P.112)

From an examination of their correspondence, a discourse analysis of *Civilization and Its Discontents*, and an interpretation of Freud's 1936 paper "A Disturbance of Memory on the Acropolis: An Open Letter to Romain Rolland on the Occasion of His Seventieth Birthday," it is conceivable that Freud viewed Rolland as one of the special few, marked off from the masses by his sensibility and his gifts. Freud considered him a man of encyclopedic knowledge and wisdom, who had a powerful commitment to research and learning. Moreover, Rolland posed tough and significant questions; he knew what questions really mattered. Rolland represented those men who did the work of civilization, who knew how to discipline their imaginations, who worked steadily, who led a regular life, who kept visitors and diversions away, and who appreciated the psychological necessity of intellectual work.

Rolland was Freud's unnamed friend in the first edition of *Civilization and Its Discontents* who saw a gap in the psychoanalytic explanation of religion, a gap which perplexed Freud and provoked him to rethink his previous position. In his life and work Rolland refused to be parochial, self-serving, or narrow-minded. He was an exceptional man, whose sincerity and tolerance never interfered with his courageous articulation of dissenting opinions (he took public stances in favor of the doctrines of pacifism, Gandhism, and antifascism, and was known to be sympathetic to communism). In the first paragraph of *Civilization and Its Discontents*, Freud refers to Rolland in glowing terms as someone who does not use false standards of measurement, who does not seek power, success, or wealth for himself or admire them in others. The tenderness of this description underlines Freud's esteem for the French writer, whom he viewed as an exemplary figure. The reverential tone and substance of *Civilization and Its Discontents* is congruent with the opening paragraph of "A Disturbance of Memory on the Acropolis."[29]

For Freud, Rolland had evolved into more than a famous man of letters. He had become a contemporary idealist and prophet, in short a writer with a priestly world view. Conceiving of his role and mission with arch-seriousness, Rolland offered inspiration and consolation to his countless readers, presenting them with strong culture heroes (Michelangelo, Beethoven, Tolstoy, Gandhi) upon whom they could attach themselves. Rolland had moved beyond the confines of being a novelist, cultural critic, and historian to make universalist pronouncements to his audience, to speak on all issues in the name of higher wisdom. He conceived of the writer in a sacerdotal manner, as if he had a divine authority and a highly moral agenda.

However, Freud's veneration for Rolland covers a repressed tendency to compete with and devalue his friend. As early as the first paragraph of *Civilization and Its Discontents*, Freud qualifies his admiration for Rolland with sentences which soften, check, and self-criticize (p.64). The full nature of Freud's ambivalence toward Rolland is revealed in the third paragraph: "The views expressed by the friend who I so much honor, and who himself once praised the magic of illusion in a poem" (pp.64-65). To praise illusion is tantamount to defending self-deception. In a letter to Rolland, Freud wrote: "A great part of my life's work (I am ten years older than you) has been spent [trying to] destroy illusions of my own and those of mankind."[30] Age, experience, maturity, world-weariness, and psychoanalytic experience all encouraged Freud to be wary of the bad faith and blind alleys connected with wishful thinking.

On the last page of the essay, Freud announces his firm refusal to play the role of prophet, sage, revolutionary, or religious leader (p.145). In brief, he rejects the full spectrum of Rolland's public roles and Rolland's style of intellectual life. All he can be is what he is: an impartial man of science, a theory-builder, committed to the search for and the expression of the truth. Freud saw himself as a demystifier of magical and metaphysical explanations about man and his relationship to the world. In contrast to Rolland, he refused to offer his audience consolation or easily digested images of themselves. In opposition to Rolland's tendency to exalt the intellectual, Freud assumed the therapeutic stance of desacralization. The psychoanalytic critic of culture, he tells us explicitly, offers interpretations, not fixed meanings. This is a responsible posture, for such insights can be modified, revised, and reassessed, while grandiose claims of omnipotence persuade by their appeal to our need for faith, hope, certainty, grandeur, and happiness. Rather than bestow upon his readers a lofty system of moral teachings, linked to a transcendent realm, Freud presents them with a critical method of inquiry, and with a model which demands that they proceed with their inquiry in a nonjudgmental, analytically neutral, detached, yet empathic manner.

In all of Freud's writings to or about Rolland, there is a pronounced tension, a wavering between affection and genuine esteem on the one hand, and strain, envy, and bitterness on the other. This tension stemmed from Freud's oscillation between uncanny feelings of familiarity with Rolland and his sense of unalterable separation from him. On an unconscious level, Rolland may have represented a rival, a ten-year-younger, gifted sibling, a contentious but private opponent of psychoanalytic theory and practice, an object of competition, envy, and hostility—someone, in brief, to be replaced, argued with, or to be cleared out of the way.

Rolland was Freud's Double. Freud felt a kinship with Rolland for his capacities as a realistic writer, as a novelist and playwright with psychological probity; he identified with the French writer's ability to penetrate beneath social conventions. Freud felt attracted to artists who handled language deftly and who playfully tapped the imagination. Rolland had provided his readers with moments of pleasure, comfort, and exaltation. He was an artist with a vast public, with enormous contemporary resonance; that is, he was a maker of high culture who spoke a language accessible to the masses.

Rolland's capacity to communicate with and move the masses was highly problematic in Freud's eyes, however, especially given Freud's view of the mass public as uncritical, lazy, careless, unreliable, easily deflected by the pleasure principle, easily manipulated by intoxicating substances and religious sedatives and narcotics. Mysticism and idealism were addictive and dangerous on these grounds. Moreover, Rolland's ability to mediate between high and popular culture reminded Freud of his own isolation, unpopularity, and vulnerabilities. Freud, the secluded scientific investigator, had reached his insights only after long and laborious effort, after detours and a lifetime of investigations. As founder of psychoanalysis, he had given expression to disturbing and unwanted truths about the human mind. Humanity had often repaid him for his labors by treating him unkindly or by totally ignoring him.[31]

To be sure, Freud's admiration for Rolland as a creative writer, humanitarian, pacifist, and conciliator of mankind existed side by side with envy and distrust of him. What is attractive in Rolland is highlighted by Freud's perception of their dissimilarities: "I may confess to you that I have rarely experienced that mysterious attraction of one human being for another as vividly as I have with you; it is somehow bound up, perhaps, with the awareness of our being so different."[32]

If Rolland represented Freud's Double he was also the Other.[33] As Freud's Double, Rolland was a brother in the cultural enterprise: he was irrepressibly honest, had the courage of his dissenting convictions, understood individual psychology and the role of instincts, defied social conventions, and combined his individual integrity with artistic ability. As Freud's Other, Rolland was the unreachable love-object, a symbolic object of temptation and seduction, a desire that remained eternally unfulfilled. His differences from Freud were striking. It is quite possible that Freud saw in Rolland, as Double and as Other, long suppressed aspects of his own personality, such as a susceptibility to mystical ideas, a craving for success and recognition, creative aspirations, and a desire to serve humanity.

In *Civilization and Its Discontents*, the scientist, artist, and intellectual are the prototypes of the sublimated man. Freud delineates sharp oppositions between artistic activity and the work of science.[34] I would like to suggest that Rolland is one of the principal, but invisible representatives of artistic and intellectual sublimation in the essay, and that Freud approaches him with a characteristic double-edged sword: with appreciation on the one hand; and with a consciousness of the risks involved in too much sublimation on the other hand—the inference being that Rolland could no longer serve as a realistic model for emulation.

Freud recognized the self-discipline and years of self-sacrifice that went into the creation of literary masterpieces. Rolland was an "unforgettable man"[35] because he knew how to suffer, how to endure hardship, and how to give altruistically to humanity. He not only embodied will power, but also channeled his psychic energies in constructive directions. In his relationship and debates with Rolland, Freud was forced to revise his earlier a priori views of the artist as passive, given over to fantasy, slightly feminine, out of touch with the reality principle—a dreamer and romantic. Rolland had demonstrated that cultural work emanated from the artist's self-mastery. Unless the impulses were tamed, the cultural products themselves could not be transformed into vehicles for the transfer of energy between the artist and his public. Committed to the creation, reinvention, and interpretation of beauty, Rolland's life and work took on meaning in the production of useless yet highly prized artistic objects and ideas (pp. 82-83). The word "useless" is intended neither to denigrate culture nor to confer meaning on cultural objects; rather, Freud is referring to a biological and material concept of necessity. Artists like Rolland had to survive through compensatory forms of gratification. They derived sustenance from the pleasure of steady mental work, from the narcissistic pleasure of giving birth to beautiful creations, a joy not unlike those which parents derive from their children; and from the mild intoxications that come with solving mental problems or perfecting one's craft.

Freud reasons in *Civilization and Its Discontents* that too much sublimation can result in grave dangers to the artist himself. To deprive the instincts of direct gratification is to court the possibility of frustration and mental disorder; it may even warp the perspective of the artist, or impair his ability to complete projects. According to Freud's theory of the economics of the libido, the life of regimen and restriction can give rise to a severely stunted personality. Overly sublimated artists like Rolland lived like horses without oats;[36] they ignored or obliterated instinctual demands. They often loved ideas or humanity in an abstract and disembodied sense; they withdrew from the cities and from social relationships; they lived a hermit's existence; they mortified the flesh; they craved rest, isolation, and solitude; and they were unable to achieve or to sustain mutual, intimate, heterosexual love relationships (pp.79-81, 102).

Thus the poignant situation of the makers of civilization is that those who apparently gave the most to society and to posterity received very little in return. According to Freud's perception, Rolland was a perfect symbol of the overly sublimated, ascetic, self-abnegating man of culture, the martyr who knew how to give gifts, yet who seemed constitutionally or psychologically incapable of permitting human reciprocity. Within the Freudian conceptual framework, Oedipal man is guilt-ridden, while narcissistic man is tragic. Rolland thus served Freud simultaneously as a symbol of the achievements of civilization and an example of the dangers of excessive sublimation.

For the second edition of *Civilization and Its Discontents*, Freud added several footnotes, one sentence to an existing footnote, and the concluding line to the text. I suggest that these seemingly trivial editorial corrections refer directly and indirectly to Rolland, that they are a parallel text that reflects Freud's continual ambivalence toward the French writer, and that they require interpretation. They are part of the debate on the oceanic feeling, and they continue the polemic, further illustrating Rolland's presence throughout the text of *Civilization and Its Discontents*.

After mentioning but discreetly not naming his "friend" four times in the text (five if we infer that the reference to "another friend of mine" who experiments with yoga is also Rolland), Freud abruptly ends the confidentiality, identifies Rolland by name, and then cites three of his works: "Since the publication of his two books, *La Vie de Ramakrishna* and *La Vie de Vivekananda*, I need no longer hide the fact that the friend spoken of in the text is Romain Rolland" (p. 65, n.1). The word "hide" is striking; one wonders about Freud's mixed motives in concealing his information, especially given his methodological interest in exposing latent psychological relationships and meanings.

While discussing the mental satisfactions of concentrated intellectual or artistic activity, Freud adds the following note on narcissistic forms of self-sufficiency: "No discussion of the possibility of human happiness should omit to take into consideration the relation between narcissism and object libido. We require to know what being essentially self-dependent signifies for the economics of the libido" (p.84, n. 2). This passage shows that to Freud there was a real, if not fully articulated, connection between Rolland's radical isolation from society and from others and Freud's theoretical speculations about narcissism. We watch Freud opening up a path for further research, urging the psychoanalytic researcher to investigate narcissistic disorders from the point of view of object relations, that is, by analyzing how the individual relates to significant others, beginning with his mother.[37]

To link the concept of virtue and a punitive conscience, Freud adds a footnote in chapter 7. In citing Mark Twain's story "The First Melon I Ever Stole," Freud is once again casting one literary sensibility against another, siding with Twain against Rolland as he had done earlier with Heine. His purpose is to signal the dangers of overly strict moral stances. To answer Rolland's righteousness, to refute the French moralist's defense of a severe conscience, Freud juxtaposes Twain's light, sarcastic musings on melon stealing. The melon is a sexually evocative symbol, and to engage in melon stealing is to fulfill a proscribed but universal wish. Twain wonders out loud: "*Was* it the first?" And Freud replies: "The first melon was evidently not the only one" (p.73, n.2). Thus Freud himself steals the metaphor to indicate in a gentle way that virtue often cloaks underlying aggressive and erotic tendencies. Like Heine's, Twain's honesty is refreshing and funny; Freud was delighted by Twain's ability to lift the censorship which surrounds pilfering and other "immoral" acts. He viewed this admission as a disruptive activity which carried an important psychological significance.

Finally, the last sentence of the second edition of *Civilization and Its Discontents* can be viewed not as an afterthought, not simply a presentiment of the rise of Nazism, but rather as a deliberate effort to counter the optimism connected with the supposed return and victory of Eros in the perpetual struggle between life and death: "But who can foresee with what success and with what result?" (p.145). This interrogative mode suggests that Freud's method and critical theory is fundamentally dissimilar to Rolland's oceanic metaphysics. Freud's technique and conceptual apparatus do not necessarily lead to wisdom, progress, happiness, or optimistic conclusions. To end the second edition on a measured note of doubt is to restate the cautionary stance of psychoanalysis. Enlightening man about his unconscious processes and his psychosexual development may take generations. Nor is Freud more sanguine about the tangible results of his own methodology in analyzing cultural patterns, in providing answers to man's "ultimate concerns," or in guaranteeing the triumph of Eros over Thanatos. It may also be that he wanted to reply to Rolland's oceanic sensation one last time: by criticizing oceanic optimism, Freud ends his most synthetic essay poignantly, with modesty and uninhibited skepticism.

The history of the psychoanalytic movement is intimately related to Freud's personal and intellectual history. In a dramatic way Freud was his own most persistent patient. And throughout his life, he continued to interpret his dreams, to free-associate, to analyze jokes, slips, memory disturbances, in short to apply his techniques to himself with the evenly suspended attention he called for in the treatment of patients. Rieff has described Freud's directness and candor, and his adherence to the ethic of honesty in psychoanalytic theory and practice; the overriding psychoanalytic rule, after all, is to say what comes to mind. Freud's discourse on culture in *Civilization and Its Discontents* does precisely this: and with results that are stunning, surprising, and majestic.

As a diagnostician of culture, Freud is not always logically consistent, conceptually precise, or philosophically systematic. His arguments are not always crystal clear, his mediations are often insufficiently elaborated. In reading him we have to beware of his sloppiness, his occasional use of nonreferential material, and his ahistorical tendency to rely on poorly defined temporal and spatial categories. This early pioneer in the psychohistory of culture often lacks historical specificity.

Freud's restless, curious mind is perpetually searching for significations; he could not tolerate meaninglessness. If Freud errs in any direction, it is in his tendency to overinterpret, which, in turn, reflects his desire for closure, for posing solutions to problems. Frequently these solutions are tentative, speculative, and shifting, while the issues being scrutinized seem pressing and urgent. But if he overintellectualizes, he also displays remarkable ease with contradiction, ambiguity, and mixed meanings. He not only appreciates the process of delay involved in building theory and in conducting research, but he also calls for periodic reassessments of working hypotheses in the light of new data.

In initiating psychoanalytic discourse on culture, Freud brought to his researches a militantly atheistic and secular point of view. This is totally opposed to the world view of Romain Rolland. For Freud the accent is always on man himself, as he is, without metaphysical or sentimental embellishment. Psychoanalysis is not formulated as a religion; it neither provides a fully integrated world vision, nor offers answers to the riddles of the universe. We have seen how Freud sets up psychoanalytic constructs as a stable, scientific theory differentiating them from less reality-bound endeavors, such as literature, music, mysticism, or revolutionary politics, all of which Rolland practiced, and which are likely to instigate or perpetuate illusions. Yet his own writing is often literary, metaphorical, evocative, mobile, wandering, and subversive. Freud tapped his own fantasy life in his writings, and his very best writing is playful, imaginative, and self-critical. In *Civilization and Its Discontents*, he even played with the notion that civilization itself might be overvalued, that cultural production may not be worth the sacrifice and demands it entails for the individual creator.

Extending the psychoanalytic stance of technical neutrality toward the patient, Freud remains neutral toward past and present forms of culture. Such neutrality allows both for empathic understanding and for self-reflexive interpretations. Freud thus consciously avoids speculating about the value of human civilization. Unlike Rolland, he deliberately refuses the role of prophet, makes no predictions about the future of mankind, presents no coherent scale of values or particular set of priorities to his public.

Instead of mindless hope or religious consolation, instead of ecstatic fusion with humanity or narcissistic fantasies of amorous bonding, Freud offers the qualified program of an irreligious education to reality, informed by psychoanalytic insights and methods. In the twentieth century, he implied, only the ignorant can afford to bypass psychoanalysis. Such an education aims at subverting naive or antipsychological prejudices, at eroding rigid ethical codes and outdated moralisms, in order to establish a more sober approach to the perennial question of freedom and necessity.

The psychoanalytic outlook on culture stresses how society, through language, symbol, ritual, institutions, and the family, imposes itself on our impulses. Freud's point of view in *Civilization and Its Discontents* mirrors his therapeutic posture: both the analyst in the clinical setting and the psychoanalytic culture critic endorse the voice of the reality principle, opposing simultaneously the unrelenting demands of the id and the false idealism and destructive demands of the superego. In contrast to oceanic forms of merger, the reality principle presupposes that the self can keep distinct the line where the self ends and the external world and the world of objects begins; that is, it requires paying attention to the real world. The ego needs to be both protected and fortified; it is fragile, easily ensnared, easily decentered. Part of the condition of being neurotic in modern society means the impossibility of achieving mental synthesis. The ego develops defensive and adaptive tendencies to cope with this absence of psychic and social harmony. Paul Ricoeur argues that for Freud the reality principle is closely linked to an ethical idea of prudence. The individual learns how to endure pain, loss, separation, lack of success, unpleasure, without giving way to despair or destructive deflections, and without "acting out."[38]

Writing neither as an indignant enemy of nor as an apologist for civilization, believing neither in imminent social apocalypse nor in some static model of the individual's conflict with society, Freud refrained from a priori ethical judgments and prescriptions. He is a system builder who appreciated the inconclusive quality of lived experience, of disruptions that could not be circumscribed by systems. He is a moralist who refrains from moral preaching, a teacher who eschews didacticism. Truth-seeking is elevated into a process of comprehending the individual's situation in society. The suspension of value judgment is thus a step toward self-knowledge, toward truly critical forms of cultural inquiry, for it liberates the mind from infantile modes of thought. It is also a way of releasing the individual from violence and self-destructiveness, without imitating or internalizing the aggression. Ethical neutrality makes it possible for the reality principle to dominate the pleasure principle in the development and deployment of human consciousness. Consciousness—"de-emotionalized reason"[39]—becomes indispensable in Freud's view of cultural continuity and rupture; it, alone, provides the individual with the tools by which he can master nature and move gropingly toward control of aggression, guilt, and his own self-destructiveness. Consciousness becomes crucial in lifting the censors, in moving toward self-fulfillment in one's work and in one's love life.

Freud, then, presents psychoanalysis as more than a synchronic discourse which comments on other discourses in an artificial and ahistorical manner. Psychoanalytic culture criticism attempts to integrate theory and practice, while working at the points of convergence of the individual's life in society; it is oriented toward the individual's mastery of infantile modes of thought and behavior without denying the complexities of lived experience.

To read *Civilization and Its Discontents* is to recognize that the psychoanalytic interpretation of culture may be as fundamentally interminable and enriching to the reader as psychoanalytic treatment is to the patient. The essay's own self-reflexive form and ambiguous meaning prepare us for the long process of remembering, associating, and working through that is involved in the mastery of the Freudian instrument of liberation. The ideal reader and teacher of *Civilization and Its Discontents* would be one with a tolerance of delay, detour, and postponement in the search for answers to meaningful questions. Such a reader would be open to psychoanalytic culture criticism as a research strategy, or at least would be willing to suspend his disbelief. An audience of such readers would be unafraid to draw on their reservoir of personal emotions, desires, memories and fantasies as well as on their intellectual faculties. Such an audience would, above all, try to emulate Freud: in using one's own psychic conflicts and ambivalences creatively in order to fertilize one's relationship to the cultural process—as both a creator and recipient of that culture.

Notes

1   Michel Foucault, *Madness and Civilization: A History of Insanity in the Age of Reason* (New York, 1973), translated by Richard Howard, pp. 198, 277-278; Foucault, *The History of Sexuality* (New York, 1978), translated by Richard Howard, pp. 53, 56, 150, 158-159; see my review of Foucault's *Histoire de la sexualité* in *The Journal of Psychohistory* (Winter 1978), pp. 481-486.
2   Michel Foucault, "What is an Author?" in *Language, Counter-Memory,*

Practice: Selected Essays and Interviews (Ithaca, 1977), translated and edited by Donald F. Bouchard, pp. 131-136; Foucault, *The Order of Things: An Archaeology of the Human Sciences* (New York, 1970), pp. 373-376.

3   Provocative readings of Freud's texts can be found in Jacques Lacan, *Ecrits: A Selection* (New York, 1977), translated by Alan Sheridan, pp. 114-178, 292-325; Lacan, "Desire and the Interpretation of Desire in *Hamlet*," translated by James Hulbert, *Yale French Studies*, no. 55-56 (1977), pp. 11-52; Samuel Weber, "It," *Glyph*, 4 (1978), pp. 1-31.

4   Roy Schafer, "Narration in the Psychoanalytic Dialogue," *Critical Inquiry*, 7 (1980), pp. 29-53; Leo Bersani, "The Other Freud," *Humanities in Society*, no. 1 (1987), pp. 33-49; Peter Brooks, "Freud's Masterplot: Questions of Narrative," *Yale French Studies*, no. 55-56 (1977), pp. 280-300; Peter Brooks, "Fictions of the Wolf Man: Freud and Narrative Understanding," *Diacritics* (1979), pp. 72-81.

5   For a full discussion of this debate, see my "Sigmund Freud and Romain Rolland: The Terrestrial Animal and His Great Oceanic Friend," *American Imago*, 33 (Spring 1976), pp. 1-59; also see David S. Werman, "Sigmund Freud and Romain Rolland," *International Review of Psycho-Analysis*, 4 (1977), pp. 225-242; Irving B. Harrison, "On the Maternal Origins of Awe," *The Psychoanalytic Study of the Child*, 30 (1975), pp. 181-195; Irving B. Harrison, "On Freud's View of the Infant-Mother Relationship and of the Oceanic Feeling—Some Subjective Influences," *Journal of the American Psychoanalytic Association* 27, no. 1 (1979), pp. 309-421; and J. Moussaieff Masson, *The Oceanic Feeling: The Origins of Religious Sentiment in Ancient India* (Dordrecht, Holland, 1980), pp. 33-50.

6   Romain Rolland, *Essai sur la mystique et l'action de l'Inde vivante: Le vie de Ramakrishna* (Paris 1929), and *Essai sur la mystique et l'action de l'Inde vivante: La vie de Vivekananda et l'evangel universel*, 2 vols. (Paris 1930).

7   Sigmund Freud, "A Disturbance of Memory on the Acropolis: An Open Letter to Romain Rolland on the Occasion of His Seventieth Birthday" (1936), *Standard Edition of the Complete Psychological Works of Sigmund Freud*, vol. 22 (London, 1964), pp. 239-248.

8   Letter from Freud to Lou Andreas Salomé, 28 July 1929, in *Sigmund Freud & Lou Andreas-Salomé Letters* (New York, 1972), edited by Ernest Pfeiffer, translated by William and Elaine Robson-Scott, p. 181. For an interesting reply to Freud's analysis of the oceanic sensation, see letter from Lou Andreas-Salomé to Freud, 4 January 1930, ibid., pp. 182-183.

9   Letter from Romain Rolland to Freud, 5 December 1927 in Romain Rolland, *Un beau visage à tous sens: Choix de lettres de Romain Rolland (1886-1944)*, Cahiers Romain Rolland, no. 17 (Paris, 1967), pp. 264-266; for an English translation, see Fisher, "Sigmund Freud and Romain Rolland," pp. 20-22.

10   Letter from Freud to Romain Rolland, 14 July 1929, in *Letters of Sigmund Freud* (New York, 1960), hereafter cited as *Freud Letters*, edited by Ernst L. Freud, translated by Tania and James Stern, p. 388. It may not be accidental that Freud wrote Rolland on Bastille Day, the most important secular holiday for the French, and also the title of one of Rolland's most celebrated plays, *Le Quatorze Juillet* (1902).

11   Robert R. Holt, "On Reading Freud," *Abstracts of the Standard Edition of the Complete Psychological Works of Sigmund Freud* (New York, 1973), edited by

Carrie Lee Rothgeb, pp. 3-73; also see Roy Schafer, *A New Language for Psychoanalysis* (New Haven, 1976).

12   All citations are to Sigmund Freud, *Civilization and Its Discontents*, translated by James Strachey, vol. 21 of *The Standard Edition of the Complete Psychological Works of Sigmund Freud* (London, 1961.)

13   Philip Rieff, *The Triumph of the Therapeutic: Uses of Faith after Freud* (New York, 1960), p. 80.

14   Letter from Freud to Romain Rolland, 19 January 1930, *Freud Letters*, p. 392.

15   Ibid.

16   Freud cited a passage from Virgil's *Aeneid* for his epigraph to *The Interpretation of Dreams*: "If I cannot bend the Higher Powers, I will move the Infernal Regions."

17   Letters from Freud to Romain Rolland, 20 July 1929, *Freud Letters*, p. 389.

18   Margaret S. Mahler, Fred Pine, Anni Bergman, *The Psychological Birth of the Human Infant* (New York, 1975), p. 44, state: "From the second month on, dim awareness of the need-satisfying object marks the beginning of the phase of normal symbiosis, in which the infant behaves and functions as though he and his mother were an omnipotent system—a dual unity within one common boundary. This is perhaps what Freud and Romain Rolland discussed in their dialogue as the sense of boundlessness of the oceanic feeling."

19   Erik H. Erikson, "The Life Cycle: Epigenesis of Identity," *Identity, Youth, and Crisis* (New York, 1968), pp. 102-103, 106. Post-Freudian etiological criticism avoids reductionism by seeing the oceanic feeling as more than an infantile experience; ego psychologists argue that the sensation can also generate hope and trust in the future. The experience may encourage an adolescent or adult to persevere in adverse circumstances, to struggle assiduously to bring his efforts to fruition. Erik Erikson links faith to the development of trust, which stems from the "attainability of primal wishes," and he incisively suggests that these wishes are attained in the child's earliest trust in his mother.

20   Letter from Freud to Romain Rolland, 19 January 1930, *Freud Letters*, p. 393.

21   Ernest Jones, *The Life and Work of Sigmund Freud: The Last Phase 1919-1939* (New York, 1957), pp. 148, 339-342, 345-348.

22   Romain Rolland, *Printemps Romain: Choix de lettres de Romain Rolland à sa mère (1889-1890)*, Cahiers Romain Rolland, no. 6 (Paris, 1954); Romain Rolland, *Retour au Palais Farnèse: Choix de lettres de Romain Rolland à sa mère (1890-1891)*, Cahiers Romain Rolland, no. 8 (Paris, 1956).

23   Romain Rolland, *Les origines du théâtre lyrique moderne: Histoire de l'opéra avant Lully et Scarlatti* (Paris, 1895).

24   See Carl E. Schorske, "Politics and Patricide in Freud's *Interpretation of Dreams*," *Fin-de-Siècle Vienna: Politics and Culture* (New York, 1980), pp. 189-193, 199, 202-203.

25   Romain Rolland, *La vie de Michel-Ange* (1906) (Paris, 1964); Sigmund Freud, "The Moses of Michelangelo" (1914), *Standard Edition of the Complete Psychological Works of Sigmund Freud*, vol. 13 (London, 1953), edited by James Strachey, pp. 211-238.

26   Letter from Freud to Romain Rolland, 19 January 1930, *Freud Letters*, p. 393.

27   Letter from Freud to Romain Rolland, 4 March 1923, *Freud Letters*, p. 341.

28   Letter from Freud to Romain Rolland, 15 June 1924, cited in Fisher, "Sigmund Freud and Romain Rolland," p. 10.

29   Freud, "A Disturbance of Memory on the Acropolis," p. 239.
30   Letter from Freud to Romain Rolland, 4 March 1923, *Freud Letters*, p. 341.
31   Lorin Anderson, "Freud, Nietzsche," *Salmagundi*, no. 47-48 (Winter-Spring, 1980), pp. 3-29; Françoise L. Simon-Miller, "Ambivalence and Identification: Freud on Literature," *Literature and Psychology*, 28, no. 1 (1978), pp. 23-39; 28, no. 3-4 (1978), pp. 151-167; Lionel Trilling, "Freud: Within and Beyond Culture" (1955), *Beyond Culture: Essays on Literature and Learning* (New York, 1965), pp. 77-102, and "Art and Neurosis" (1945, 1947), *The Liberal Imagination: Essays on Literature and Society* (New York, 1976), pp. 160-180.
32   Letter from Freud to Romain Rolland, May 1931, *Freud Letters*, p. 406.
33   See letter from Freud to Arthur Schnitzler, 14 May 1922, *Freud Letters*, pp. 197-198, for Freud's thoughts on his doubleness with a prominent Viennese writer. For a psychoanalytic reading of the problem of otherness, see Lacan, "Desire and the Interpretation of Desire in *Hamlet*," pp. 11-52; Jacques Lacan, "The Function of Language in Psychoanalysis," in *The Language of the Self* (Baltimore, 1968), translated by Anthony Wilden, pp. 3-87; Anthony Wilden, "Lacan and the Discourse of the Other," ibid., pp. 137-311; Herbert I. Kupper and Hilda S. Rollman-Branch, "Freud and Schnitzler—(Doppelganger)," *Journal of The American Psychoanalytic Association* (1959), pp. 109-126.
34   J. Laplanche and J.-B. Pontalis, *The Language of Psycho-Analysis* (New York, 1973), translated by Donald Nicholson-Smith, pp. 431-433.
35   Letter from Freud to Romain Rolland, 29 January 1926, *Freud Letters*, p. 364; this is the opening line of Freud's tribute to Rolland on his sixtieth birthday.
36   Sigmund Freud, *Five Lectures on Psycho-Analysis* (1910), *Standard Edition of the Complete Psychological Works of Sigmund Freud* (London, 1957), edited by James Strachey, vol. 11, p. 55.
37   This suggestion has recently led to creative results in the psychoanalytic works of Heinz Kohut, *The Analysis of the Self* (New York, 1971), and of Otto Kernberg, *Borderline Conditions and Pathological Narcissism* (New York, 1975).
38   Paul Ricoeur, *Freud and Philosophy: An Essay on Interpretation* (New Haven, 1970), translated by Denis Savage, pp. 279, 302-309, 326.
39   The term is taken from Frank E. and Fritzie P. Manuel, *Utopian Thought in the Western World* (Cambridge, Mass., 1979), p. 791; the Manuels read *Civilization and Its Discontents* as "the most trenchant and devastating attack on utopian illusions—what he [Freud] called the lullabies of heaven—that has ever been delivered," p. 788.

6

Psychoanalytic Culture Criticism
and the Soul

*I should like to hand [analysis] over to a profession which
does not yet exist, a profession of lay curers of souls who
need not be doctors and should not be priests.*

—Freud to Oskar Pfister
25 November 1928

Bruno Bettelheim belongs to the finest tradition of European and psychoanalytic culture criticism. Whether he is explaining the group dynamics of Jewish prisoners in concentration camps,[1] unmasking the sentimental popular appeal of the Anne Frank diary,[2] undermining satirically Philip Roth's spoof of psychoanalysis in *Portnoy's Complaint*,[3] distinguishing between survival and resistance in dealing with the literature and films of the Holocaust,[4] or deciphering the unconscious roots of fairy tales, Bettelheim has been at the cutting edge of critical discourse for the past forty years. His works stimulate and irritate. Even his redundancies shake us from our complacency. He does not take the consensus viewpoint. His creativity requires that he be the outsider, taking well-timed shots at various establishments, piercing the conformist point of view. His writings invariably challenge the readers' received ideas. Bettelheim's audience is invited to reply, to get angry, to enter into dialogue with him, to see, as it were, if his tone of authority is based on substance, or if it simply expresses an authoritarian personality.

Bettelheim lived a long and eventful life, producing a substantial and evocative body of work, sixteen books in all, not to mention a prodigious number of articles, prefaces, book reviews, and journalism. For over thirty years, he taught at the University of Chicago, directed the Orthogenic School for emotionally disturbed children, supervised mental health professionals, and carried on a psychoanalytic practice.[5] Since his semi-retirement in 1973, Bettelheim wrote an additional six books, including some of his best, and continued to teach, lecture, and supervise.

I view Bettelheim as if he took the impassioned argument of Freud's 1926 *The Question of Lay Analysis* as his life's mission. Because he occupied a privileged position among contemporary lay analysts, and because Bettelheim's name is practically synonymous with lay analysis, I intend to extrapolate a few thoughts from Freud's text to assess what he achieved as a psychoanalytic culture critic.

In outlining the qualities most appropriate to the practice of psycho-analysis, Freud insisted that "doctors have no historical claim to the sole possession of analysis." With particular opposition to the American scene and the emerging trend toward the medicalization of psychoanalysis, Freud spoke plainly: "We do not consider it at all desirable for psychoanalysis to be swallowed up by medicine." Instead, the recruitment and training of analysts ought to focus on the intrinsic trustworthiness of the individual; on the individual's capacity to acquire knowledge and understanding of the inner lives of other human beings; and on the individual's readiness to gain valuable experience in depth psychology through a personal training analysis, through supervised study at a psychoanalytic institute, and through sustained efforts at introspection. Practicing lay analysts are not "any chance collection of riffraff, but people of academic education, doctors of philosophy, educationists." In order for psychoanalysis to fulfill its own internal developmental possibilities, in order for it to resist bureaucratization and rigidification, Freud urged that psychoanalytic training remain open to the nonmedical laymen. He emphasized the acquisition of expertise in the fields of the history of civilization, mythology, the psychology of religion, and the science of literature. Always attuned to the potential for cross-fertilization of disciplines, Freud proposed that the application of depth psychology to history, philology, education, and literature might be methodologically pertinent in solving fundamental problems in those fields. He also anticipated the creative possibilities of lay analysis in the understanding of normal and emotionally disturbed children, in educating educators, and in informing parents how to bring up children.[6]

Bettelheim's achievements are precisely in the areas that Freud mentions. He made major contributions to our understanding of contemporary history, having developed a unique and original perspective on the Nazi Holocaust; he devoted his life to the project of integrating his educational and therapeutic concerns; he dedicated himself to the understanding and treatment of children, all of which stems from his advocacy of the helpless child; he produced a seminal and inspirational book on fairy tales; he developed a nuanced appreciation of language and its use and abuse in all interpretative work.

Bettelheim's work is characterized by an astonishingly broad range of interests, where he applied a variety of perspectives that cut across disciplinary boundaries. If he entered different universes of discourse, he came prepared, bringing with him a distinctly European sensibility and a high level of cultivation and erudition. Yet he has also demonstrated a capacity to write both for professionals and for a wide literate audience. His prose is clear and accessible, never convoluted or Germanic. Whenever possible, he avoids technical or jargon-ridden terminology. His best writing is simultaneously perspicacious, trenchant, caustic, and playful. He is one of a handful of classically trained lay analysts who emerged as a public intellectual in America; that is, as a social and cultural critic who influenced a wide audience and who commands attention for the power and originality of his ideas.[7]

Bettelheim's books sell; they sometimes win prizes. *The Uses of Enchantment*, for example, won both the National Book Award and the National Book Critics Circle Award in 1977. *A Good Enough Parent* sold 100,000 copies in French translation alone and Bettelheim appeared on French television four times consecutively in prime time, no mean feat for a foreigner. His name, face, and accent became representative of psychoanalysis. Perhaps this became certified by Bettelheim's role in the 1983 Woody Allen film *Zelig* in which he played himself as a spokesman on psychoanalysis. When he told me of the Woody Allen escapade, he mentioned with a twinkle in his eyes that he did the scene in only one take.

Bettelheim belongs to the history of psychoanalysis as an outsider; his creativity demanded independence; consequently, he deliberately chose to belong to no single school. He is loyal to the authority of Freud as a critical thinker; he is a Freudian who maintains an irreverent, probing, self-analytical stance, committed to the expansion and revision of psychoanalytic concepts and practice. Like Freud's, the corpus of Bettelheim's writings are symphonic and he has never departed from the methodological and humanistic underpinnings of Freud's work. As a Viennese who witnessed the birth and hegemonic victory of ego psychology, Bettelheim never embraced—nor was embraced by—the leading Austrian and American theoreticians and practitioners of ego psychology, many of whom were his teachers, associates, and friends.

He was an exemplary representative of the psychoanalyst as university professor, succeeding in a milieu that has been hostile and resistant to psychoanalytic modes of thinking and research. He spent many of his best years at a great university, where he interacted with outstanding scholars, had access to a first-rate library, and assimilated the cultural life of a distinctly American city. Professorial responsibilities allowed him to draw a salary to support his family; he eventually gained tenure, liberating him from the economic and practical pressures of the private psychoanalytic clinician; he had minimal anxiety about referrals, about earning a living, about networking, about credentializing with the local institute, or about being recognized and being offered legitimacy by the American Psychoanalytic Association. Instead of therapy or professionalization overwhelming the science, he concentrated on investigating, on thinking, on posing questions, and on passionately engaging with some of the most pressing issues of the day. Bettelheim also resisted the temptation to publish highly technical works aimed at a relatively tiny coterie of specialists. He did not academicize his research or his mode of touching his audience. Bettelheim's psychoanalytic culture criticism is intentionally communicative and dialogic.[8]

Bettelheim explicitly fashioned his writing to resonate with the hearts and ultimate concerns of his educated public. His pieces have appeared in *The New Yorker, Harpers Magazine, The New York Times,* and *The Times Literary Supplement* of London.[9] He did not play it safe or avoid controversy. He was an outspoken, authoritative, and opinionated man, frequently pugnacious and acerbic in style. Like Freud, whom he approached as a master thinker, he could be polemical when an issue of integrity was at stake. Bettelheim was not afraid to oppose and to criticize official establishments, including the conservative psychoanalytic mainstream; outsider status represented a continuous pattern of critical thinking throughout his life. He represents an old, somewhat vanishing European tradition of the psychoanalyst as a nonconforming and free-thinking intellectual. It should also be said that he has been lambasted by the mainstream in tendentious, ad hominem, and often sneering articles, articles that often psychologize, dismiss, or assassinate his character rather than deal with the content of his ideas.[10] The old Bettelheim did not "mellow out" or become Californianized; he remained just as contentious and just as incisive; nor had he become more patient with sloppy, mystified, and slogan-ridden forms of thinking.

Bettelheim's writings on the Holocaust and the Nazi concentration camps emerged directly from his own experiences in Dachau and Buchenwald where he was imprisoned during the year 1938-39. Theodor Adorno once suggested that after Auschwitz there could be no poetry. Bettelheim approached this atrocity to illustrate that there could be memory and reparation, even after Auschwitz. He addressed the genocidal tendencies of modern civilization by assigning meaning to the historical and existential experience of surviving. His analysis of the greatest crime of this century enables individuals not to be rendered helpless, not to be silenced, not to be overwhelmed by what he called "the unfathomable horror of mass death." Without the historical and psychological understanding that he provided, there would be fewer means of resisting future forms of barbarism.

Psychoanalysis in the post-Holocaust world owes a huge debt to Bettelheim; he courageously argued against the banalization of this history, against the cheapening of the Holocaust by sensationalizing it, sentimentalizing it, against diluting it with comparisons; he opposed the ideological or propagandistic uses of it; likewise, he spoke persuasively of the dangers of forgetting, emphasizing the creative and therapeutic possibilities of remembering. His writings on the Nazis stem from a moral vision: the profound conviction that survivor guilt and anger can become a source of ethical and historical insight, rather than a trauma leading to unending resignation and victimization.

His 1943 paper, "Individual and Mass Behavior in Extreme Situations," is the most famous and controversial report on the concentration camps in the existing literature. In observing and describing the structure of the camps, Bettelheim clearly indicated the techniques and goals of the Gestapo and related their actions to the prevailing Nazi ideology. The concentration camps were explicitly set up to shatter the morale of the individual prisoner; to spread terror; to provide the Gestapo with a training arena; and to torture, torment, and break the body and spirit of the inmates.[11] Although his report is a classic, Bettelheim's article was rejected summarily by prestigious East Coast psychoanalytic and psychiatric journals; they alleged that the author lacked objectivity in the writing about these issues; that his slant was unfair to the Germans; and that the author, himself, a Jew, psychoanalyst, and social democrat, was suffering from paranoid delusions. It was published in the *Journal of Abnormal and Social Psychology*, a journal read primarily by teachers and researchers in social psychology. Almost immediately afterward, the perspicacious left-wing social critic, Dwight Macdonald, appreciated its value as a conceptual breakthrough and he reprinted it in his journal, *Politics*. This opened Bettelheim's work to an audience of nonprofessionals, inaugurating a career of culture criticism.[12]

Bettelheim realized that the concentration camps represented something entirely new for the victims and the victimized. Along with other members of his generation, like Hannah Arendt, Franz Neumann, Arthur Koestler, and George Orwell, Bettelheim connected the Holocaust to a critique of totalitarianism. He emphasized the psychological dimensions of this terrifying relationship of master and slave. The deepest lesson of the concentration camps was the ways in which modern mass society, with its scientific and technological resources, could extinguish a sense of individuality, could demolish an individual's sense of self. The degree of psychic trauma and regression which the prisoner in the camps underwent unveiled the terrible vulnerability of the self in extreme situations. For the prisoner, the main drama was the struggle to maintain his selfhood intact, to fight off personal disintegration, to keep a moral sense and a sense of dignity intact. Further-more, the concentration camp experience was not unique. Bettelheim warned that genocidal possibilities existed in all technological soci-eties, leaving contemporary man threatened not only by massive alienation and domination, but also with the loss of his autonomy.[13]

If Bettelheim's writings on the Holocaust display the psychoana-lyst's capacity to speak out publicly and to introduce the element of resistance to the passive participation in mass death, his work on children testifies to his unrelenting commitment to resonate sensitively with the lived experience and internal and external struggles of the young. Bettelheim's clinical philosophy insists that the therapist be warm, spontaneous, and establish an emotional closeness with the child. His interest in children and in infant autism began in Vienna before the experience of fascism, the concentration camps, and exile ruptured it. It resumed after his emigration to the United States, continuing into the present. Many of his conclusions about parenting are summarized in his 1987 book, *A Good Enough Parent*.[14]

After surviving the concentration camps, Bettelheim was motivated by his anger about the shameful and pathetic waste of the lives and spirit of emotionally disturbed children. They existed in a confused and anxious state of abysmal misery. Like a prisoner in the camps, an emotionally troubled child remains completely at the mercy of others who believe they know how he should live. Bettelheim's therapeutic approach refused that notion. The orientation of the Orthogenic School pivoted on the deep empathic understanding of the child, defined as the therapist's vicarious experience of feeling himself into the mind and the skin of the other. While taking on the treatment of supposedly untreatable and hopeless cases—including schizophrenic, anorexic, antisocial, and autistic youngsters—Bettelheim advocated the sustained personal investment of the therapist in the play, learning, and the inner world of the child.[15]

His direction of the Orthogenic School anticipated by decades the psychoanalytic understanding of the optimal therapeutic milieu; he stressed the need to respond to the child's demands for prolonged safety and comfort; he pointed out the necessity for a humane concern with space and living conditions, with the therapist providing a secure, stable residential center. He also designed his training of the personnel to be simultaneously cooperative and therapeutic, but without room for the infantile and grandiose rescue fantasies of the staff.[16] Bettelheim's case studies also directly addressed the issues of the therapist's countertransference, especially its uses in generating empathy and in deepening one's connection to the other. These audacious proposals pioneered the addressing of such material in the clinical literature, which previously was considered inappropriate.[17]

Bettelheim, to be sure, was no stranger to the dark side of man: his aggressivity, his selfishness, greed, and death anxiety, his capacity to do and to think evil things. Preoccupied with the exploration of unconscious conflicts, he also recognized that the unconscious was varied, multi-layered, chaotic, ambiguous, and ill-defined.

If he directly experienced horror and clinically immersed himself in the horrific life histories of the severely disturbed, the fairy tale text abounds in the author's sense of delight and astonishment in the poetic and imaginative inner world of the child. For the child, fairy tales entertain, arouse curiosity, stimulate the imagination, enlighten, clarify emotions, and resonate with their anxieties, depressive states, and conflicted aspirations. They accomplish something that realistic or didactic stories fail to do: namely, to take seriously the drama and enormity of the child's psychological and developmental dilemmas. They do not devalue the child's struggle for meaning in his life. Bettelheim invites parents and educators to follow the child's lead, to let the child determine which fairy tale will be most important at a specific phase of life. The task of the adult is to not be alienated from the subjective experience of the child's world. As the security of the extended family ended, the enormous pressure on the nuclear family increased, and the well-integrated community ceased to function, a historical situation emerged increasing the contemporary child's separation anxiety and annihilation anxiety. These anxieties require an appropriate sensitivity on the part of the parents; parents must give up their own self-centeredness in order to respond to the child's legitimate needs, affirming the child's sense that his experiences, desires, and fantasies are justified by his psychological situation. The reading aloud of fairy tales not only affirms the tender affection of the parent for the child, but it sets in motion a flexible, subjectively rich interpersonal relation. This close, affect-laden interaction between parent and child facilitates the child's subsequent growth, prompting psychological independence and moral maturity.[18]

Freud and Man's Soul (1983), his thirteenth book, focuses on another vital area of inquiry in the human and social sciences today, language. More specifically, it addresses the elusive issue of Freud's language, the content and spirit, the surface structure and significant latencies, of Freud's texts.

In this jewel of an essay, Bettelheim restores the concept of the soul to the psychoanalytic corpus. In differentiating the soul from the mental apparatus, he is not referring to a concept which is religious, supernatural, metaphysical, or mystical. The soul is the life principle in man; it represents that part of man's nature which is spiritual and emotional, the human being's most prized possession. As a psychological concept, the soul symbolizes a deeply hidden seat of the mind and the passions that is hardly accessible to investigation. It is worth investigating in the context of a collaborative psychoanalytic dialogue because all that is precious, worthy, and human in man is influenced by it.[19]

Bettelheim makes a number of pronouncements about psychoanalytic theory and practice in this text. First: what it is not. Psychoanalysis is not about making life easy; it is not about the amelioration of isolated symptoms; it is not about adjustment to the existing social or political status quo; it is not a system of intellectual constructs or abstractions; it is not the sole prerogative of the physician or the medical and biological disciplines; it is not a religion; it is not about the purveying of an esoteric or revealed body of truth; it is not a positivistic or pragmatic form of knowing whose results can be replicated, predicted, or statistically measured.[20]

For Bettelheim, psychoanalysis is first and foremost a science of the spirit, part of a tradition of hermeneutics, that is, an introspective form of self-understanding that relies on the exploration of unconscious and symbolic meanings. As an ideographic science, psychoanalysis belongs to the human sciences where the method is historical, archeological, and, above all, interpretative. Psychoanalytic insight threatens our narcissistic image of ourselves; it reveals that the "I" is not the master of its own house, thus injuring our self-love and our self-esteem. Profound self-knowledge always turns on the exploration of the individual's most shameful, most incestuous, and most destructive internal forces. Above all else, Bettelheim argues that psychoanalysis is part of an endless process where an individual resumes a stunted developmental course, attaining or approximating psychological maturity. Its insights enhance the capacity of an individual to acquire a moral education, learning how to act and behave ethically. In attempting to wring some meaning out of our existence, psychoanalysis accepts the problematic and tragic nature of life without being defeated and without giving in to escapism.[21]

Freud's writings, Bettelheim argues, have been misrepresented by his translators in *The Standard Edition*. Why does he raise these issues about a distorted translation? The culture critic cannot disregard these inaccuracies because Freud's ideas have radically shifted the twentieth-century perception of humanity. Freudian terminology has penetrated into everyday speech. Freud's words have evolved into a universe of their own; his language has decisively shaped our conception of subjectivity, despite its uncertain destiny. Language is central in understanding Freud's theoretical orientation; the repercussions of Freud's words are vast for those engaged in therapeutic endeavors and in humanistic enterprises. Thus, how Freud was translated can largely determine how he is read and how his ideas are applied. The strategy of Bettelheim's book is to indicate selectively crucial mistranslations of Freud's work from the German to the English. He is uniquely qualified to perform this task. He entered adulthood in Freud's Vienna in the 1920s and 1930s. His cultural, educational, ethnic, and linguistic background resembles Freud's (the most important contrast would be the absence of medical and neurophysiological training in Bettelheim's formation).

Bettelheim alerts us to the outright errors, esoterism, and clumsy technical jargon in *The Standard Edition*. This obstructs the process of making Freud's words accessible to the reader. The translators failed to engender a sense of the implications of psychoanalytic concepts. He emphasizes how Freud, an ingenious and inventive writer, rarely borrowed from Latin and Greek usage; rather the major sources of his writings came from ordinary spoken German, as well as from the existing psychological and psychopathological literature of his day.

Bettelheim hammers away at several overlapping themes: that Freud sounds more abstract, more scientific, more dispassionate, more mechanistic in English than in German; that the recourse to specialized vocabulary in the English version covers up imprecise, often soft, thinking and deflects the reader from emotional associations; that

Freud frequently opted for the most simple word in German without striving for consistent or systematic meaning every time he used a given term; that Freud's language was explicitly chosen to sound an intimate note, that is, that he built theory in order to strike his audiences' private register. In short, reading Freud ought to invite a process of familiarity, akin to the spontaneous, empathic feelings of closeness experienced in confronting what is human in oneself. Reading Freud ought not to be conducted at too great a distance, ought not to be experienced with the feelings of strangeness or detachment. Freud's sublime gifts as a writer allow his audience to return to themselves both emotionally and intellectually. The corpus of his work stands as an extended invitation to explore one's inner depths; it encourages a deeper understanding of one's unconscious and of the unconscious modalities of others.

Although he does not cite his predecessors, Bettelheim's critique of the faulty translations in *The Standard Edition* is not new. Lacan, among the most penetrating, railed against erroneous conclusions based on erroneous translation for years.[22] In the introduction to the superb *The Language of Psychoanalysis* (1967), Daniel Lagache called for more "faithful translation" of Freud's work.[23] English translator James Strachey mentioned the "deficiencies" and the "irremediable" faults of his efforts in the 1966 "General Preface" to *The Standard Edition*. Strachey was aware of the untranslatable verbal points in Freud's writings, especially in the autobiographical works like *The Interpretation of Dreams* and *The Psychopathology of Everyday Life*. He mentioned that Freud's German editions were often untrustworthy.[24] Moreover, Ernest Jones alerts us to Freud's "cavalier" attitudes about foreign editions of his writings; Jones, nevertheless, predicted that the English translation would be more accurate than all previous editions.[25]

At first glance, Bettelheim seems harsh in criticizing the Herculean enterprise of making Freud's complete psychological works available in English. Perhaps the best that any individual could accomplish should be a sustained structure with a unified thematics. This, it seems to me, Strachey accomplished. Bettelheim would disagree, strenuously. He is attacking a sacred cow by calling into question *The Standard Edition*, which scholars and the general public have gratefully used since its publication between 1953 and 1974. The extensive annotations, explanations, cross referencing, and its official authorization by the Freud family and the psychoanalytic establishment, have made it a chief source of reference for those seriously committed to studying Freud's work. Bettelheim irreverently reveals gaps in the translation, glaring errors of fact, and untenable misinterpretations of Freud's major texts, including the titles of his works.

For Bettelheim, *The Standard Edition* does a disservice to Freud because it distances the reader from his own unconscious conflicts, barring access to his own deepest desires. Freud modernized the injunction to know thyself by inviting his audience to confront what is darkest, ugliest, most untamed, most disordered in themselves. Freud's insights, Bettelheim contends, injure modern human beings' narcissistic image of themselves as civilized, rational, perfectible, loving, progressive, dutiful, and harmonious. Misleading and incorrect translations subvert Freud's humanistic intentions; consequently, his translators are responsible for a "perversion of the original," proving, once again, how the translator is a "traitor to the author."[26]

Bettelheim explains the betrayal of Freud by his—admittedly—self-chosen translators. When psychoanalysis was presented to English and American audiences, the analytical side was given a privileged position over the psychical side. Psyche, Bettelheim reminds us, means soul, emotion, and the human conceived in an unscientific sense. To comprehend the psyche, Freud held that one had to know and deal with one's unconscious strivings, unconscious fantasies, and symbolic representations. This form of knowing required interpretation, a sustained effort to get beneath the surface of things, to restore the psyche to its latent layers of meaning. *The Standard Edition* distorts the spiritual side of psychoanalysis by overemphasizing analysis, the scientific effort to break down and to dissect the mind. Scientists tend to approach the mental apparatus from the outside from an apparently objective or detached point of view, thus disregarding the nuances, metaphorical quality, poetic and imagistic contents of the soul. For Bettelheim psychoanalysis unquestionably belongs to the humanistic disciplines, not to the natural sciences. This was Freud's intention.

The determining influence of Goethe on Freud's intellectual development and methodology can be seen, Bettelheim contends, in the syntheses of his late, cultural texts. Unfortunately, Freud's translators blunted the emotional impact of what Freud was conveying in order to make the scientific component of his discourse palatable to the "positivistic-pragmatic" branch of scientific study so dominant in England and America, especially in psychiatric milieus. The clarity and definitiveness of Freud's writings in English camouflage the contradictions and ambiguities of the German original. *The Standard Edition* obscures the spirit as well as the content of Freud's ideas by transforming what is essentially a human science (a branch of knowledge much closer to hermeneutical-spiritual knowing) into something that approximates natural science.

Bettelheim detects two motives that underlie the mistranslations: the desire to make psychoanalysis acceptable to a medical and psychiatric community in England and America; and the unconscious wish of the translators to detach themselves from the emotional impact of the unconscious. Countering recent efforts to debunk Freud by characterizing him as an unoriginal, anachronistic, nineteenth-century man of science, Bettelheim claims that Freud evolved from a biologist to a theoretician of the soul. For evidential value, he observes that Freud rarely cited scientific or medical literature, while often referring to or paraphrasing literary, artistic, and philosophic works. Freud wanted the psychoanalytic profession to be ideally composed of "secular ministers of souls,"[27] that is, something between the physician and the secular priest. There is no doubt that Freud borrowed from and contributed to psychology, but to a form of psychology far removed from the banalities of Anglo-Saxon behaviorism or the gross obviousness of academic psychology. He was unconcerned with predictive or readily replicated empirical science. Rather, Freud's psychology was tied to a hermeneutical branch of philosophy devoted to unraveling the meanings of the deeper, buried, fragmented, and many-layered nature of psychic reality.

Bettelheim's most telling illustration of mistranslation is his exegesis of the concept of soul (in German: *die Seele*). Freud clearly and distinctly meant soul and not mind or mental apparatus (as *The Standard Edition* has rendered it). Bettelheim has rehabilitated the concept of soul for the psychoanalytic profession, while affirming a militantly secular and humanist version of this metaphor. He does so without muting Freud's lifelong atheism and his unwavering distrust of wishful or delusional thinking. The soul ought not to belong exclusively to the universe of discourse of religious thinkers, Jungians, or mystics.

By soul Bettelheim means people's common humanity, their essence, their most valuable traits, their spiritual core. Soul cannot be comprehended precisely without collapsing its emotional and vitalistic resonances. Soul cannot be defined or pinned down. The soul is one of those border concepts straddling psychology and language; it is a metaphor that Freud employed self-consciously as a metaphor. It evokes both an intellectual and an affective response. It has nothing whatsoever to do with the supernatural, with a religious deity, with salvation, or with immortality. As a secular discipline, psychoanalysis can legitimately be concerned with spiritual endeavors. The good psychoanalytic researcher investigates the underworld of the soul. If he treats the soul as the human being's most prized possession, he also knows that the soul requires a care and respect—a love—not to be mistaken with the medical orientation of therapy and cure for the body. Bettelheim contends that Freud never wished psychoanalysis to be a subspecialty of the medical profession. The text he cites most often by Freud is the much neglected *The Question of Lay Analysis*.[28]

Bettelheim offers other tasty examples of incorrect English constructions of Freud's seminal concepts. As an adherent of the structural model, he shows that the English version of id, ego, superego radically falsifies Freud's original German, transforming these living aspects of the soul into cold, reified, teleological, and reductionistic agencies of the mind; this totally blunts the affective impact on the reader. Freud selected personal pronouns to name these concepts; Bettelheim restores the it (for id), I or me (for ego), and above-I (for superego); he suggests that the personal pronouns relate directly to the individual's experiences, thereby arousing his associations, memories, fantasies, and desires. The personal pronouns allow the reader to get inside the psychoanalytic process itself; they allow his I or me to borrow from, coexist with, achieve rational control over the it. He retranslates the famous line ("Where id was, there ego shall be.") from Freud's thirty-first lecture in *The New Introductory Lectures on Psychoanalysis* (1933) as "Where it was, there should become I." The I, in brief, does not unseat, ride, or obliterate the it, but rather the I labors to change itself in significant ways in order to achieve or perpetuate culture.[29]

There are other semantic rectifications in the Bettelheim volume. "Free association" is not free at all and he urges us to translate it as an idea or image that spontaneously comes to mind. He translates fending off or parrying for "defense," occupation for "cathexis," and lapse for "slips of the tongue." He reveals a double error in the title of the 1914 essay, "Instincts and Their Vicissitudes," and substitutes "Drives and Their Mutability." For *Civilization and Its Discontents,* an inspired title in my judgment, Bettelheim prefers a more literal *The Uneasiness Inherent in Culture*—a title consistent with the underlying intention of the text to be sure, but unconnected to the artistic underpinnings and imaginative structure of the essay.

However, I found it dubious, even a bit illogical, for the translators of *The Standard Edition,* James Strachey and Anna Freud, to be held responsible for the positivistic, empiricist, and medical-biological slant of these twenty-four volumes. Historically, both Strachey and Anna Freud were lay analysts, both were analyzed by Freud, and both were deeply trusted by Freud and members of his estate. Ultimately, Bettelheim's indictment of the translators of *The Standard Edition* is exaggerated. Perhaps purposefully. From their own published writings, it is clear that Strachey and Anna Freud sought to anchor psychoanalysis in a biological framework based on Freud's early energy model. It was not bad faith or unconscious motives that made them reject Bettelheim's version of psychoanalysis as an interpretive science with its own laws and techniques, its own, primarily hermeneutical, sense of exactitude and research strategies. That is, Bettelheim's Freud is subjectively different from the Freud of Strachey and Anna Freud; different, in that his conception of psychoanalysis is more literary, more historical and archeological in methodology, more enamored of prehistory and mythology, more preoccupied with securing psycho-analysis a place of honor in cultural history, less interested in establishing its scientific verifiability and experimental or clinical validity. For Bettelheim psychoanalysis is more exciting as a general theory of culture, not (as for Anna Freud and Strachey) as a refined instrument of therapy. Bettelheim appreciates the complexity in Freud's thought by explicating his gifts as a writer: his ability to operate on many levels simultaneously, his deft choice of allusions and references, his capacity to touch his readers affectively and intellectually.

Every translation is a rewriting and a reinterpretation. Certainly, there are critical inaccuracies, pretensions, and linguistic problems in *The Standard Edition;* often the multiplicity of meaning, inconsistencies, the earthiness, the wit, the Jewish humor, and the poetry of Freud's writings are not sufficiently fleshed out.

If Bettelheim makes errors in emphasis, he compensates for them by his candid and intransigent humanism. He does not tediously lament the current crisis or decline of the humanities. Instead, he makes a strong case for psychoanalytic humanism. In the process, he recruits Freud to a pivotal position in the modern humanist tradition, albeit a hermeneutical-spiritual one. Bettelheim's humanism is oriented toward the dynamic of self-discovery, toward integrating the hidden and narcissistically injurious truths about one's inner world. His is a demystifying and critical humanism which attempts to lay bare the psychosexual and aggressive roots of human beings' psyche and behavior. This form of humanism is neither mawkish nor akin to the belief in Santa Claus. Bettelheim firmly understands the determining role of unconscious conflict in symbol formation, inner and outer representations of reality, and in the multiple ways in which individuals deceive themselves. Bettelheim practices a polemical kind of psychoanalytic culture criticism. He discloses the errors, sophistry, idiocy, dangers, opportunism, and silliness (sometimes all of the above) in his opponent's views. Bettelheim writes with a strong point of view and he willingly argues it. He is prepared to generalize, to take risks, to give offense, in order to stir up his audience.

Despite its negations, I read his *Freud and Man's Soul* as essentially an affirmative work. It is written in defense of culture, more specifically it depicts how conflict works both to generate and to allow the individual to comprehend cultural creation. Bettelheim sees no end to the individual's antagonistic relationship to his environment, no end to intrapsychic conflict. He accepts these struggles as part of humanity's existential curse. Rather than be wished away, struggle ought to be embraced. It is not accidental that the feisty Bettelheim published this essay first in *The New Yorker*, the weekly that analysands read. It appears he decided tactically to influence the psychoanalytic community by uttering his thoughts through the back door; analysts would hear his irreverent message via the analysand's words from the couch. There is controlled anger in his writings, a certain glee in standing apart, a pride in pointing out the deficiencies and shallowness of American culture, including American psychoanalytic culture. Bettelheim's tendency to repeat himself, a characteristic flaw in all of his writings, suggests a frustration at not being listened to, an exasperation at not being understood—the recurring complaint of all polemical writers.

Despite its weaknesses, its self-righteous and strident tone, Bettelheim wrote a spirited essay, which posits that knowledge of the self and that the search for the truth are at the center of the psychoanalytic project. He wrote from an independent and free thinking position, one which indicates his debt to and identification with Freud, especially the late Freud, and his animus toward establishment psychoanalysis in America. Psychoanalysis, he emphasized, was never designed to move in the direction of social accommodation or adaptation to the prevailing opinions, values, or anxieties of any civilization. In the midst of the contemporary malaise of psychoanalysis, the essay is an eloquent testimony to the need for humaneness, truthfulness, compassion, and courage on the part of the psychoanalytic researcher and practitioner in pursuit of the buried meanings of humanity's inner life. Bettelheim, finally, enjoins us to return to the soulful letter and spirit of Freud's writings with the same tragic skepticism of the late Freud. Such a voyage into the realm of humanity's soul is surely interminable, but Bettelheim, with his dialectical love of process, is undeterred. He would agree with T.S. Eliot in enjoining us to launch and sustain the journey:

We shall not cease from exploration,
And the end of all our exploring
Will be to arrive where we started
And know the place for the first time.[30]

Notes

1   Bruno Bettelheim, "Individual and Mass Behavior in Extreme Situations" (1943), in Bettelheim, *Surviving and Other Essays* (New York, 1979), pp. 48-83.

2   Bruno Bettelheim, "The Ignored Lesson of Anne Frank" (1966), in ibid., pp. 246-257.

3   Bruno Bettelheim, "Portnoy Psychoanalyzed" (1969), in ibid., pp. 387-398.

4   Bruno Bettelheim, "Surviving" (1976), in ibid., pp. 274-314.

5   For biographical information, see Morris Janowitz, "Bettelheim, Bruno," in *Biographical Supplement to International Encyclopedia of the Social Sciences* (New York, 1979); Lewis A. Coser, *Refugee Scholars in America* (New Haven, 1984), pp. 63-68; Anthony Heilbut, *Exiled in Paradise: German Refugee Artists*

and Intellectuals in America from the 1930's to the Present (New York, 1983), pp. 203, 209-210, 295. For some autobiographical data, see Bruno Bettelheim, *Freud's Vienna and Other Essays* (New York, 1990), pp. 24-38, 98-111.

6   Sigmund Freud, *The Question of Lay Analysis* (1926), in *The Standard Edition of the Complete Psychological Works of Sigmund Freud*, vol. 20 (London, 1959), edited by James Strachey.

7   I am borrowing the concept from Russell Jacoby's *The Last Intellectuals: American Culture in The Age of Academe* (New York, 1987), although Bettelheim is unmentioned in the text.

8   See Mikhail M. Bakhtin, *The Dialogic Imagination* (Austin, 1981), translated by Caryl Emerson and Michael Holquist; Tzvetan Todorov, *Mikhail Bakhtin: The Dialogical Principle* (Minneapolis, 1984), translated by Wlad Godzich.

9   For a comprehensive bibliography, see David James Fisher, "Bruno Bettelheim's Achievement," *Free Associations*, Spring, 1991.

10 See Terence Des Pres, *The Survivor: An Anatomy of Life in The Death Camps* (New York, 1976), pp. 61-63, 88-94, 182-187, 189-194; for the representative psychoanalytic dismissals, see Stanley J. Coen, "How to Read Freud: A Critique of Recent Freud Scholarship," *Journal of the American Psychoanalytic Association*, vol. 36, no. 2, 1988, pp. 487, 489-491; Darius G. Ornston, "Review of *Freud and Man's Soul*," *Journal of the American Psychoanalytic Association*, vol. 33, supplement 1985, pp. 189-200.

11 Bruno Bettelheim, "Individual and Mass Behavior in Extreme Situations," in Bettelheim, *Surviving*, pp. 48-83.

12 Bruno Bettelheim, "Behavior In Extreme Situations," *Politics*, August 1944, vol. 1, no. 7, pp. 199-209.

13 Bruno Bettelheim, *The Informed Heart: Autonomy in a Mass Age* (New York, 1960).

14 Bruno Bettelheim, *A Good Enough Parent: A Book on Child-rearing* (New York, 1987).

15 Bruno Bettelheim, *Truants From Life: The Rehabilitation of Emotionally Disturbed Children* (New York, 1955); Bruno Bettelheim, *The Empty Fortress: Infantile Autism and the Birth of the Self* (New York, 1967).

16 Bruno Bettelheim, *A Home for the Heart* (Chicago, 1974).

17 Bruno Bettelheim, "On Writing Case Histories," in Bettelheim, *Truants From Life*, pp. 473-478.

18 Bruno Bettelheim, *The Uses of Enchantment: The Meaning and Importance of Fairy Tales* (New York, 1975); also see Ruth B. Shapiro and Constance L. Katz, "Fairy Tales, Splitting, and Ego Development," *Contemporary Psychoanalysis*, vol. 14, no. 4, October, 1978, pp. 591-602 for a balanced critique.

19 Bruno Bettelheim, *Freud and Man's Soul* (New York, 1983).

20 Ibid., pp. 6-7, 16, 40-41, 43, 53, 107.

21 Ibid., pp. 33, 35, 43, 57, 76-77, 102-103, 109-110.

22 Jacques Lacan, "The Freudian Thing, or the Meaning of the Return to Freud in Psychoanalysis" (1956), in Lacan, *Ecrits* (New York, 1977), translated by Alan Sheridan, pp. 114-145; Jacques Lacan, *The Four Fundamental Concepts of Psycho-Analysis* (1973) (New York, 1978), translated by Alan Sheridan, pp. 44-46.

23 Daniel Lagache, "Introduction" (1967), in J. Laplanche and J.-B. Pontalis, *The Language of Psychoanalysis* (New York, 1973), translated by Donald Nicolson-

Smith, p. viii.

24 James Strachey, "General Preface" (1966), in *The Standard Edition of the Complete Psychological Works of Sigmund Freud*, vol. 1 (London, 1966), pp. xiii-xxii; Strachey dubbed his translation a "blurred reflection" of Freud's thoughts and words, calling himself a "contriver" see, ibid., p. v.

25 Ernest Jones, *The Life and Work of Sigmund Freud: the Last Phase 1919-1939* (New York, 1957), pp. 9-10; also see Ernest Jones, *Free Associations* (New York, 1959), p. 169.

26 Bettelheim, *Freud and Man's Soul*, p. 101.

27 Ibid., p. 35.

28 Ibid., pp. 33-34, 35, 36, 37, 6-61, 71.

29 Ibid., pp. 61-64.

30 T.S. Eliot, "Little Gidding," *Four Quartets* in *T.S. Eliot: The Complete Poems and Plays 1909-1950* (New York, 1952), p. 145.

7

A Final Conversation with Bruno Bettelheim

*I wondered all the time whether man can endure so much
without committing suicide or going insane.*

—Bruno Bettelheim, 1943

Bruno Bettelheim committed suicide on 13 March 1990. He left behind a distinguished and original body of work, consisting of sixteen books and copious other writings. He was one of the world's foremost psychoanalytic humanists.

The transcript of this conversation with Bettelheim is taken from two discussions I had with him, the first on 27 July 1988, and the second on 28 November 1988. They took place at his apartment overlooking the Santa Monica Palisades and the Pacific Ocean. He was living there alone, cared for by a housekeeper. Bettelheim requested that I not publish the interview until after his death due to the confidential nature of some of the material, particularly the section on suicide.

The text covers a good deal of ground, including his ideas on old age, his children, Los Angeles, on the concentration camps, on suicide, on his experience in the 1930s around the Vienna Psychoanalytic Society, his reflections on lay analysis, on Freud, his memories of his analysis with Richard Sterba, and on the treatment of severely disturbed children. I have selected and edited the material to allow Bettelheim to speak in his own voice.

A poignancy and sadness pervade the text; it is as if Bettelheim was continually wrestling with the idea of suicide and of ways to defend against taking his life. Here is the late Bettelheim summing up and reflecting on the themes that mattered most to him. It may be his last in-depth interview.

D.J.F.   Let me begin with a question on Simone de Beauvoir's book on old age. She says old age exposes the failure of our entire civilization, and she advocates a more generous old age policy, including higher pensions for the elderly, decent housing, medical care, and organized leisure. Tell me your particular thoughts about old age.

B.B.   Don't reach it! I think that what de Beauvoir suggests is perfectly reasonable. Although, in my opinion, these do not go to the heart of the matter, at least not from my perspective. What I have experienced is a deterioration of physical strength and energy, which I find very hard to take. It is depressing. I see no compensation for it, unless one wishes or desires to see one's grandchildren grow up because I am curious about them. I know that I am too old to see them grow up, so I will not know what they are going to do. I wish them well, naturally. But what will happen to them in the future is not going to be of interest to me. My children no longer need me. I feel that I have done my life's work, and I am fairly satisfied with it. But I feel a weakness that makes it very difficult, if not impossible, for me to go on in ways in which I was accustomed to go on. And that is the great narcissistic hurt which I find very difficult to cope with. It's nothing unusual or unexpected. It's nothing that doesn't come with the course of old age, but I don't like it. What I fear, of course, is what everybody my age fears. What happens to some of my age mates is that they become completely incapacitated and live in such a state for a number of years, then they invest in nursing homes from which the best subsequently die.

D.J.F.   There have been significant personal changes in your life recently, including the death of a spouse, a move to Los Angeles, a minor stroke, difficulties in swallowing, anxieties about an incapacitating illness, and fears of death.

B.B.   No, not fear of death. Only of a painful death. Fear of a prolonged death. What I really wish for is a fast and easy death. That's easy to wish for.

D.J.F.   You are now a man in your mid-eighties and, if you will permit me, I would like to ask an Eriksonian question about your experience of the life cycle. Are you experiencing the conflict between despair and self-defeat versus integrity or the acceptance of one's life?

B.B.   Let me put it this way. This is only referring to ideal types. He doesn't give any indication at all of the statistical frequency of this ideal. It's very easy to pull ideal types out of one's own head without really checking the frequency or infrequency of the case. For example, he starts with basic trust and basic distrust. Although these are very good categories, how many children or infants really experience basic trust?

D.J.F.   Or degrees of basic trust?

B.B.   That's right. Actually, what we are talking about, at best, are degrees. And degrees are frequently statistical concepts.

D.J.F.   Let's talk personally. He's really thinking of overcoming disgust, misanthropy, chronic contemptuous displeasure with life, and achieving what philosophers used to call wisdom and what psychoanalysts call integrity. Does that tally with your own experience? Forget about statistics for a second.

B.B.   I had lunch today, before you came, with two prominent members of the faculty of the University of California. They were both highly intelligent and accomplished people, as prominent as they each can become in their profession. The conversation was often uninteresting, but a couple of years ago, I would have found it extremely stimulating. Today, I thought the conversation could have been stimulating, only I was really physically too tired to fancy it. Not that I didn't enjoy it, not that I didn't find it interesting, but it revolved around the subject of who was going to be the new chairman of psychiatry. Quite frankly, whoever that might be no longer interests me, whereas ten years ago, that would have been of great interest to me. This is because I have a realistic assessment of how much time I have, which isn't very much.

D.J.F.   What does interest you?

B.B.   As one grows older, the areas of interest shrink, at least in my case this is so. Now, of course, there are some people who have been able to retain that ability to be creative and hold interests. When I compare today to four years ago during the national elections, I was very interested in seeing one of the candidates win. Today, this topic really doesn't interest me.

D.J.F.   Are you alluding to a physical sense of exhaustion?

B.B.   It's very hard to say. It is a deterioration of interests in life. To be very personal, I have essentially two interests in life. One is to see my younger daughter who is pregnant give birth, and the other is to try to finish another book of mine on ethics. I hope to finish at least the introduction to this book. So, you see, when one is young, one desires many things for the future. But when one becomes as old as I am, one desires only to finish a few things.

D.J.F.   I want to get your general impressions and perceptions of Los Angeles.

B.B.   I never wanted to live here. My other daughter used to live in Pasadena, so I visited from time to time. I am going to make a very quick, prejudicial statement. I saw changes in my own daughter from the girl she was in Chicago to the woman she became once she made her home in Los Angeles, which in terms of my values, was an undesirable one. Now, I cannot blame it on the city. It might be her personally. It might be what drove her to move here. I cannot sort it out. I'm much too close to her. There is a concern with possessions which I consider external. But I would have liked to see her develop other qualities that might not have developed in any degree. There were many misgivings about Los Angeles despite being warned by my other two children. I moved here because she invited me, and I had no other opportunities. It was by no means my first choice. I explored other possibilities; each one had its problems. Here, at least, I had a daughter. I was hopeful for a good relationship, but it didn't turn out the way I hoped for. And I guess it didn't turn out the way she hoped for. This is hardly surprising or new. I wish her well. When she was a child in Chicago, we had so many common interests together; she had many values in common with me, and now the opposite was true. Now, wasn't I developed then, wasn't she developed then, or was it the city?

D.J.F.   You've mentioned to me in previous conversations that you find a sense of superficiality in Los Angeles, a materialism, leading frequently to a trivialization of culture, to a sense of bad values, to a flamboyance and narcissism of everyday life here.

B.B.   Let me put it this way. I know about the concentration of the entertainment world. Its importance in society here seems to be very different than in other places.

D.J.F.   What are your impressions of the influence of money and of the trendiness of the Hollywood industry on the psychoanalytic community in Los Angeles?

B.B.   I really don't think that I know enough about the analytic community in Los Angeles to give you a judgment about them.

D.J.F.   You can give me an impressionistic judgment.

B.B.   There are many analysts in the Los Angeles area. Some who are very respectable, some who are very serious about it. Let's face it, there are some who are in it for the money and the prestige. I don't think it's any different from anywhere else. We are talking about degrees, and for that, we need to study it statistically, which I haven't done.

D.J.F.   Can a European intellectual like yourself ever "assimilate" into the United States? Have you become "Americanized"?

B.B.   I can answer that in an uncomplicated way. When I retired from the University of Chicago, my wife and I very seriously considered retiring in Switzerland, Southern Switzerland. Finally, we decided we have three children who live in the United States. We didn't want to be very far away from our children. Within a few years of reaching our decision, two of our three children went to live in Europe.

D.J.F.   Your American children have become Europeanized.

B.B.   Certainly one of them, very much so. Very much becoming Anglophiles.

D.J.F.   Do you think of yourself as American, or do you still regard yourself as primarily a European, a European intellectual, or someone who bridges both cultures?

B.B.   As an analyst, you know the amazing background of so many of us from Europe.

D.J.F.   I want to turn to Buchenwald and Dachau and the concentration camp experience. We were talking about Primo Levi's sense of the poignant burden of the survivors. He says that the experience of the concentration camps cannot be understood historically or psychologically by those who did not live it, that it is impossible to convey that experience. There is a paradox for the survivors of the camps, that is, the need to make that incomprehensible experience remembered. Can you comment on that?

B.B.   It's an experience that is so overwhelming, so full of contradictions really that it's very hard to cope with. I think that anybody who spent time in a German concentration camp—it does not necessarily have to be an extermination camp—never gets rid of the feeling of guilt and shame. It is such a degrading experience that you feel obliged not to suffer it, but to fight back your guilt. You have to suppress your normal reactions in a life threatening situation. The problem is that you feel no one really understands what you went through. Some people repress it, some try to go on with life as usual as if nothing had ever happened. That's a very empty way to deal with it.

D.J.F.   Can you make it a little more specific? Do you agree with Primo Levi who says that the drowned and the saved are the same? He points out a degree of rage and shame among the Holocaust survivors. He insists on the need not to sentimentalize or idealize the past. In talking about this question, you mention that very revealing story of your cousin in Dachau. Would you talk about him again?

B.B.   He was already in Dachau when I arrived there. He gave me some good advice. The advice is whenever you have a chance to sleep, sleep; whenever you have a chance to eat, eat. I found this to be very good advice because some of the prisoners, particularly Jewish prisoners, were very spoiled; they couldn't eat the kind of junk they presented us with. If you didn't eat it, you lost all power to survive. You had to force yourself to eat this junk in order to survive. You also needed only short sleep, so whenever you had ten or fifteen minutes to rest, you tried to sleep. Now the interesting thing are the dreams. In the concentration camp, I rarely dreamt about imprisonment or captivity. I dreamt of happy occasions, about...

D.J.F.   Wish fulfilling dreams?

B.B.   Yes, and they were very helpful. On the other hand, when you were liberated, you dreamt that you didn't get out. These were anxiety dreams. So the interesting thing was that in the camp, you didn't have these anxiety dreams because you wouldn't be able to cope.

D.J.F.   You had enough realistic anxiety.

B.B.   That's right.

D.J.F.   Now tell the story—I know this is painful—of the lineup and when your cousin was assaulted.

B.B.   As for my cousin, he wasn't assaulted; he just collapsed. He became unconscious and fell down. And then he was, of course, kicked by the S.S. and so on, and I couldn't come to his rescue.

D.J.F.   No one could have come to his rescue.

B.B.   One has to restrain oneself from doing what is so tempting to do. It is a very difficult experience. Very shameful. It goes with the feeling that so many people who were as good as you, maybe better, were murdered. It gives rise to deep feelings of guilt and shame.

D.J.F.   To have helped him out would have put your own life in jeopardy.

B.B.   That's right. Very much so. Without really helping him.

D.J.F.   And that particular episode comes back as an example of the ambiguity of the morality in the camps?

B.B.   Yes, well, in order to survive in the camps, you needed to be a good comrade because you always needed someone to help you. People wouldn't help you unless you had done the same. There is one experience which becomes very troublesome for me—the "Muslims." They were the living corpses, unable to act on their own behalf; they all died very soon. What I've seen in some of the old age nursing homes is so much like the camps, the same psychological conditions.

D.J.F.   Let me ask you about your views on the chapter in Primo Levi's *The Drowned and the Saved* called "The Intellectual in Auschwitz." It's basically about the philosopher Jean Améry. Levi talks about the morality of returning the blow, how the concentration camp experience pushed an individual to the limits of the spirit, into the realm of the nonimaginable. We know that Levi himself had an inability to trade punches, to respond to violence with violent forms of self-defense. Is that a particular legacy of the intellectual who survived the camps, or is that something that is universal?

B.B.   Yes, I would like to talk about the intellectual. The important thing was that you demonstrated to yourself that your mind was still working. It meant a great deal, it provided some self-reassurance, and it allowed one to hold onto certain ideas and to certain hopes. The main thing was not to lose hope.

D.J.F.   Would an intellectual have a different kind of relationship to the issue of hope than a nonintellectual?

B.B.   That is hard to say. I had to act so if I wanted to survive. Although I knew the odds against it were very high. But if you adopted hope that you would survive, you wouldn't suffer all the regulations. You could finish your life. It was very easy—all you had to do was run into the electric wire.

D.J.F.   Was the cultivated man worse off than the uncultivated man? Did the man of culture have a deeper sense of humiliation, destitution, and lost dignity?

B.B.   That's a hard one to answer because I cannot jump out of my skin. I can only talk from my own experience. I don't really know how the uneducated person took it. I had very little contact with the uneducated person because one tried to remain within one's circle. I can tell you what the old prisoners told us when we arrived in Dachau. They said, if you survive the first months, you have a good chance to survive the first year; if you survive the first year, you have a good chance to survive the whole time. There were certain adjustments which had to be made practically immediately. One was that we had to accept the degradation without being in a continuous state of fury, which would drain you of all mental energy. So, I was observing Dachau, while being in Dachau. It was as if we technically were separated from the experience in Dachau. Sometimes you acted as though you were observing a stranger rather than yourself.

D.J.F.   You had to live a kind of split-off existence?

B.B.   That's right. A split in the ego.

D.J.F.   Primo Levi talks about the memory that he had in the camp of verses by Dante, which had great value, which reestablished his link with the past, which saved culture from oblivion and reinforced his identity. You mentioned a memory of *Fidelio*. How important were those episodes or events, and how did that allow you to distinguish yourself from the Muslim, the worn-out man with the dead or dying intellect?

B.B.   One had to hold onto whatever had given meaning to one's previous life, even if it was nonsensical in the camp situation. You had to hold onto it to survive. One becomes afraid when one stops thinking and feeling; one wanted to reassure oneself that one hasn't given up.

D.J.F.   And your memory of that *Fidelio*?

B.B.   It was a Sunday afternoon when one of the officers, a camp commander, piped in some area music. Suddenly, there was a *Fidelio*, which was an overture. A blast of trumpets which marks the liberation; I felt strongly that it was the voice of freedom from Buchenwald.

D.J.F.   Not the meaning they wanted the music to have, but clearly that's the power it had for you on a personal level.

I want to get your speculations on the burden and the shame the survivors of concentration camps have, specifically, the potentiality of suicide. I'm thinking again of Primo Levi and of his apparent suicide. And I'm wondering about the existential and psychological proximity to death that survivors of the camp have as a legacy.

B.B.   I don't want to reflect theoretically. The experience in the camp plays havoc with the ego because the ego can no longer protect one. One's ego becomes deficient. To every sensitive person, there was a very serious weakening of the ego, or, shall we say, it becomes difficult to contain the death drive. One no longer trusted the ego to be able to function.

D.J.F.   Why would that experience continue to have, especially amongst people who have written about it, who have borne witness, and who have attempted to perpetuate a memory of it, such power even after thirty or forty years of working it through?

B.B.   That's right. After all, to write about it, to think about it, is to remember it. One remembers how deficient one's ego was; it is a painful and disturbing experience to study and remember this. I am reexperiencing this now as I read about the fantasies of the Free Corps, for an essay I am preparing for the *Times Literary Supplement*. My point is that when one was in this experience with so many murderous fantasies, somehow or another the death drive was so overwhelmingly hostile. It was a destructive experience.

D.J.F.   Even as a victim?

B.B.   That's right. Even as a victim. Studying it causes one to expose and to see how overwhelming the death drive is and how weak the defenses are against it.

D.J.F.   To the extent that it could lead to suicidal inclination?

B.B.   That's right. That's right.

D.J.F.   I want you to speculate on the burden and the shame of the survivors of the camps, and in particular, the inclination to commit suicide. Is there an inevitable loss of a defense against death?

B.B.   This is always a very personal thing: the propensity to think of suicide in a realistic sense. In the past, I had something very important to live for. But now, with age, particularly since the loss of my wife, there is this wish or the idea of suicide. I don't want to publicize it.

D.J.F.   You have written about the limits of the psychoanalytic perspective in an extreme environment, one of physical, mental, and material deprivation. Yet, you have also talked about, in *The Informed Heart*, the strength of psychoanalysis as an instrument of understanding, even in impossible situations. Do you still hold to that?

B.B.   Yes, the explanatory value of psychoanalysis is beyond question, always. Other aspects of psychoanalysis, the introspection, the self-criticism, are not very useful in an extreme situation. The explanatory value is always there.

D.J.F.   I want to turn now to your psychoanalytic training and to ask you how you first came to psychoanalysis.

B.B.   [*laughs*] Well, it was a Sunday in the Viennese woods. I belonged to an
           organization, the Jung Wandervogel. It was based on the tradition of the old
           German youth movement, but it was no longer as nationalistic as the original
           youth movement had been. It was very much antiwar, pacifistic, and leftist.
           Anyway, we met in the morning and went to the Viennese woods for a day of
           talk and play. On this particular Sunday, a young man, Otto Fenichel, dressed
           in military uniform, joined me and the person I considered my girlfriend.
           They started to talk about dreams and dream interpretation and the sexual
           meaning of dreams and all that. He was fully immersed in it all because he
           attended the University of Vienna the last time Freud lectured there, which
           would become *The Introductory Lectures on Psychoanalysis* of 1917 or 1918.
           As he talked about it, my girlfriend became fascinated—not that I was
           fascinated, but, I didn't want my girlfriend to become attracted to this man. As
           the day went on, I became more and more furious; later, we separated and I
           had a sleepless night. I decided that if this soldier on leave to finish his
           medical studies at the University of Vienna could talk about psychoanalysis,
           so could I. The next morning I had to go to school. As soon as school let out, I
           went to the one bookstore in Vienna that sold psychoanalytic literature and
           also published it. That was Deuticke. I bought all the psychoanalytic literature
           that I could buy. This included *The Psychopathology of Everyday Life* and
           some articles and journals, and I started to read it. I became more and more
           fascinated by it. But the origin of it was my anger at Otto Fenichel who had so
           impressed my girlfriend. The next Sunday, when we met again, I started to
           talk about psychoanalysis. At that time my girlfriend said, well that's enough
           for one Sunday, let's talk about something else, let's talk about us. It was a
           great relief to me, but anyway, I got hooked. Since then I have been reading
           psychoanalytic articles and everything Freud had written.

D.J.F.   It's a charming story.

           I want to ask you about your earliest memories of the Vienna Psychoanalytic
           Society. I know it was like a second family to you.

B.B.   I don't really have any memories of this Society, but rather of those who
           attended it. Because, you see, I was not yet a member. I was very friendly
           with Wilhelm Reich and, I've already mentioned Fenichel, who also became a
           good friend, and others. I got reports of what happened.

D.J.F.   Let me ask you about the period when you were a candidate and your memo-
           ries about how the candidates were treated: were they infantilized, were they
           nurtured, were they treated as loyal apprentices? What was the general climate
           there in terms of the general training period?

B.B.   I can only speak from my own experience. It was a very friendly and encour-
           aging experience because I was interviewed, as all candidates at the time

were, by Anna Freud and [Paul] Federn. I forgot who the third interviewer was; there were three. And when I was interviewed with Anna Freud, her father entered the room and she introduced me to him, to which he replied, "A Bettelheim does not need any introduction to me!" He had, as a student, frequently come to the house of my grandfather, and he became friendly with an uncle of mine who shared military service with him. He knew the family. And then he asked about my background. I told him I studied art history, literature, and philosophy. Freud said, "that's exactly the kind of person we need in this Society to counterbalance the dominance of the medical people who do not have broad culture and interests." So that was very encouraging to me; everyone was very encouraging to me.

D.J.F.   Do you have memories of whether there was toleration in Vienna for critical debates where there could be challenges to orthodoxy, and was research and independent kind of thinking promoted?

B.B.   I know that Freud permitted deviation.

D.J.F.   Tell me about it.

B.B.   Freud was a very skeptical man who could be very kind, but who could also be very cutting because he did not suffer fools easily. I can tell you one thing that happened. It was described to me by Willie Reich, who at that time was one of the leading members of the Viennese School. During a discussion held at the Society, someone suggested that it might be of benefit for all of humankind if all leading statesmen would be analyzed. There was a lively debate. Freud didn't talk much then; he was sick. Finally, they turned to him. He said he was pleased that his students had such a high opinion of psychoanalysis. He stopped for a while and looked around the room. And he said, "when I look around this room and think that all of you were analyzed, I cannot help but be skeptical." This was typical.

D.J.F.   There was an atmosphere that was pervaded with Freud's skepticism. But that did not get in the way of certain forms of research and of critical thinking as long as one did not deviate too far from Freud's own theoretical model?

B.B.   I don't know. I always had the suspicion that Freud would never have accepted child psychoanalysis if it had not been started by his daughter. You know, obviously with children, you can't put them on the couch and just analyze them. You have to play with them and be active, something that Freud didn't think was very appropriate for analysis. There were personal reasons that he permitted deviations from the classical model.

D.J.F. I'm curious to know what your own perception was of lay analysis in Vienna. Your story of Freud is revealing, but I want to know if there was a particular kind of receptiveness to it. Was there a comraderie amongst the lay analysts?

B.B. Yes, there was a comraderie between all of us. It was a beleaguered group that had to stick together and support each other. I think that the question of lay analysis was not a strong issue because there were many lay analysts, and I just told you how Freud responded to my training.

D.J.F. Was there a hierarchy amongst the lay analysts? For example, was Ernst Kris always regarded as someone of exceptional or special status?

B.B. No, no. I think there was [Theodor] Reik who was very close to Freud. Kris was relatively important because he married Marianne, the daughter of Dr. [Oskar] Rie who was a pediatrician in the Freud family and a close friend of Freud's. [August] Aichhorn was also one of the leading lay people and nobody questioned it.

D.J.F. Another question about Freud's role in Vienna and the period when you were there. Was Freud someone who played the role of a powerful and germinating father, or was he someone who curtailed creativity?

B.B. He encouraged creativity if it didn't challenge his theories. He liked it if one of his students or members of the Society anticipated things he later said; however, he always needed to discover things on his own.

D.J.F. In other words, it was dangerous to be a little too innovative or original.

B.B. Not dangerous, but one met with criticism.

D.J.F. You've told me privately that Richard Sterba was your training analyst. Do you have some specific memories about the analysis? Beginning with the length of time, how a didactic analysis was distinguished from a therapeutic analysis in those days?

B.B. During the therapeutic analysis, one was not supposed to read psychoanalytic writings. One might have read them before. In the didactic analysis, one was encouraged to read.

D.J.F. Do you recall whether or not your training analyst reported on you as a candidate? Or did they maintain confidentiality?

B.B. I had just started the training analysis before the Nazis marched in.

D.J.F.   So it really was never finished. Tell me what memories you have of the analysis with Sterba.

B.B.   They are only isolated bits, fragments of memory.

D.J.F.   He is still alive; he is 90 now.

B.B.   He's in bad shape. I remember one day, there were binoculars on his desk, and I asked him, what are the binoculars doing here? He said that there was a beautiful young lady living across the street, and I like to watch her. And then he added, "Don't you do the same?"

D.J.F.   And that made an impression on you.

B.B.   Yes, that he had the freedom to permit himself to do this and he openly admitted it.

D.J.F.   I know the Beethoven volume that Richard Sterba wrote, but I knew that he was not Jewish. Was that an important feature of your analysis?

B.B.   It played a part in my selecting him because I had grown up with all the contemporaries, Edith Buxbaum, Wilhelm Reich, and Annie Reich; I had grown up with them. It was difficult to find someone who I did not know well and someone who could be impartial; so I came to Richard.

D.J.F.   Was that a problem in terms of the degree to which your identity, your ego, your sense of self was bound up with being a Viennese Jew?

B.B.   No, not at all. It was very clear that Richard was very friendly with many Jews, and there was no inclination of anti-Semitism among Richard and Editha, his wife. Both were gentiles, Catholics. It didn't come up at all.

D.J.F.   You've mentioned a number of times that Wilhelm Reich was your friend; you call him Willie. You've often commented on his originality and creativity, especially in the period from the twenties into the early thirties until about 1933, the period of *Character Analysis* and *The Mass Psychology of Fascism*. What were the features of Reich's psychoanalytic mind that made him a very crucial figure in the history of psychoanalysis?

B.B.   What impressed me most was his vitality. He was full of spirit. He got excited about things, and he was a very vital guy.

D.J.F.   And the people around him also were vitalized by him?

B.B.   Yes.

D.J.F. Tell me of your own views of the impact of Anna Freud on the Vienna group in the early and mid-1930s, after Reich was excluded. Was it known that she had been analyzed by her father?

B.B.   It was known, but it was kept a secret. Although it was known, it was very much kept a secret that she was analyzed by her father. But, on the other hand, in those early days, children of analysts were often analyzed by their parents; it was not that uncommon.

D.J.F. And her impact? Did she grow in stature when Reich was excluded? And as she began to move toward the publication of *The Ego and the Mechanisms of Defense*?

B.B.   The trouble is, I don't think *The Ego and the Mechanisms of Defense* would not have been written if Reich had not published his *Character Analysis* before. Although it has never been acknowledged.

D.J.F. Do you feel that in some way it is her answer, her more moderate version, of *Character Analysis*?

B.B.   No, it's not a moderate version, but the whole idea of the analysis of resistance in her book were alleys opened up by the seminars where Willie Reich talked and where she was a student.

D.J.F. The clinical seminars?

B.B.   That's right.

D.J.F. What is your own sense of the comparisons and contrasts of the status of lay analysts in Vienna, and then the period you spent in Chicago?

B.B.   As I told you, my training was interrupted very early at the beginning by the invasion of Austria by Hitler. When I came to Chicago, I talked to [Franz] Alexander, who was Director of the Institute, about my background and so on. He said, you just ought to become a member of our Chicago society; you know more than our candidates know.

D.J.F. The candidates or the faculty?

B.B.   I know. I meant the faculty. He did the same with Gerhard Piers who also did not complete his analysis in Vienna.

D.J.F.   In Vienna, how many years of seminars did you finish? Did you have formal seminar training as well?

B.B.   No, I had just started.

D.J.F.   You had just started and then 1938 ruptured it?

B.B.   Yes. I had just completed my own analysis in '36 and was asked to wait a while before applying so that it was sure that it was not transference that resulted in my desire to be an analyst. The requirement was to wait more or less two years.

D.J.F.   What about those Americans who came to Chicago who didn't have European connections? How were they treated?

B.B.   I think that there were very few lay analysts who were in Chicago. What was clear was that Alexander and the Institute preferred medical candidates, and I can't remember any lay person besides the Europeans. There were very few lay analysts. But, on the other hand, I didn't feel that there was any animosity against me. I was well accepted.

D.J.F.   Did you actually teach on the faculty of the Chicago Psychoanalytic Institute?

B.B.   I taught some courses for teachers and extension courses.

D.J.F.   You never joined the faculty?

B.B.   No.

D.J.F.   Back to Vienna for one second. In the thirties, classical meant Freudian, not ego psychology. I know that you have a certain critique of Hartmann and still consider yourself to be a classical Freudian. What's the distinction?

B.B.   Well, I can only say what Freud said about Heinz Hartmann. He said Heinz has to put on his glasses which change all clinical experience into adaptive statements. In some way, Freud was critical.

D.J.F.   Hartmann was also his analysand, wasn't he?

B.B.   That's right.

D.J.F.   In sum, you object to it because it is too theoretical and too distant from clinical experience?

B.B.   It seems to me, that's right. I like to stick closely to the clinical experience.

D.J.F. Is there something objectionable about the idea of neutralization and adaptation? You never entirely subscribed to ego psychology.

B.B.   I have no reservations about ego psychology, only that I feel that psychoanalysis is an art and not a science. I am critical of the efforts to make it an objective science when it is an art.

D.J.F. Which is what Hartmann tried to do?

B.B.   Right.

D.J.F. Based on your experience, would you say that the future of psychoanalysis ought not to be in the hands of clinicians alone, but rather in the hands of independently minded researchers and intellectuals?

B.B.   Well [laughs] after all, I would have to speak against me and my own experience. I felt that the university is a very important place for freedom of thought and generosity in the acceptance of deviant opinions, which I think is a very significant element in the future development of any discipline. But psychoanalysis as such doesn't lend itself too well to the academic career. On the other hand, I think that the humanistic trends that you can find at a great university are very advantageous to psychoanalysis.

D.J.F. If psychoanalysis and psychoanalytic associations remain dominated by private practice clinicians, by people who are not committed to thinking, or to contributing to the literature and conducting serious research, is the discipline in danger?

B.B.   I think that development in psychoanalysis has to be based on clinical experience. Whether one is a medical doctor or not doesn't determine whether one learns from one's own clinical experience. I always felt that to be a full-time practitioner of psychoanalysis is a difficult task because one gets caught up too much in one's patients. One spends all one's time with the patient hours and it leaves no time to do one's own thinking. Freud could do that: to see patients all day and then at night write these papers; but there are very few Freuds around. Progress in psychoanalysis will come from people who have time to cogitate on their experience.

D.J.F. You have described your years in Chicago as the happiest and most creative in your life. Yet the assignment you took on was one of the most difficult, if not impossible, namely the understanding of the inner world and the psychological processes of autistic children. What was your inner need to work with the most elusive of cases?

B.B.   [*laughs*] That's a complicated story. It really began in Vienna where Anna
        Freud saw an autistic American child. A mute American child. She thought it
        would be interesting to find out what psychoanalysis could do for such an
        abnormal child. But, in order to be effective, the child would have to live in a
        home that is completely psychoanalytically organized. One hour a week, six
        hours a week wouldn't do it; it would have to be day and night. Through a
        complicated configuration of circumstances, this mother then came to us, my
        [first] wife and I. We took this child into our house as an experiment for a few
        months; this experiment lasted for seven years till the Anschluss. It was a
        fascinating experience to live and work with this child. I tried to help her to
        begin to talk and to learn in school. It was a fascinating experience.

D.J.F. What was your motivation? Why did you want to take on therapeutic work
        with the incurable?

B.B.   It was one way for me to cope with the experience of the concentration camp.
        It was the opposite of that experience in the concentration camp, which was
        deliberately personality destroying to learn to rehabilitate personalities.

D.J.F. With this particular population of patients, how does one evaluate what is a
        clinical success, a cure?

B.B.   When you start out with hopeless cases, you can never cure them; you can
        only rehabilitate them so they can function in society. They retain certain odd
        characteristics. Although some of the students with whom I worked have
        really been completely healed, but they are the exceptions I would say.

D.J.F. It there such a thing as a cure or a therapeutic success even for a so-called
        normal neurotic.

B.B.   [*laughs*] I'll leave that one up to you!

D.J.F. At the Orthogenic School no one could get in without permission and anyone
        could leave at any time. Some people have called that a noble experiment with
        a utopian concept, not used in a denigrating but rather in the descriptive sense.
        Would you agree with that description?

B.B.   No, I think that what we did is what the patients required. I don't think that it
        is utopian to do right by the patient. It seems to be the only thing that is
        appropriate.

8

Homage to Bettelheim (1903-1990)

I came to know Bruno Bettelheim in the waning years of his life. Many things separated us; many things united us. If I did not and could not share his mother tongue, his classical education at the University of Vienna, his age, his unique historical experiences, the Holocaust, his emigration to the United States, and his singular work with severely disturbed children, I could and did share with him a visceral antifascism, a commitment to lay analysis, a fascination with psychoanalytic hermeneutics, a concern with grasping contemporary history, and an interest in asking mordant questions.

There was a spirit of gravity about him, an intellectual seriousness and an emotional depth, most of which stemmed from the force of his personality, much of which resulted from the tragic weight of his historical consciousness—above all his memory of German fascism and the concentration camps. I always found him to be courteous, formal in an European sense, a bit remote; yet there was always a compelling presence about him, a personal dignity, a twinkle in his eyes, an ironic sense of humor, an intolerance of the foolishness and stupidity of human beings, a capacity to be self-deprecating and self-critical. His toughness was legendary; he also directed that toughness on himself, as evidenced by his remarkable work discipline and by the prolific quality and quantity of his publications.

Bettelheim once confessed to me, poignantly, that he wished I could have known him ten years ago. Yet until the end of his life, he maintained a spark of intellectual vitality, focusing his vast storehouse of erudition on contemporaneous issues of real concern to his public. In our talks together, he frequently made a gesture of touching, almost massaging his head, when he spoke; this was a man who clearly had a narcissistic investment in the mind, and when he could no longer generate fresh and original ideas, he no longer wished to live.

In the years I knew him he was depressed, often suicidally depressed. He spoke candidly, almost clinically, about his suicidal intentions. It became clear to me that he had researched, thought through, and convinced himself that this was the only courageous way out, the only dignified path for him at his stage in life. He knew that he had completed his creative and scholarly work. He had grown despondent after the illness and death of his wife in 1984, his companion for over forty-three years. He was terribly bitter and resigned about the rupture of his relations with his daughter, his hopes shattered after living with her in Santa Monica. A mild stroke had disabled him to the extent that writing and typing became major chores for him; it was sad to watch him labor over autographing copies of his books when I asked him to lecture before my class on Freud's Cultural Writings at UCLA. When I last saw him in January 1990, I observed how signing his recently published book, *Freud's Vienna and Other Essays* (1990), required a major expenditure of effort.

Bettelheim was a philosopher of psychoanalysis who spoke a fluent, ordinary language that was not condescending to his audience. That language resonated with a large, influential, international public because it touched people in their profoundest depths; he targeted his writings to appeal to the heart and intellect simultaneously. Like a finely trained European intellectual, he knew how to raise elusive questions about history, ethics, psychoanalysis, children and parenting; he knew how to research, how to read texts, how to investigate and explicate the psychological and emotional nuances of things, often grasping the meaning of things between the lines. He was determined not to get bogged down in highly technical or overly specialized questions, not to write in jargon. He developed a distinct style and a discernible voice in which he communicated on a visceral level with human beings, responding soul to soul, much of which emanated from a source of empathic sensitivity in his own psyche.

He produced a distinguished and varied body of writings that demands a radical distinction between authentic feeling and cheap sentimentality, between rigorous analysis and reciting established pieties, between realistic confrontations with difficult choices and an objection to positions flowing from denial, avoidance, or reaction-formation. Most of his texts abound with a sincere humanity, compassion, and care, especially those devoted to comprehending the inner lives of the severely disturbed child; yet his works also served to deromanticize and demystify. In short, his humanism was not simple-minded, soft, overly optimistic, nor oblivious to reality considerations.

For Bettelheim the privilege of being a psychoanalyst and of practicing, teaching, transmitting, and modifying psychoanalytic theory and practice, consisted in a deeply ingrained respect for the human being, for his or her own privacy, individual uniqueness, his struggles, his quest for truth, his aspirations toward personal forms of liberation, creativity, and playfulness. These values may reflect his identification with Freud and with the classical liberalism of the Viennese Jewish bourgeoisie of the interwar years. He was one of the last truly independent voices in the world of psychoanalysis, one of those irreverent iconoclasts who never concerned himself about establishment institutions or psychoanalytic institutes, having considerable disdain about regional, national, or international psychoanalytic doctrinal quarrels. He regarded these quarrels as beside the point.

As a self-assured, critical voice, he spoke his mind—often in a combative, acerbic, intolerant way, but always thoughtfully, succinctly, pungently. I learned quickly that on certain issues it was futile to debate with him; more than once I found him to be opinionated, authoritarian, rather harsh in his judgments—for instance on the politics of the antiwar movement in the 1960s, on the critique of American foreign policy, on the theoretical attempt to link Marxism with psychoanalysis. However, even in his decline, dialogue was possible with him; he could be astonishingly disarming and empathic about problems that he knew were existentially and psychologically pressing.

Bettelheim was a man full of stories. If one caught him in the right mood, he was ready to reminisce. For him psychoanalysis was not an impossible profession, it was a "spooky" profession, practiced by a gallery of rogues, geniuses, shamans, priests, false prophets, narcissists, exhibitionists, functionaries, and occasionally spooks. However, when all was said and done, he maintained a pride about psychoanalysis, finding it intriguing, impossible to pin down, and endlessly evocative. Bettelheim, himself, could be a little spooky.

He had fond and extraordinarily favorable things to say about Wilhelm Reich, whom he knew in Vienna as a young man, regarding him as "the" seminal psychoanalytic thinker and clinician of the century. Whenever he spoke of him, he always noted Reich's vast vitality and unquenchable thirst for knowledge. I sensed that Bettelheim identified with Reich because he, too, felt marginalized and ostracized by official psychoanalysis, at least in America. For Bettelheim, Reich's *Character Analysis* (1933) represented the birth of modern psychoanalytic theory and practice. He had penetrating, if often biting, anecdotes about other luminaries in the psychoanalytic movement, including Margaret Mahler, Anna Freud, Heinz Hartmann, Kurt Eissler, D.W. Winnicott, Melanie Klein, Franz Alexander, and Heinz Kohut.

On my last visit with Bettelheim, I asked him for his clinical advice on persistent problems I was having with several patients who were children of Holocaust survivors. Bettelheim generously urged me to be patient, kind, sensitive, calm, to remain the master of my own anxieties, to learn to tolerate better the extended process of not knowing, to not rush into interpretations that reconstructed memories or fantasies of the Holocaust, to tough out the often ferocious negative transferences (which he considered the most difficult task to learn and to assimilate in psychoanalytic technique), and to consider and to reflect on the countertransference as an authentic way into the mind and soul of the patient. Then he paused and said with a shock of painful recognition: "You know, *my* children are children of a Holocaust survivor." This is the Bettelheim I remember: helpful, incisive, caring, yet always personal, affectively attuned to the emotional and historical interplay of all interpersonal encounters.

My favorite image of Bruno Bettelheim remains the one with his arm around the shoulder of a female child in the hallway of the Orthogenic School; it's a powerful image, with his back to the camera, capturing a man who was self-assured, protective, reassuring, sensitive, exuding self-confidence, capable of bearing his own doubts and the terrible weight of his own historical and psychic experience with dignity and courage.

Publications of Bruno Bettelheim

"Individual and Mass Behavior in Extreme Situations," *Journal of Abnormal and Social Psychology*, 38 (October 1943), pp. 417-452.

Love is Not Enough: The Treatment of Emotionally Disturbed Children, New York, The Free Press, 1950.

Symbolic Wounds: Puberty Rites and the Envious Male, New York, The Free Press, 1954.

Truants From Life: The Rehabilitation of Emotionally Disturbed Children, New York, The Free Press, 1955.

The Informed Heart: Autonomy in a Mass Age, New York, The Free Press, 1960.

Paul and Mary: Two Cases From Truants From Life, New York, The Free Press, 1961.

Dialogues With Mothers, New York, The Free Press, 1962.

Social Change and Prejudice, New York, The Free Press, 1964 (with Morris B. Janowitz).

The Empty Fortress. Infantile Autism and the Birth of the Self, New York, The Free Press, 1967.

Children of the Dream, New York, Macmillan, 1969.

A Home for the Heart, New York, Knopf, 1974.

The Uses of Enchantment: The Meaning and Importance of Fairy Tales, New York, Knopf, 1977.

Surviving and Other Essays, New York, Knopf, 1979.

On Learning to Read, New York, Knopf, 1982 (with Karen Zelan).

Freud and Man's Soul, New York, Knopf, 1982.

A Good Enough Parent, New York, Knopf, 1987.

Freud's Vienna and Other Essays, New York, Knopf, 1990.

9

Thoughts on Michel Foucault's *History of Sexuality*

> *The degree and kind of a man's sexuality reach up into the ultimate pinnacle of his spirit.*

> —Friedrich Nietzsche
> *Beyond Good and Evil*, 1886

Some may be dazzled by his works, others may find them unnecessarily obscure, still others perverse. While his intellectual style eludes facile classification, Michel Foucault was an imaginative and audacious thinker. Culture critics and historians would do well to reflect on his dense book, *The History of Sexuality: An Introduction* (1976).[1] In it Foucault examined the shifts in Western man's perception of sexuality over the past three hundred years. He focused on *mentalité*—the shared myths, norms, joys, anxieties, and suffering connected with sexual practice, but above all, with codes of thinking and attitudes related to sexuality.

This history of sexuality, he postulated, is the history of discourses on sexuality. Discourse analysis differs from conventional literary explication of the text. Foucault delved into the strategic dimensions of language; who the speaker is and why the speaker says what he says in a specific situation is as important as what he says. Similarly, what is not said, what is omitted because of internal prohibitions or because of external constraints, becomes central to his interpretation. The job of the philosophical historian of sexuality is to bring these relations to light, to lay bare continuities as well as ruptures. The author uses discourse analysis to develop his thesis: that there is a dynamic network between sexuality, knowledge, and power.

In his earlier works, Foucault (1926-1984), who was a professor at the Collège de France until his death, and possibly France's most prominent critical theorist, examined the history of social outcasts with emphasis on the various repressive modes of exclusion. While studying madness, delinquency, adolescence, matricide, and criminality, he unmasked the relationships between the excluded figures and the administrative and ideological modes of disciplining these perceived pariahs. He sensitively probed the ways in which those in power legitimized the isolation and silence of confined figures.[2] He originally planned a subsequent five volumes in *The History of Sexuality,* but failed to continue this line of inquiry with empirical data on the sexually oppressed. Foucault's project was to explore this history of children and masturbation, women and hysteria, homosexuality and the condemnation of nonmonogamous, nongenital forms of sexuality, and lastly, the complicated question of population control.

Foucault overthrew the Marxist thesis that Western societies have systematically repressed sexual desires for economic reasons. The development of modern, industrial capitalism has not produced more restrictions or interdictions of sexuality, nor has it led to the rigid organization and harnessing of nonreproductive sexuality. Instead, there has been a multiplication of—in fact a veritable "explosion" of—curiosity and writings about sexuality.

Foucault claimed that the will to explore the secrets of sexuality represented the foundation of all forms of inquiry and independent research; it links bodily pleasure to the pleasure of knowing. With its Nietzschean echoes, he subtitled the volume "The Will to Knowledge," speculating that there is an integral relationship between man's need to speak about sexual intimacy and the search for the truth. Discussions of sexuality have gradually, and often unintentionally, served to undermine prejudices and obsolete codes, including the Christian repudiation of the body. Since the classical age there has been an increasing spiral of questioning and disseminating information about sexuality. This he partially explained by Western man's mania for confession, itself springing from the association of sex with sin (or crime) and the search for penitence. Discussions of sexuality have grown increasingly less discrete, less regulated by strict codes of decency, less hypocritical. But the quantitative increase of discourse does not necessarily mean the decrease of sexual misery; sexual discourse often plays a manipulative role, itself resulting in a subtle form of repression.

No historian of sexuality can avoid a confrontation with Freud and with the psychoanalytic psychology of sexuality. Foucault's relationship to Freudian psychoanalysis was not only highly ambivalent, but it shifted over the years. In an manner paralleling his allusions to Marx, he discussed Freud's work as if it were a coherent, fully elaborated psychological system; he discounted periodization in Freud's life; he did not bother to quote passages directly or to cite texts. This may be irritating to some scholars and raises side issues about the handling of the ambiguities, modifications, and the dialectical complexity of Freud's thought. He did not deal with Freud's metapsychology and the later modifications of psychoanalytic theory by the object relations theorists, neo-Freudians, and ego psychologists. He appeared not to be familiar with the psychohistorical literature on the history of the family. He valued Wilhelm Reich's "historico-political critique of sexual repression," but did not follow Reich's lead in his own study.

In *Madness and Civilization* (1961), Foucault praised Freud for reestablishing a dialogue with unreason; Freud accomplished this by returning to madness at the level of language, that is, by allowing the mad to speak and by developing a method of listening. He appreciated Freud's opposition to positivistic medicine, acknowledging Freud's alertness to material normally excluded from scientific investigation and polite conversation. He also credited Freud with having rigorously investigated the physician-patient relationship.

According to Foucault, Freud exaggerated the importance of the psychoanalytic relationship. In its clinical application, the analyst allegedly assumes an almost "quasi-divine status," becomes the ultimate arbiter, the judge with a capital "J." Exploitation of this unequal relationship by the analyst puts the patient at a disadvantage, strips him of his autonomy, limits his ability to make independent decisions, and makes his treatment turn on regressive behavior. The psychoanalytic relationship, in short, recapitulates the power relationships in the asylum. The analyst is the crucial authority figure because he has mastered the psychological science and is not mad; he assigns guilt, makes judgments, and operates as if he were a miracle worker.[3]

In the first volume of *The History of Sexuality*, Foucault revised his critique of Freudian psychoanalysis by suggesting that Freud's understanding of sexuality remained seminal, but that it required a critical and historical assessment in order to be surpassed. His approach is more nuanced and less polemical than that of the French antipsychiatry school of Deleuze and Guattari.[4] Foucault agreed with Freud in urging man to know about sex and to place that secular knowledge in an analytical frame of discourse. Freud shattered romantic and Victorian myths about sexuality; he unravelled disturbing truths about infantile desire, bisexuality, aggression, and incest. Like Freud, Foucault had no use for illusions, for consolation, for prophesy, or for revolutionary posturing, and he clearly supported the psychoanalytic injunction to investigate and remedy the sources of intrapsychic repression. Politically, he held that psychoanalysis should be "honored" for its antiracism and antifascism.

Foucault faulted psychoanalysis for inheriting and perpetuating the tradition of the medicalization of sex. While observation and classification of sexual normality and deviance can often result in new forms of surveillance and arbitrary judgment, the establishment of a scientific apparatus (styles of writing, research strategies, logic, causality, presentation of evidence) can function to hide the truth about sex. Such "scientific" techniques serve to obliterate dialogue. Just as Foucault questioned the role of the psychoanalyst as miracle worker in various therapeutic settings, particularly with regard to the understanding and treatment of psychosis, so he also questioned the accuracy of psychoanalytic knowledge outside of the clinical situation. He vehemently contested the judicial abuses of psychology, recognizing the ways in which psychological "insights" can be transformed into a new institutional system of control. He proposed limiting psychiatric pronouncements on criminality and temporary insanity. In 1977 Foucault stated: "[Psychiatry] is incapable of knowing if a crime is an illness, or of transforming a delinquent into a nondelinquent."[5]

After establishing the connection between sex and knowledge, Foucault complicated his model by introducing the dimension of power, the individual's relationship to political, social, legal, and institutional forms. In rambling and involuted passages, he proposed that power is "the multiplicity of relations of force." Power is omnipresent in society, but is usually concealed; its pressure is felt in unequal degrees and in shifting strategic patterns. Ultimately, Foucault's concept of power turned on the notion of cultural hegemony. Nontotalitarian societies regulate sexuality through the control of information and knowledge concerning sex, that is, how we think about the body and sexuality, in establishing rules of what is thinkable. That control is never exclusive and never entirely parochial, but it embraces the whole of society. It sets limits. Western man also carries "power" in his head, through the impact of symbolic representation, internalization, acceptance, and interdiction. External constraints are superfluous since we police and survey ourselves.

With regard to sex, Foucault held that those in "power" exercise their political prerogatives by examining, watching, and urging its citizenry to confess or transform sexual curiosity into "true" forms of discourse and application. This in turn means following the models of dominant medical, legal, biological, psychiatric, and pedagogical texts, those regarded as the canon at any given moment. These paradigms are stamped upon us in the family and schools, or through the medical profession and the courts. The family, organized around patriarchical lines, plays a key mediating role in transferring the individual from one system of institutional discipline to another. Those who control the production and distribution of discourse, then, have the ability to normalize, tutor, punish, reeducate, and moralize, often in the name of science. Such control over discourse often stems from the ability to assign guilt. Since those in control usually adhere to the conformist values of a given society, specifically those connected with the family, work, science and morality, renegade or polymorphous forms of sexuality are often excluded from the social norm.

Throughout the text, Foucault did not balance his discussion of "power" with particular illustration and amplification. The author was abstract, often needlessly so, swept away by his own conceptual structures, slightly intoxicated by his metaphorical modes of expression. Foucault's discursive analysis referred backward or forward to other discourses. We seldom know how and why he selects his sources, or how representative they are. French sources predominate; historical context is often missing or insufficiently fleshed out. While covering the long duration of four centuries provides an overview, this periodization collapses concrete tensions and details about epochs. The reference to texts often obscures particular sexual practices and the relationship between sexual discourse and practice. Foucault did not adequately develop the tensions between sexual mores and class, or between the mutability of the sexual drive itself and the possibilities for cultural or social achievements. Finally, it remains unclear who those in power are, what their agencies of control are, how decisions are made, how forms of institutions or governments alter power structures, how the French Revolution or Industrial Revolution transformed power relations.

Foucault was not spinning out value-free theory. His ideas about the interlocking network of pleasure-knowledge-power were grounded in what he candidly called an "ethico-moral choice," the author's opposition to power. This antiauthoritarianism placed him much closer to anarchist thought, or more precisely, to the leftists of May 1968, than to classical Marxism or to the left Freudians. He said "power is evil, it is ugly, it is poor, sterile, monotonous, dead."[6]

Foucault saw his function as primarily an intellectual one, but with social and political implications. He contributed to alternative strategies of resistance by mapping out the ideological means by which men's minds and bodies are controlled. He recognized that the mechanisms of discipline were often puerile and transparent, often cynically justified, but were manifestly potent. Unless they were known, strategies for changing them could not be implemented. As Foucault aphoristically put it: "Where there is power, there is resistance."[7] For him theory building and philosophical investigation were a committed form of action, for his form of critical theory was constructed in conflict to power. Foucault viewed his theoretical works as "tool boxes"—the androgynous sexual metaphor is evocative—for all those who find power intolerable. He argued that the contemporary struggle against power extended beyond, while being linked to, the activities of the exploited proletariat. He saw conscious women, prisoners, soldiers, mental patients, homosexuals, and students playing avantgarde roles in the cultural assault on power; and he himself interceded to protect their rights or to publicize their causes.[8]

Foucault was not a sexual utopian in the manner of Charles Fourier, Wilhelm Reich, or Herbert Marcuse. To talk about nonrepressive sexuality was not equivalent to realizing such liberty. But it may be necessary. At bottom he was relatively optimistic that libertarian forms of discourses on sexuality could help to loosen repression, subvert prejudices, and erode obsolete codes. Language, he argued, could play a vanguard role, anticipating future possibilities of freedom. In short, language became both the fundamental unit of analysis and the mediating agency for radical change—not traditional mass political movements, not psychoanalytic methods. Foucault's stance restored the philosopher to a prominent place; his skeptical search for the truth became indispensable in deciphering the pleasure-knowledge-power triangle. Without his analysis society will remain stalemated, the individual lost in a series of interlocking, institutional systems of discipline. He did not speculate about the shapes, coloration, or limitations of that future sexual freedom, and in fact, counseled intellectuals to abandon their prophetic pretensions.

Foucault's guarded optimism contrasted with Freud's pessimism. Freud insisted that the sexual instinct was at odds with the demands of culture, and that the sexes themselves were almost permanently embittered. He thought that the theoreticians of unrestrained sexual liberty were behaving irresponsibly by misleading their readers and overlooking the various obstacles to free sexual expression. Freud's prognosis was gloomy about reconciling these tensions, about removing the obstacles to unfettered sexual liberty. It is too early to scrutinize Foucault's qualified hope about the end to or amelioration of sexual misery. He took his stand on the side of freedom, or at least, against the perpetuation of sexual oppression and ignorance. Interrogation was his means of contesting power. Foucault argued that he was posing the key philosophical question since 1789; namely, whether revolutions, sexual as well as political or social, were desirable and worth the risk of unleashing violence or of giving up one's life.[9]

Notes

1   Michel Foucault, *The History of Sexuality: An Introduction* (New York, 1978), translated by Robert Hurley; subsequent volumes in Foucault's *History of Sexuality* include *The Use of Pleasure* (New York, 1985), translated by Robert

Hurley and *The Care of the Self* (New York, 1986), translated by Robert Hurley.

2   Michel Foucault, *Mental Illness and Psychology* (New York, 1976), translated by Alan Sheridan; Foucault, *The Birth of the Clinic: An Archaeology of Medical Perception* (New York, 1973), translated by A.M. Sheridan Smith; Foucault, ed., *I, Pierre Rivière, Having Slaughtered My Mother, My Sister, and My Brother ... A Case of Parricide in the 19th Century* (New York, 1975), translated by Frank Jellinek; Foucault, *Discipline and Punish: The Birth of the Prison* (New York, 1977), translated by Alan Sheridan.

3   Michel Foucault, *Madness and Civilization: A History of Insanity in the Age of Reason* (New York, 1973), translated by Richard Howard, pp. 277-278; Foucault, "L'Asile illimité," *Le Nouvel Observateur*, 28 March 1977, pp. 66-67, a review of Robert Castel's book, *L'Ordre Psychiatrique*.

4   Gilles Deleuze and Felix Guattari, *L'Anti-Oedipe: Capitalisme et Schizophrenie* (Paris, 1972); "Anti-Oedipus," *Semiotexte*, vol. 2, no. 3, 1977.

5   "L'Angoisse, de juger," *Le Nouvel Observateur*, 30 May 1977, p. 121; this summarizes a debate on capital punishment between Foucault, Robert Badinter, and the French psychoanalyst, Jean Laplanche.

6   Foucault, "Non au sexe roi," *Le Nouvel Observateur*, 12 March 1977, p. 113; this is an interview with Foucault after the publication of volume one of *The History of Sexuality*.

7   Ibid., pp. 113, 124; "Entretien sur la prison: le livre et sa méthode," *Magazine Littéraire*, no. 101, June 1975, p. 33.

8   "Les Intellectuels et le pouvoir," *L'Arc*, no. 49, 1972, pp. 3-10; this was a conversation between Foucault and Gilles Deleuze.

9   Foucault, "Non au sexe roi," *Le Nouvel Observateur*, 12 March 1977, pp. 105, 130.

10

On French Structuralist Theory and Practice

The New Yorker recently published a debunking piece on the Parisian cultural scene. The reporter characterized contemporary French thinkers as exhibitionistic, faddish, and lacking humor. Just as ideas have lost all integrity in Paris, so, too, has the Parisian intellectual evolved into a superficial virtuoso. Thinkers construct theories about "reality" while keeping an eye on marketplace fluctuations. The popularizers in the media and the press package and diffuse the product. The French intellectual cultivates his image as glamorous, learned, theoretically dazzling, quotable, one with an instant opinion on any subject. The more outrageous the posturings, the more the public adores him. His sex appeal and his performing abilities make him equivalent in America to popular culture heroes such as the entertainer, the rock star, and the quarterback.

Thinking in France is eroticized. Recently, thinking "otherwise" has given rise to perverse, self-reflexive and promiscuous verbal performances. Such modes of cultural research and production are more than sublimated forms of sexual curiosity; the sexualization of the mind updates, makes modernistic, a French romantic tradition of celebrating genius, nonconformity, and the brilliant display of one's semantic abilities. *The New Yorker* reporter portrayed French thinkers as rhetorically excessive, self-serving, self-aggrandizing, overly pious,

191

192 Cultural Theory and Psychoanalytic Tradition

and given to the indiscriminate trafficking in ideas. And traffic they do: French social thought reproduces itself rapidly and opaquely. New techniques of analysis beget not only abstract vocabularies in the human sciences, but also "innovative" scientific disciplines such as grammatology, psycholinguistics, the archaeology of knowledge, semiology, and structural anthropology. The literati and the master thinkers—even if the former reject systems, even if the latter construct an anti-system—constitute a privileged, classically educated caste, removed from the real centers of power in the state bureaucracy or in the military-industrial-labor complex, protected from the pockets of material suffering in France and the rest of the world.

The Parisian intelligentsia create and discard ideological systems with equal ease. Eloquence for the sake of eloquence has replaced the fetishistic worship of pure art, abstract art, pure reason, pure shock appeal, or pure alienation. Discourse in Paris thrives on self-reference and impunity. (Barthes, in a half-mocking, half-desperate piece of narcissism, reviewed his own autobiographical study, *Barthes on Barthes*.) Language and speech give rise to ever increasing concentric circles with no identifiable center. Language studies have developed into a spider's web with no spider, no insects to be caught, and no apparent way out. Just as eloquence has replaced clarity and morally resonant committed thought, so too has social thought become confused with verbal sleight of hand. Gimmicks have substituted themselves for the honest working through of complex human problems, of problems that require more than ingenious interpretations of texts.

The Parisian cultural sector (perhaps easily defined as the half million readers of *Le Monde*; perhaps, more complexly, composed of liberal professionals, managers, technocrats, teachers, and students) reinforces the illusions and hyperbolic quality of its celebrated thinkers. Taking positions in Paris has long been a necessary, if nuanced art, a way of being *au courant*, a ritualized way of inserting oneself into the nexus of Parisian cultural politics. The cultural public consumes, mirrors, and imitates; it defines itself for or against rhetorical chapels, absorbing the latest book osmotically, gobbling up advanced aesthetic movements and imbibing scientific methodologies as if they were vintage wines contained in the newest, flashiest bottles.

One need not view *The New Yorker* as the last word on the cultural and political habits of the Parisians. To be sure, *The New Yorker* takes a part for the whole, the manifest form for the latent content. Much of the hyperbolic and histrionic side of contemporary Parisian thought stems not from the seminal structuralist thinkers but rather from the excesses of the New Philosophers, the unsubstantiated claims of French antipsychiatry, the posturings of ultra-leftist chapels, and some unserious journalistic writings.

Structuralism is synonymous with language and with excess. Structuralists examine language, directing their inquiries into its labile forms and functions. Since language is conceptualized as movable, its essence can never be pinned down. They assume that meaning can be infinitely multiplied, that texts have plural significances, that language is displaced endlessly in series. Structuralists establish dynamic relations in terms of textual difference and multiplicity. They reject the ideas of identity or similarity as stale metaphysical and nonverifiable notions. Structuralists reject philosophical systems. Interpretation involves putting together a coherent combination or deriving laws about series. Structuralists oppose all methodologies that posit a center, a conducting thread, or a unifying ideational content in a text. They view the postulation of a whole or autonomous subject as a chimera. Instead they see the subject as wandering, dispersed, nomadic, disordered, in the process of permanent transformation. Ego psychology is dismissed as a false construct, a wish fulfillment. A structuralist hero, if not a complete contradiction in terms, would be one without identity, perfectly schizoid.

Structuralist critics move from destabilized discourses to incomplete, unstoppable, discontinuous formulations about thinking. A text, in turn, becomes a void: the reader or critic is assigned the task of filling that emptiness. The project is ultimately vain because structuralists hold that all interpretations are tentative, hypothetical, simultaneously probable and improbable. At its most trivial, structuralism is a radical form of relativism refusing absolute or supreme values. As an antidote to rigidity or to simplistic dualisms, it is a sweeping indictment of dogma and of nonreferential synthetic thinking. Most structuralist thinking is antiauthority, while most practitioners are classically authoritarian. Lacan, for example, played the role of irreverent master thinker in French psychoanalytic circles for almost four decades, without tolerating criticism of his doctrine or practices.

A text can never be saturated. Structuralist criticism works by erecting interlocking antitheses: to define emptiness in terms of plenitude; absence in terms of presence; the said in terms of the unsaid. The elaboration of these paradoxes circulates words, produces new texts, mini-paradoxes, which function to elucidate old ones. A discourse has no final or definitive meaning. It contains infinite possibilities and myriad meanings. Structuralists do not pose ultimate questions. Truly dense texts—a Freudian case study reworked by Lacan, a kinship rite deciphered by Lévi-Strauss, a Balzac story decoded by Barthes—cannot be reduced to a single essence; one cannot assign a unified truth to it. Truth, if not altogether banished from the structuralist canon, is viewed as fragmentary, fleeting, or a potential instrument of domination—a denial of desire, freedom, silence, pleasure, or difference. Thus, no totalizing synthesis can be achieved, no dialectic produced, which can account for the ensemble of structures in the universe, even if that universe is restricted to texts, bracketed off from material reality and social existence outside of language. Consequently, as a method of knowledge, structuralism repudiates the ideals and subverts the expectations of humanists, moralists, historicists, and individualists.

John Sturrock's volume, *Structuralism and Since: From Lévi-Strauss to Derrida* (1979), focuses its attention on five representative French structuralist thinkers. His book provides short, succinct essays on the main proponents of the structuralist ideology over the last thirty years. This is a useful publication, even if slightly outdated now that several prominent thinkers have died while Lévi-Strauss seems to be in eclipse or decline, and now that Derrida seems to be beleaguered by the Paul de Man affair and assaults on deconstructionism. Structuralism deserves a critical scrutiny because of its uneven influence on a variety of disciplines from anthropology to literary criticism, from philosophy to psychoanalysis, from the analysis of popular culture to the discussion of cooking.

These new "prophets of Paris"—Lévi-Strauss, Barthes, Foucault, Lacan and Derrida—all lived, worked, taught, wrote, and thought in Paris; all were prophets in spite of themselves. They eschewed the priestly pretensions of the intellectual, preferring the apparently more humble task of decentering, destabilizing, desacralizing, demystifying, and deconstructing. Most would, and have, refused the label structuralist. As discourses about discourse are disseminated, the old virtues of clear prose and of conceptually precise formulation have been radically revised. Structuralism has served as an invitation to offend established canons, including the deification of lucidity. The awkward "And Since" from the work's title refers to Derrida, the youngest of the group (born in 1930), and the one most commonly thought of as "post-structuralist."

Each essay is written by a well-informed scholar who is generally sympathetic to the structuralist method and assumptions. The critics follow the structuralist approach; typically, they provide only a perfunctory biographical sketch (two or three sentences at the end of the essay, hardly more than a parenthetical remark). No effort is made to situate a particular thinker into the cultural or political context of Paris, or some other social, economic, or psychological framework. Thinking is discussed almost as if the individual thinker did not matter. The artificiality and antihistorical nature of structuralism is embraced. Cross references are restricted to earlier or later textual productions by the given writer. No connections are drawn between structuralist perspectives and internal debates in Paris, the events of May 1968, the disillusionment of the 1970s, or to reactions to earlier cultural and intellectual developments.

Despite its weaknesses, Sturrock's book provides a condensed overview of recent structuralist thinking. The figures he includes are or have been controversial. However, there are some significant omissions. French structuralism borrows from, creatively misreads, several older intellectual traditions. All of the thinkers in this volume have been profoundly influenced by the Swiss linguist, Ferdinand de Saussure, himself a contemporary of Freud. Sturrock should have included an introductory, expository essay on the fundamental ideas and contradictions of Saussure's work. This would also help the reader grasp the seductive quality of his linguistic theory, as well as understand the divergences of Saussure's system with that of analytic philosophy or transformational grammar. Just as French existentialism derived partially from the nineteenth-century writings of Kierkegaard and Nietzsche, so French structuralist theory is also a return to the past. Lacan has transformed his return to Freud into a slogan, a banner, upon which he hoped to build his legitimacy. Lévi-Strauss has generously indicated his debt to Durkheim, Freud, Marx, and Rousseau. Foucault, sometimes obliquely, sometimes transparently, reveals his fidelities to Roussel, Artaud, Nietzsche, and anarchistic thought. Barthes emerged as the cultural antennae of his age for the last thirty years. A contemporary intellectual history of Paris could be written by tracing his itinerary. Derrida himself has only "advanced" our knowledge by returning to German phenomenology; his first book was a translation of Husserl's *Origin of Geometry*.

Similarly, Sturrock's volume excludes an essay on Louis Althusser and the ambiguous penetration of structuralist thinking into Marxist, Maoist, and leftist circles in France. Because of the current crisis of Marxism, the apparent death of Western and Eastern communism, and because of the highly tragic events in Althusser's personal life, we would have welcomed a critical article on his contribution. It might have clarified the extent to which structuralism impoverishes or deepens our understanding of Marxism. Reading Marx's texts rigorously, at least according to the Althusserian method, may push the scholasticizing of Marxism to an extreme limit, thereby making antiseptic its critical philosophy and its revolutionary practice.

As a synchronic method of analysis, structuralism may not be applicable to realities that are extralinguistic. However, there is no reality that can be perceived, thought about, and communicated that does not involve language. Opponents of structuralism have pointed out that not all human antagonisms can be compressed into textual interpretation. Social existence, intrapsychic conflict, nonverbal experience, the modalities of lived experience in concrete, social circumstances, all these processes have a texture and a vital quality ignored by structuralist theory. The insurgent students of May 1968 intuited the poverty of this ideology, exclaiming that "a structure cannot descend into the streets"; that is, that real people live, suffer, and make their own history in situations not of their choosing, but both the environment and the will to resist are real. When I paraphrased that piece of poetic graffiti at a scholarly conference, trying to insist that events, unhappiness, and resistance could not be collapsed into the terms of discourse analysis, a wag in the audience replied: "A street is a structure."

Dan Sperber's essay on Lévi-Strauss makes several important points about the French anthropologist. He finds Lévi-Strauss attractive because of his versatility and eclecticism, his authentic openness to perceptions from a variety of disciplinary perspectives. In Lévi-Strauss the artist coexists with the scientist, the classifier with the synthesizer, the poet with the ethnologist, and the surrealist with the Marxist. In what other major thinker does one find the geologist concerned with psychoanalytic innovations? Sperber suggests that we translate *la pensée sauvage* as "untamed thinking," rather than savage, bestial, uncivilized mental activity. Lévi-Strauss' work leads to a reevaluation of the concept of the primitive, having mapped out the modalities of untamed thinking in so-called primitives. It is no longer possible to see primitives as children or underdeveloped specimens. Rather, they think abstractly, complexly, morally, and metaphysically. His perspective questions traditional Western ideas of scientific progress, making us more skeptical about how far we have advanced in symbolic, mythical, and folkloric forms of thinking. Sperber grasps the breathtaking grandeur of Lévi-Strauss' project: to understand thoroughly the psychic unity of humanity. Of course, Lévi-Strauss is a first-generation structuralist, and somehow he has retained a relatively sanguine and tidy view of the possibilities of human knowledge. Such methodological optimism and universalism are not shared by the subsequent generations of structuralists.

John Sturrock presents Barthes as a charming, intelligent, sophisticated but essentially unoriginal cultural critic. What is seductive about Barthes the man of letters is his capacity to bridge the gap between creative writing and academic scholarship. Readers of Barthes rightly find his prose coquettish, precious, versatile, clever. The ensemble of his work is the articulation of a sensibility. His writing contains flashing insights, sparkling formulations, witty perceptions, and a visual component. He is weakest when he tries to be systematic and rigorous. He is strongest when he writes as the hedonist, approaching a text as a gourmet would relish a fine meal. If reading is equivalent to the enjoyment of a good couscous, then Barthes also showed that a discourse can be a verbal festival—an unlimited garden of earthly delights. Late in his life, he insisted on the erotic relationship between writer, text and reader, with the body being the mediating agency between that triangular structure. To map out a text, following Barthes' example, is to engage in an exercise in the arbitrary.

All of Barthes' writing can be seen as a sum of destructions; and he always claimed that his project meant the exploration of the artificial rationality of language. Barthes himself recognized no single truth, no set of privileged relations, no absolute hierarchy, in his personal scale of values. His critical method involved decomposing and deforming a text. This is best illustrated in *S/Z*, where the will to disintegrate saturates the work to the extent to which the writer, Balzac, becomes almost dissolved. Barthes' universe is one where harmony and synthesis are excluded, having been replaced by discontinuity and rupture. His hatreds became notorious: he detested naturalism and realism, all forms of bourgeois idealism, biography as a genre, the psychoanalysis of authors (not texts), and all didactic art forms (not Brecht). Reading Barthes requires an appreciation of his technique of dispersing, of breaking up concentration, of denying the integration of the subject, and of ridding oneself of received opinions. Sturrock depicts Barthes as a pluralistic and centrifugal critic, as the last of the appealing eclectics. Historically, he provided legitimacy to structuralism within the realm of the Parisian literary left.

Hayden White's essay on Foucault is characteristically perspicacious. It is a model of the "tropological" perspective on intellectual history. White emphasizes Foucault's deep skepticism about words and language. Foucault distrusted the ability of words to represent accurately things, thought, or people. From his archeological assumptions, from his view that all knowledge is fleeting, from his fascination with the surfaces, vertical structures, and ruptures, Foucault wrote with great empathy and compassion for the excluded and oppressed victims of history. He resurrected the forgotten and silenced from the dustbin of the archives, the overlooked chronicle, the never-read historical narrative. It is not accidental that Foucault's major works deal with deviants, criminals, the insane, and the persecuted. His philosophical-historical treatises documented and interpreted the ways in which these groups have been deceived and duped by the establishments (scientific, legal, criminological, medical) of their day. He wrote from a powerful libertarian and antideterministic bias, embodied in the spirit of the rebellious students of May-June 1968.

Power, according to White, was Foucault's real interest; and in his *Discipline and Punish* (1975) and volume one of *The History of Sexuality* (1976), he has relentlessly unmasked the disciplinary apparatuses of ethical systems and systems of knowledge that serve to classify, restrict, police, normalize, and observe vast (ostensibly dangerous and marginal) sectors of the population. Foucault demonstrated the multiple ways in which language has contributed to social control over the last three hundred years. From linguistic modes of understanding, he believed that strategies for resistance to power could be elaborated. White points out how Foucault's radical doubt has increasingly given way to a love of facile paradox and "negative apocalypse." White concludes his essay on a devastating note, by mentioning that Foucault's methodological and epistemological approach is grounded in an eighteenth- and nineteenth-century form of rhetoric, which is now discredited and outmoded. He wonders why Foucault did not examine his own theoretical repertoire with the same analytical skills he has deployed on other disciplinary apparatuses.

Malcomb Bowie's study of Lacan steers clear of the French psychoanalyst's most controversial stances: his version of psychoanalytic technique, his clinical perspective, and his ideas on analytical training at institutes. Bowie grudgingly admits, but deemphasizes, that Lacan's intellectual style smacked of the buffoon. He insists that we appreciate Lacan's rethinking of Freud without being deflected by his personal arrogance and grandiosity, that we tolerate his obscurantist prose and his cult of theory.

Bowie situates Lacan at the cusp between Freud and Saussure, the effect of which is a major reinvention of both psychoanalysis and linguistics. Lacan abandoned Freud's desire for psychoanalysis to be subsumed under science; Lacan's generalizations cannot be tested for predictability or verifiability according to traditional empirical strategies. Rather, his theories were confirmed by the methods of structural linguistics. The return to Freud also resulted in many radical departures from contemporary psychoanalytic theory and practice; Lacan, for instance, repudiated typologies, diagnostic categories, characterology, and current psychoanalytic wisdom about ego development for their static and puerile conceptual function. He polemically rejected the idea of the ego constituting an autonomous or conflict free zone, viewing it as an illusion; for him the ego was the realm of defensiveness, the repository of absence, depletion, and unreliable knowledge. Lacan's writings on the subject posited a permanently decentered self, fragmented, split, empty, and mobile; he practiced psychoanalysis with no expectation of providing coherence, cure, or reliable strength to the ego.

Most of Lacan's writings were first delivered as speeches or verbal presentations. His style of writing is close to speech, to poetry, to the rhetorical and stylistic modes of automatic speaking. His writings were illogical, nonsensical in a form paralleling an analysand's free associations and the freely suspended attention of the analyst. Such contradictory forms of speech do not make sense to the uninitiated in psychoanalytic method. To be initiated, in turn, means having access to Lacan's version of the unconscious as a creation of language. Words make man. Man is a creature who speaks. If the unconscious is structured like a language (according to Lacan's famous dictum), then that structure makes sense only if one grasps its endless displacements, its disobedience, its disruptive quality. The unconscious is the discourse of the other insofar as we carry lacks, deficiencies, and permanently unfulfilled desires in us all the time.

Lacan claims that contemporary Anglo-Saxon psychoanalytic theory mistakenly attempted to tame the primary process by rendering it in a closed and mechanistic system. He asserted that the unconscious cannot be reified, categorized, or immobilized. Part of Lacan's project was to liberate psychoanalytic discourse from the arbitrary constraints of Freud's followers and codifiers. Returning to Freud meant returning to the unconscious at the level of language. Within speech one thinks genuinely, one's desires oscillate between symbolic absences and presences. By language Lacan was referring to the signifier, or to the sound realm of speech. The signifying chain is the best guide to unconscious ideation, along with the study of metaphor and metonymy. In Lacan's theory, consequently, he experimented with word plays and witty reworking of speech patterns. This approach was consistent with his postulation of the linguistic unconscious as displaceable, uncodifiable, and unstoppable. Emulating his surrealist precursors, Lacan's id was poetic, polyphonic, and overdetermined. Because the unconscious does not recognize negations, much of Lacan's theory played on contradiction and self-contradiction. Many readers are dismayed by his style, without realizing that for him nonsense is determined, never accidental, but rather that it represented a form of abundance. The unconscious haunts us with its unknowable quality of mystery and otherness; its existence precludes limits, special considerations, and finite endings. Here indeed everything is possible, including the senseless. For Bowie, finally, Lacan's importance lies in his creative reinterpretation of Freud's texts and in his attempt to revaluate psychoanalytic discourse by focusing on the linguistic components of the "talking cure."

Jonathan Culler argues that Derrida's method relies on a rigorous application of negative paradox. Derrida has established a decentering style of reading literary texts and philosophical discourses. He has set himself up as an opponent of all theoretical, metaphysical, and hierarchical systems; his strategy of interpretation works by critically intervening to illustrate holes, gaps, inconsistencies, and blind spots in a given piece of writing. Such a technique, Culler holds, is essentially negative: it involves a complicated process of undoing, of deciphering thought, the mobilization of linguistic modes of double readings and oppositional constructions. Deconstructing a narrative is a way of affirming the multiplicity of difference and of displacement in language. Meaning can never be reduced to a single principle or essence, but is constantly disseminated.

While playful in his best critical pieces, Derrida tends to attribute to the deconstructing critic more insight and knowledge than the author in question. Every text, almost by definition, contains implicit contradictions and blind spots. The task of undoing these paradoxes involves elaborate semantic dispersals, the working through and breaching of contradictions from within theoretical frameworks. Thus, language production is unstoppable, everything is in movement. Derrida also delights in questioning, if not displacing, his own categories and critical maneuvers. Deconstructing forces the critic to return to language as the key to all difference and signification. For Derrida, Culler explains, language can be exceeded but never dispensed with. Language determines and makes possible all events in the universe, even though writing produces an ambiguous access to the writer, and at best, an undecidable interpretation of truth. Prior structures—language—give rise to new events (that is, texts). New events can best be comprehended by double readings, supplements, and strategic interventions that invert, displace and destabilize writing.

The 1960s and 1970s in Paris were a period of flamboyant theorizing. For two decades philosophers and philosophical critics replaced the novelist and the politically *engagé* intellectual, usurping their influence in French cultural life. A famous French cartoon, dating from July 1967, caricatured Lévi-Strauss, Barthes, Foucault and Lacan (Derrida had not yet emerged). The four leading structuralist philosophers were pictured in a tropical setting topless, clad in grass skirts. In this variation on paintings by Gauguin and Manet, the four Parisian structuralists were portrayed talking, listening, reading, presumably holding forth on their theories. The structuralist luncheon on the grass endured for over twenty years. One wonders how much of a party it has been. The self-confidence, arrogance, and verbal facility of those French thinkers is apparent. That they are intoxicated with language and exegesis is quite plain. But their lasting contribution remains unclear. There is a great deal of facile paradox in structuralist thinking, in addition to a massive dose of formalistic posturing and of taking things apart. Surely that is a sign of the times, part of the post-modernist response to and negation of intellectual life.

The structuralist professors of Paris—whether in grass skirts or velour suits—have revealed the infinite possibilities of textual interpretation. Structuralism at its best demonstrated the truly subtle and impressive penetration of contemporary Paris' most self-reflexive thinkers. The five structuralist thinkers of Sturrock's volume, despite their differences, write at the interface of disciplines. All have developed erudite and powerful techniques of exegesis. All claim to have incorporated what was valid, discarded what was invalid, in the methodologies of linguistics, psychoanalysis, Marxism, and Nietzschean culture criticism. All are committed to the project of re-examining the assumptions, presumptions, and consequences of the human sciences. Their work, in contrast to the decline of the humanities in America, and in contrast to the increasingly marginal quality of theoretical work in the social sciences, has demonstrated the primacy of historical, anthropological, literary, and psychoanalytic studies in France. The structuralists play the culture game with a dubious, perverse, and altogether problematic attitude toward preserving and surpassing the culture. Their form of philosophizing may result not only in the end of philosophers but ultimately in the dissolution of philosophical discourse.

Nevertheless, structuralist method sterilizes historical process, impoverishes social and psychological theory, while disseminating increasingly sophisticated and abstract forms of hermeneutics. In spilling a great deal of ink about discourse, they have forgotten, or chosen to neglect, the points of intersection between criticism and action, theory and human fate. This is a severe limitation, one that truly deep and humble thinkers have always remembered, and which is perhaps summed up best in Hamlet's reminder to his friend: "There are more things in heaven and earth, Horatio, than are dreamt of in your philosophy."

Part III

Psychoanalytic History

11

The Question of Psychohistory

*We cannot leave history entirely to nonclinical observers
and to professional historians who often too nobly immerse
themselves into the very disguises, rationalizations, and
idealizations of the historical process from which it should
be their business to separate themselves.*
—Erik H. Erikson,
Young Man Luther, 1958

In 1958, psychoanalytic psychology was suddenly and rather unex-
pectedly given legitimacy as an auxiliary science of history. It was in
that year that Erik H. Erikson published his *Young Man Luther,* bringing to his researches a vast storehouse of clinical acumen and therapeutic experience, especially into the defensive, adaptive, and creative
conflicts of adolescence; Erikson also came to history as an innovative
theoretician, drawing on his pertinent concepts of the life cycle and of
identity crisis and identity diffusion. As a nonprofessional historian,
Erikson, who in fact has no higher academic degrees, subtitled his
essay, *A Study in Psychoanalysis and History.*[1] His work was explicitly designed to uncover, unmask, and deidealize much of the source
material and interpretative strategies that most academic historians
gloss over, and incidentally, that is glossed over by the curriculums of

most graduate programs in history.

In that same year, William L. Langer, a serious and rather conservative diplomatic historian at Harvard University, editor of a prestigious series of books in "The Rise of Modern Europe" collection (which generations of history graduate students had to plow through to pass their doctoral examinations), published his Presidential Address to the American Historical Association. Despite its pedantic title, "The Next Assignment" audaciously announced the need for the historian to investigate and integrate the extensive literature, methodological approaches, and theoretical possibilities of depth psychology—psychoanalysis—into their own conceptual repertoire.[2]

Remaining true to his artistic past, the intuitive and imaginative Erikson did not consider the need for psychoanalysts to receive formal training in research oriented doctoral programs in history; Langer, for his part, urged younger historians to acquire the requisite education by entering psychoanalytic institutes for systematic training in the clinical and theoretical aspects of depth psychology: "for many years young scholars in anthropology, sociology, religion, literature, education, and other fields have gone to psychoanalytic institutes for special training, and I suggest that some of our younger men might seek the same equipment."[3]

The chapter that follows will discuss the work of two prominent academically trained historians who both invested the time, money, emotion, and intellect to undergo a comprehensive psychoanalysis and to follow a rigorous course of training in a psychoanalytic institute. Peter Gay and Peter Loewenberg have emerged in the 1980s and 1990s as psychoanalytically engaged historians. While their orientation, approach, and styles differ, it will be illuminating to see what their versions of psychohistory (a term that Gay dislikes but that Loewenberg embraces) has contributed to the historical discipline and to the existing discourse of cultural and intellectual history.

Gay's *Freud for Historians* (1985)[4] is a quirky, inconsistent, rather contentious essay that replies to standard dismissals of psychoanalysis and psychohistory by historians. In the text, "Freud" actually functions as a code not for Freud himself and his contribution, but rather for classical psychoanalytic ego psychology, actually launched by Freud in his 1923 text, *The Ego and the Id* and refined and elaborated by figures such as Anna Freud, Heinz Hartmann, Ernst Kris, David Rapaport, and Rudolph Loewenstein. Gay has not drawn on the ideas and methods of the English object-relations school, the findings of psychoanalytically oriented developmentalists, the self-psychological followers of Heinz Kohut, nor the perspectives of Lacanians or neo-Lacanians; these competing and often divergent psychoanalytic schools of thought are banished from his psychoanalytic pantheon in all but the most rhetorical fashion.

Gay's allegiance to and identification with ego psychology may give his audience of contemporary historians a misleading, unhistorical impression; it tends to blunt the edge of major, often acrimonious theoretical and clinical disagreements within psychoanalysis for the past forty years and gives a false idea of consensus; it neither takes into account debates within psychoanalysis about the validity of Freud's assumptions nor controversies about the concept of the "ego." Gay adheres to a conservative, anachronistic position in that ego psychology represented a dominant trend in American psychoanalysis in the 1940s and 1950s; it is no longer the prevailing contemporary view. Gay's summary of the achievements of the English object-relations school reveals his balancing act: "But in concentrating on the pre-oedipal relations of the infant with the mother, the object-relations analysts extended, and further complicated, Freud's range of vision without materially altering it."[5] Gay's apparent attempt to assimilate divergent ideas into Freud's conceptual framework (extended, complicated, but not altered) trivializes the discrepancies in how the clinical material is seen and worked over, thereby discounting the differences between an ego psychological and an object-relations analyst.

Graciously written and immensely readable, Gay's book makes an elegant and at times convincing case for what historians might gain by grasping the modalities of unconscious mental process, particularly the role of instinctual impulses, psychosexual development, the predominant role of early childhood on character formation, the defensive and adaptive maneuvers of the ego, and the multiple vicissitudes of anxiety in human behavior and mental life. He not only argues for the cogency of a psychoanalytic history, but demonstrates that the historical and the psychological can be combined "in one."

Psychoanalytic insights will enhance a historian's knowledge of the unrelenting demands of the unconscious, the role of compromise formation in the individual's struggle with his primitive urges and his environment, thus sensitizing him to the complexity and subtleties of the inner world. Not least, psychoanalytic method will alert the historian to the precise working of defensive mechanisms, above all repression. Without collapsing the clear and distinct boundaries between psychoanalysis and history, Gay insists in a number of conciliatory passages that the two can go together fraternally, even felicitously. Both disciplines belong to the science of man in that they approach their subject matter skeptically; both reject absolute or dogmatic assertions about knowledge; both are oriented toward retrieving, reconstructing, and preserving memory; both have a critical function of piercing through commonplaces and deceptions that obstruct a nonillusory and nonsentimental grasp of human experience.

As a full professor of history with an endowed chair at Yale University, having earned a distinguished reputation as a specialist on the European enlightenment, and after contributing a prodigious body of publications on the history of modernism, cultural history, and historiography, Gay entered the Western New England Psychoanalytic Institute in 1976; he apparently opted for two thirds of the training offered there: he received a full training or didactic analysis and he attended the full spectrum of seminars and course work at the Institute, usually lasting a minimum of four to five years. The one piece of psychoanalytic training that Gay did not receive was long-term clinical work with patients with Gay as psychoanalyst, conducted under the close supervision of senior analysts at the Institute; Gay probably had little access to patients, perhaps he had some vicarious clinical contact while conducting (or observing) in-take interviews in a New Haven clinic or hospital. Unfortunately, he does not indicate the reasons for not undertaking a full psychoanalytic education; perhaps he elected a partial training because of his commitment to his scholarship and teaching at Yale.

Gay summarizes his experience with his analytic training in relatively positive terms: it was "fascinating, laborious, painful, exhilarating, immensely illuminating."[6] He reports that the psychoanalysts at his home Institute, as well as those he encountered in New York City and the umbrella credentializing organization, the American Psychoanalytic Association, welcomed him cordially and were never "condescending" toward him. Gay does not acknowledge that his reception was rare because psychoanalysts are notoriously detached, nonnurturing, and noncollegial even toward their own medically trained clinical colleagues; he does not mention the long history of official and unofficial disdain of trainees from nonclinical fields, although, in all fairness, that tradition is currently in disrepute and the climate in and around local institutes is changing, while the "American" seems intent on resisting or postponing change. He does admit, however, that many clinically oriented analysts harbor grave doubts toward applied psychoanalysis, including his project to unify history and psychoanalysis.

Professional historians, Gay argues, have approached Freud defensively and dishonestly; either they dismiss him with silence, or they banish him from serious consideration by willful misrepresentation and misquotion. Historians caricature Freud by presenting fragments of his writing extrapolated from their appropriate historical context and textual intent. The hostility, anxiety, and exaggerated doubts about psychoanalysis derive from a number of sources. One is an arrogant form of philistinism and a smug lack of knowledge about psychoanalytic theory and practice that could be easily remedied with a good-faith study of the ideas and techniques of the science; historians "parade their ignorance as a badge of professional wisdom."[7] The great refusal to study Freud systematically and sympathetically has led not only to a wholesale devaluation of psychoanalysis, but more injuriously it has led historians to reject a methodological instrument that could greatly enhance their craft. Too many historians, unwisely and imprudently in Gay's mind, reject psychoanalysis for being inaccessible, incoherent, and authoritarian. Psychoanalysts have not always helped their cause by behaving in an elitist and exclusive manner and by writing in a style that seems self-congratulatory and hermetically closed to the uninitiated.

Gay refutes the charges that psychoanalysis is dogmatic, reductionistic, mechanistic, religious, nonfalsifiable, poetic, and mythical as overstated and unjust. He does not seriously debate each charge in an elaborate or substantive way. He repeatedly reiterates Freud's deep appreciation of and commitment to the concept of overdetermination, that is, to the postulation that an individual's behavior, thoughts, feelings, fantasies, and desires have multiple causes and meanings. Without a grasp of overdetermination, it is impossible to comprehend the degree to which people are conflicted, deficient, defensive, ambivalent, and not fully conscious of their emotions or actions. The concept of overdetermination works against simplistic and monolithic explanations.[8]

Besides inaccurately representing psychoanalytic ideas, and besides avoiding a serious intellectual and emotional encounter with Freudian psychoanalysis, historians are themselves amateur psychologists, seemingly not in need of a more exacting theory or method. Gay alleges that they have assimilated a naive, superficial psychology with untested hypotheses and with rather dubious value for penetrating the vagaries of the human mind. As an amateur psychologist, the historian who lacks a solid Freudian cultural foundation relies on a banal understanding of human motivation—banal in that it is innocent, shallow about motivation, defense and fantasy, lacking self-consciousness and self-reflectiveness about the psychologist's relationship to his own theory and techniques. Gay insists that it is "unscientific to minimize or ignore psychoanalysis."[9]

Furthermore, historians make a number of psychological assumptions about human motivation that psychoanalysts would contest if not thoroughly repudiate; most historians assume that "self-interest" predominates in all human affairs and historical interactions. Such a view presupposes that man is a selfish character. The egoism, greed, and venality of human beings is thus taken for granted. Psychoanalysts, on the other hand, posit that man is a pleasure-seeking animal, thus accounting for an inevitable conflict between man's wishful desires and the demands and requirements of reality. Seeing man as a wishing animal helps to account for the power of mixed perceptions, alternating feeling states, potent fantasies, untamable desires, as well as the pervasiveness of guilt, shame, and deception in human affairs. Gay disputes the rationalism of the prevailing psychology in the historical profession, seeing it as an ideology built around a cognitive notion of self-interest; he sees self-interest as a compromise formation, not as something rational, stable, omnipresent, but as something that is frequently ill-perceived and not persistently pursued by historical actors. According to him, the psychoanalytic approach helps to illuminate the role of self-sabotage, the need to fail, the role of conflicting wishes in affairs, which a simplistic psychology of self-interest can never explain.

Gay consistently asserts that psychoanalysis is an open-ended field of knowledge, capable of revision based on new discoveries, receptive to an evolving body of research and thinking. Toward Freud himself, Gay is overwhelmingly sympathetic, but not worshipful; his immersion in Freud's writings over the years has been a rewarding and comfortable experience, not one of exceptional difficulty or self-torment. The future biographer of Freud prizes psychoanalysis without needing to make propaganda. He does not hold that psychoanalytic therapy is necessarily the most efficacious cure for all neurotic disorders (which it is not), or that Freud himself ought to be remembered as a perfect angel (which he was not). Gay does not elevate Freud into a saint or paint him as "an impeccable gentleman."

Gay originally came to Freud through the neo-Freudian and culturalist perspectives of Erich Fromm; he confesses his former deep devotion to Fromm's attempt to synthesize Marx and Freud in books such as *Escape From Freedom* (1941) and *Marx's Concept of Man* (1961). Gay has since disavowed the ideas of achieving a Freudo-Marxist unity, judging the effort to have been "a shotgun marriage with calamitous consequences for both."[10] Like many who have gone from Marx to Freud (let us remember that the young Peter Gay wrote an intellectual biography of a seminal Marxist revisionist, the Social Democratic leader, Eduard Bernstein),[11] he remains enamored of Freud's revolutionary contribution and still points to the subversive aspects of the psychoanalytic instrument of analysis.

For him, Freud's methods allow us to capture the core of human defenses and rationalizations, breaking out of abstract and mystifying speculations about human motivation; Freud appreciated not only the staggering diversity of man's inner life, but demonstrated an exquisite concern for the multiplicity of individuals urges, impulses, and apparently irrational behavior. Freud's psychology stemmed from a view of the human subject as an "individual, unique, unduplicable, thus, in his particular way, interesting."[12] Though Freud eschewed prophecy or the role of charismatic leader in building an international movement, he still emerges as a "giant," as an original thinker who stood on the "shoulders of other tall men." Gay, in short, insists that we accord Freud a monumental position in the history of the modern mind.[13]

If Freud needs to be acknowledged for his "stature" in penetrating the deepest dimensions and the unexamined secrets of the human mind, honored for the "astonishing" range of his perceptions, Gay asks historians to view Freud as an audacious, but over all a scandalous thinker. In that sense, psychoanalysis is a "subversive science," undermining shallow, reassuring, optimistic, but commonplace psychologies.[14] Certainly, Freud distrusted experimental or laboratory verification of psychoanalytic findings, preferring to listen carefully to his patients, to resonate to his own affective states and psychic struggles, and to attend to the discoveries and advances of his followers. Certainly, prediction occupies a relatively modest role in psychoanalysis. Certainly, his most rewarding ideas are indirect, inferential, and highly debatable, even speculative. Certainly, Freud's concepts are best comprehended in terms of their ability to disorient and shatter our most persistent narcissistic and rationalistic views of ourselves. Certainly, Freud was not a systematic thinker with a comprehensive or fully integrated theory, but rather was someone who constantly changed his mind, who had the courage to rethink his own formulations. Gay suggests that Freud is most fruitfully approached as if he were "an architect of stature" who constructed a fascinating and disturbing edifice of the human mind. It is most enlightening to enter his texts as if one were exploring an "imposing, sprawling castle."[15]

Where psychoanalysis achieves rigor and precision, however, is in the cooperative, dialogic venture that Freud established in inventing the psychoanalytic situation. This setting allows for minute investigation of the subjectivity of the individual, for the close and empathic observation of data, and for the ability to make discoveries about man's inner world, its contradictions and strangeness.

For Gay, the Freudian psychoanalyst is a combination Sherlock Holmes, skeptical philosopher, modern artist, and relativistic historian who pays attention to the clinical facts. The analyst undertakes his adventure in psychoanalytic detection by interpreting clues not as a master empiricist but as one engaged in a joint venture, an interpersonal exchange. He is simultaneously open and suspicious about what he hears, knowing that revelation and concealment go together. He pays attention to the devious play of transference and resistance, the role of honesty and defense, candor and deception in the analytic dialogue. Like a surrealist artist, he listens with an ear attuned to surprise, amazement, error, uncertainty and his own subjective reactions to what he hears. He knows that a pipe is sometimes not a pipe, but a symbolic representation open to a myriad of associations and significance. Because of his historical consciousness he knows that memory can be evasive and the affectively charged fragments from the past can emerge in disguised or distorted forms in the analytic dialogue. He does not dwell on the intrapsychic exclusively, always recognizing the pressures of external events, culture, religion, language, mores and objective realities from the external world.

The good analytic practitioner appreciates that interpretations function as a "small experiment," offered not to summarize or terminate an inquiry, not to demonstrate the analyst's brilliance, but to shed some light on the meaning of frightening, hitherto unpalatable, suppressed ideas, fantasies, or affects. Despite its pluralism of method and of explanation, psychoanalysis can be transmitted, learned, and acquired. Moreover, it can be rationally criticized and ratified in the light of new evidence. Gay insists that Freudian psychology is receptive to experimental inquiry and logical reflection. The psychoanalytically engaged historian needs to acquire the tact, abstinence, empathic attitude, and capacity to entertain an introspective form of reflective dialogue with his sources and subject matter; like the analytic clinician, he must be ready to be surprised, he must learn to tolerate uncertainty and not knowing, and he must suspend his own value judgments and biases.[16]

If Freud never entirely surrendered a biological orientation, he was always receptive to the role that culture and environment played in determining human character. In approaching life histories or the dynamic realm of collectivities, psychoanalysis focuses on the persistence of human wishes, the unrelenting push for gratification and discharge, and the inevitable occurrence of frustration, delay and postponement. Gay proposes that historians understand Freud's conviction about the primacy of instinctual drives. In Freud's late writings, particularly in postulating a dual drive theory of sexuality and aggression, he came to see the instinctual drives as the fuel for all human action. Once historians become alerted to the multiple ways in which drives become fused, confused, disguised, distorted and defended against; once they perceive the ubiquitous connection between drives and anxiety and drives and the generation of unconscious guilt in the emergence of compromise formations; once they develop a capacity to register the nuances and often fragmentary residues of fantasies, desires, transferences, memory traces and visual images, then they will understand that instinctual drives "make history."[17]

Based on his own sensitivity to the clinical setting, particularly his knowledge of the ubiquitousness of transference love and hatred, including its displacements, condensations, and symbolic representations, Gay does not overstate the explanatory potentialities of a psychoanalytically informed history; he cautions us to remain aware of the fallibilities, difficulties, and inconclusive aspects of the analytic instrument. Just as psychoanalytic therapy has never succeeded in achieving its clinical ideal of the completely analyzed human being, so the psychoanalytic historian can only approximate the impartiality, empathic understanding, and sustained reflection leading to an unfolding of unconsciously determined meanings. Introspective dialogue reveals more than an isolated insight. If approached as a pathway to discovery and as an open-ended method of inquiry, he argues that a psychoanalytic historian can "register the broken surfaces and sound the unplumbed depths of human nature."[18]

Understanding life histories and the bizarre, ever-changing play of wishful gratifications and frustrations is where psychoanalytic history can mediate between "couch and culture." Every good clinician knows that the separation between couch and culture is arbitrary, the two interpenetrate. Gay emphasizes the fundamentally social or triangular nature of the Oedipus complex, keeping in mind its evocative and authoritative impact on all of human experience, including aspects of political, economic, and diplomatic history that historians in those specialties frequently neglect. Gay defines culture psychoanalytically: it is an elaborate collective and individual set of defenses used to prohibit murder and incest. Psychoanalytic techniques can help to decipher the subtle interplay of love and hatred, regression and abandonment of controls, in grasping how individuals and groups cope with conflict and extreme situations, how they participate in the making of history, or are acted upon when history is being made in specific milieus.

Gay concludes his essay on a high-spirited and optimistic note; this, too, is consistent with his identification with ego psychology. He echoes the young and incisive Wilhelm Reich in calling for historians to undertake studies in the sociology of the unconscious. The next "next assignment," he proposes, is a careful and particularized history of human defenses, their "personal and social transformations." He salutes three professional historical practitioners of psychoanalytic history, for their expert, nonreductionistic use of the Freudian method. In paying such positive attention to E.R. Dodds' *The Greeks and the Irrational* (1951), John P. Demos' *Entertaining Satan: Witch-Craft and the Culture of Early New England* (1982), and Maynard Solomon's *Beethoven* (1977), Gay has inevitably slighted other scholars who are working in the field—many of who may be working in historical fields closer to Gay's own specialized interests.[19]

To be sure, one could fault Gay for being idiosyncratic, subjective, and arbitrary, in terms of the studies that he has selected or omitted; his detractors have often accused him of being heavy-handed and grandiose in his construction of bibliographical essays. Yet his criteria seems fairly straightforward: he honors the psychoanalytic historian who is not doctrinaire, who attempts to shine the light of psychoanalysis on sources or texts while appreciating the pluralism of meaning and explanation. He appreciates those who do not back away from a confrontation with the pressures of the unconscious; such historians demonstrate a rigor and sensitivity to the inner dynamics of the mind. Gay praises Dodds, Demos, and Solomon because they have read their sources from a point of view informed by an analytic understanding of free association, grasping that a chain of associations often reveals unconscious but significant linkages. Moreover, these historians are not oblivious to the often mysterious, ineffable, and astonishing role of the unconscious in mental and cultural life.

Refraining modestly from discussing or advertising his own projects to understand the "totality of human experience" for the nineteenth-century European and American middle classes[20] or to capture the complexity of Freud's life and contribution,[21] Gay admires those psychoanalytic historians who have honestly succeeded in blending the two disciplines without collapsing distinctions between the worlds of history and psychoanalysis.

He proposes, finally, that psychoanalytic history can serve as an auxiliary discipline to history because of its ability to enrich, inform, and expand historical discourse; he eschews those who wield psychoanalytic terminology wildly, who use the technique as an aggressive weapon, who overinterpret, who overemphasize psychopathology to the detriment of adaptation, creativity, and restitution; following Anna Freud, he warns against using psychoanalysis as only a key to the id or to primary process functioning, counseling us to remain equidistant from all the internal structures and functions of the mind, not to devalue the role of the ego and superego; and lastly he argues that psychoanalysis can achieve a precision and textured understanding of inner dynamics if it is practiced tactfully, compassionately, empathically, as if it belonged to a general psychology. The task is for the historian to use psychoanalytic technique and theory in order not to overlook anything, including the historian's capacity to look at himself while he analyzes historical evidence.

Gay's polemical defense of psychohistory, then, affirms the potential for this aesthetic science to arrive at new and surprising insights into the nature of the past, while the historian maintains a sharpness, suspiciousness, and perspicaciousness about penetrating the many hidden realms of human experience.

In turning to Peter Loewenberg's contribution to psychohistory, we must remember that he crossed disciplinary and professional boundaries and has taken a great deal of flack in attempting to integrate a clinically grounded psychoanalysis into academic history.

His detractors have accused him of doing bad psychoanalysis and writing bad history. Psychoanalytic practitioners have questioned the depth of Loewenberg's clinical acumen, have been skeptical of his use of clinical data, and have been quick to remind him of the obvious, that the dead do not free associate, joke, dream, or provide us with slips of the tongue the way analysands do on a couch in an analyst's office. Analysts seem reluctant to admit that a specialist from the humanities or social sciences can achieve a subtle and incisive grasp of therapeutic issues. Historians, for their part, have been unacquainted with or put off by a psychoanalytic perspective. Only recently, and quite selectively, has historical training included an immersion in psychoanalytic theory and practice. Most historians trained in America lack a Freudian cultural formation; thus they are ill prepared to entertain psychoanalytic methods of inquiry and argumentation. Historians suffering from fetishism of facts, cannot accept the untraditional forms of verification that go along with psychoanalytic interpretations of history. They are offended by analogical forms of thinking. They distrust speculative leaps about what *feels* right as opposed to what can be demonstrated conclusively did happen. In two professions so ostensibly committed to the comprehension of the past, it is not surprising that mainstream historical and psychoanalytic thinking tends to be conservative, deeply resistant to interpretative and methodological innovations. For more than fifteen years, Loewenberg has bucked misrepresentation, misunderstanding, suspicion, and downright contempt of his work. Yet, he has persevered, achieving a kind of begrudging respect and legitimacy in both communities.

As a pioneer, Loewenberg has staked out new, often unexplored territory on the frontier of psychoanalysis and history. Borders make people uncomfortable. They require a toleration for uncertainty. They cry out for a new language and a new mode of conceptualization. He is the first *fully* trained professional historian, with distinguished academic credentials, also to receive *full* psychoanalytic training at an accredited institute of the American Psychoanalytic Association. Loewenberg writes history as a practicing, licensed research psychoanalyst, as someone who has been clinically trained in the slow, comprehensive, and elusive ways of psychoanalysis. His analytic training was largely opposed by senior historians both in his field and his own department at UCLA, many of whom considered psychoanalysis unscientific, unfalsifiable, esoteric, and most egregiously of all "unhistorical." Thus, he trained at considerable risk to his standing in the historical profession.[22]

From 1966 to 1974, he trained at the Southern California Psychoanalytic Institute in Los Angeles where he was not warmly embraced; they were cautious and deliberate about training him, and presented him with a myriad of obstacles and delays in making progress toward graduation. Many members of the psychoanalytic institute resented and envied him; questions were raised about the dangers and advisability of training candidates outside of the medical-psychiatric fields; a minority opposed him on ideological grounds, insisting that psychoanalysis ought to remain a medical monopoly. Previously, there were analysts who have been well grounded in historical methodology and historiography; articles and books exist by amateurs or the proverbial history buffs. Likewise, several generations of psychohistorians have existed, varying in enormous degrees of wildness and speculative zeal, often guilty of imposing a rigid theoretical model on their material. A minority of psychohistorians have been thoroughly psychoanalyzed themselves and have interpreted their sources astutely in the light of their textured knowledge of psychoanalytic theory. But none to my knowledge has possessed the dual training, thus bringing to his research projects a twin competence.

Decoding the Past: The Psychohistorical Approach (1983), brings together the fruits of Loewenberg's labors, and consequently provides us with an opportunity to offer a preliminary assessment of his contribution. His education as a psychohistorian, every bit as arduous, and in certain ways more emotionally taxing, than doctoral programs in major research-oriented universities, has definitely limited his time for writing and research. Nor can he take off for lengthy stays in Europe and the archives because it would require him to neglect his psychoanalytic practice. While this may have diminished the quantity of his scholarship, it has not interfered with the quality nor the significance of his ground-breaking perspective. The volume consists of eleven essays, four of which are previously unpublished (a paperback edition issued by the University of California Press includes an autobiographical preface). Subtitled *The Psychohistorical Approach*, Loewenberg has extended the boundaries of meaning in historical scholarship. He has done so with a good deal of modesty, with clear prose, with a modulated passion akin to analytic tact, and with meticulous attention to documentation and evidence. He makes no grandiose claims about his methodology. He is seldom messianic or polemical.

Loewenberg's psychohistory would be more accurately understood in the plural—approaches. He has mastered a vast armamentarium of psychoanalytic theoretical perspectives and insights, beginning with Freud's classical model of instinctual drives and defenses, borrowing generously from the ego psychologists and Eriksonians who pointed to the adaptive as well as neurotic aspects of defenses; he is well aware of post-Freudian advances, including the subtle perspectives about human interactions opened by the English object-relations school and the current study of creative and pathological narcissism undertaken by Kohut and the practitioners of self psychology. While aware of the contributions of Melanie Klein, he has not incorporated her ideas and techniques in his studies, except for a brief reference to Wilfred Bion's work on group dynamics.

Just as the psychoanalyst who works with patients with vast differences in psychopathology, presenting symptoms, cultural heritage, linguistic abilities, and life experience has to be equipped with a flexible assortment of therapeutic tools and conceptual frameworks, so too must the psychohistorian come prepared to decipher the past by relying on a full assortment of psychoanalytic methodologies. Without multiple ways of understanding his subject, the historian will not be able to comprehend historical figures, mass movements, and seemingly irrational phenomena. As the scope of psychoanalysis has broadened in the past thirty-five years to include the treatment of more severely disturbed character disorders, the psychohistorian has also widened his interpretative grid to grasp more horrific historical events, such as the Holocaust and genocide. In offering his readers plausible interpretations, not definitive truths or dogmatic assertions, Loewenberg remains consistent with modern historiography that is relativistic, nonreductionistic, and opposed to one-dimensional causal explanations. Loewenberg, in short, has written a compelling form of history which reveals the underlying emotional and psychic factors which influence historical action, or inaction. Given his clinical training, he is particularly attuned to the emotional lives of his subjects, to the impact of their early childhoods, to periods of crisis, to thoughts and fantasies they expressed about their bodies, members of the opposite sex, parents, authorities, and an assortment of transference figures. Loewenberg's psychohistory is informed by a sensitivity to latencies, to the deeper layers of psychical meanings and unconscious conflicts in the lived experience of men and groups.

Loewenberg the psychoanalytic historian wrote this volume with two caps on, straddling two dissimilar universes of discourse, speaking to two different audiences. This is ultimately a strength and a weakness. He has intelligently and discerningly penetrated the interface of history and psychoanalysis. He has neither psychologized history nor historicized psychoanalysis. He never argues that the psychological "code" is the only code, or key determining agency of the historical process. Loewenberg is particularly adept at situating his case studies—whether of Austrian luminaries, Nazi leaders, or Nazi followers—in their proper historical contexts, that is, with a full awareness of political, social, and economic frameworks and of the powerful role of culture on events and human choices. For many classically trained analysts, reality is a construct, something important, but vaguely "out there," outside of the intrapsychic realm. Thus most psychoanalysts sound naive, and rather inadequate, when they speak of "reality considerations," "circumstances"—the so-called external world outside of the analyst-analysand interaction, outside the clinical competence of most clinicians.

Loewenberg grasps the subtleties of his era, primarily the 1890s to 1945, while appreciating the emotional conflicts and psychological nuances of individuals and generations presented with limited options.

Loewenberg has not, however, found the ideal kind of language which effectively bridges the disciplines. That language has yet to be invented. Preferably, it will be in plain, felicitous English, which describes unconscious symbolization, impulses, fantasies, and psychic conflicts in a manner comprehensible to a literate audience. When Loewenberg's narrative flows into analytic sections, they resemble paragraphs extrapolated from professional psychoanalytic journals. These journals are not celebrated for their prose. The psychoanalytic sections of his essays are saturated with technical language and jargon. There is no question about Loewenberg's grasp of difficult and abstract psychoanalytic terminology. He opts for this language as a short hand, to avoid lengthy expository passages. This may please his audience of analysts, while alienating his readers in the human sciences. He does not use inflated verbiage to cover confused or mystified thinking.

Scientific language, to be sure, lends authority; Loewenberg may have chosen an intellectualized, somewhat remote way to present his material in order to demonstrate to the analytic community that he was sufficiently well-versed in psychoanalytic concepts and sufficiently well-removed from his research, akin to analytic neutrality and clinical detachment. He might have risked being more personal, disclosing his own empathic immersion in his material and methodology, in a style adopted by Erik H. Erikson in *Gandhi's Truth* (1969),[23] without a loss of clarity, scholarly balance, intellectual seriousness, and insight. Such a subjective approach might have alerted his readers to another authentic way of arriving at psychohistorical modes of thinking. Perhaps in his subsequent writings, he will be less concerned about following the accepted academic and psychoanalytic style of discourse, and will be at liberty to find an idiom more appropriate to his theme, closer to his own personal voice.

In two of his "Austrian Portraits," the study of Victor and Friedrich Adler and of Otto Bauer, Loewenberg makes compelling use of both psychohistory and the history of psychoanalysis. Here intellectual history and psychohistory converge, and the convergence is illuminating. He documents "Dora's" identity as Ida Bauer, sister of Otto Bauer, one of Austrian Social Democracy's key leaders. (Dora's identity has been well known to insiders in the psychoanalytic movement for decades, most especially by those trained by the Vienna Psychoanalytic Society). Because of the recent flap over works by Jeffrey Masson and Paul Roazen,[24] the issue of disclosure and of access to documents has become controversial. Loewenberg's application reveals that such knowledge can open up vistas of understanding. Like an experienced clinician, he uses his sources critically and tastefully, without a prurient interest, with a sensitivity to confidentiality, with no hidden agenda of embarrassing psychoanalyst or analysand. If Kurt Eissler has played the role of self-appointed watchdog of the Freud Archives, and Anna Freud the role of superego of the analytic community (including its history), then Loewenberg's example provides a persuasive rebuttal. Denying competent psychoanalytically trained historical researchers access to the sources, keeping the archives closed, will ultimately work to the detriment of the psychoanalytic movement; it raises rather than resolves questions, suggesting unrealistic anxiety or cover-up on the part of the custodians of the archives; and it implies that the history of psychoanalysis exists independently of responsible forms of critical inquiry and evaluation of the available evidence.

In Loewenberg's most successful chapters he displays a sensitivity to the emotional tone of a text, to the affects either disguised in phrases or words, or hidden between the lines.

The William Langer essay, the least well realized in *Decoding the Past*, somehow lacks an emotional or intellectual resonance. Perhaps this American family, the particular American milieu, the specific individual, and his particular dilemmas remained inaccessible to the author.

Having mastered a form of psychoanalytic reading of his sources (his study of Theodor Herzl draws on diaries, autobiographical novels, short stories, and letters). Loewenberg performs a sounding on Herzl, not an attempt to unearth and answer all the secrets about the founder of modern Zionism. A psychodynamic perspective on Herzl shows a rather marked oscillation between his dismal self-regard and swelling omnipotence, which resulted in a blurring of the boundary between fantasy and reality, ideas and people, action and dream. Without deni-

224 Cultural Theory and Psychoanalytic Tradition

grating his achievement, Loewenberg's portrait humanizes and demythicizes Herzl, places him in a particular time and place, and fleshes out the inner dimensions of his life history.

Loewenberg is extremely competent in depicting and scrutinizing generational conflict. The essay on Victor and Friedrich Adler is an ingenious illustration of father-son hatred and love. Within psychoanalytic circles it has become strangely unfashionable to employ Oedipal forms of interpretation, almost as if this form of contestation of authority was no longer relevant. Loewenberg is no such slave to the fad. He argues that Fritz's assassination of the Prime Minister of Austria in 1916 can be understood as a displacement and acting out of aggressively murderous urges toward his own father. Most historians operating on a cognitive level, oblivious to the logic and power of unconscious conflict, might fail to grasp the symbolic significance of such an act of murder.

The chapters on Otto Bauer and on Heinrich Himmler illustrate Loewenberg's craft at building historical character portraits.

Personality factors in Bauer's case at least partially explain the reasons behind a prominent Socialist leader who put the brakes on social revolution, refusing to unleash the masses in a counterassault on Austrian fascism. Bauer's various forms of denial, avoidance, and intellectualization clarify his adoption of passive political tactics, and underscore how his personality dynamics reinforced a defensive political strategy in order to stop effective action.

In the Himmler study, Loewenberg depicts a depressed, unfeeling, frightened adolescent boy unable to integrate his unconscious sadism, cruelty, and severely regressed tendencies into a coherent identity. For Himmler identification with Hitler and incorporation of the anti-Semitic ideology and demonology had healing effects, while leading to horrendous consequences for European Jewry. If it is erroneous to generalize that all Nazi leaders had a schizoid personality structure with overt oral and projective mechanisms, Loewenberg's portrait gives us pause to reflect on political leaders, past and present, who overvalue toughness, who depreciate sensitivity to others, and who deny affect.

Loewenberg's Nazi youth cohort analysis is a *tour de force*. This is first-rate generational analysis of followers, an evocative, historically shrewd account of the mass psychology of the led. Cohorts are groups or collectivities who share a momentous generational experience, a prolonged traumatic episode like world war, revolution, emigration, depression, or economic dislocation. In describing the common experience of those recruited to the Nazi Party, Loewenberg draws on socioeconomic, demographic, and psychological forms of research. For German youth who came of age in the late 1920s and early 1930s, unemployment became the massive trauma. Millions of men and women found themselves helpless, confused, psychologically disorganized and fragmented. They were receptive to irrational appeals and simplistic explanations for their difficulties. It is not surprising that a clever mythomaniac like Hitler could easily fill the political and emotional vacuum. Given the context and the shattering effect of the unemployment traumas, it makes sense that his message of racial violence, revenge, and national honor could easily sweep away this generation that was so demoralized and so desperate for security. Loewenberg adeptly shows how the Fuhrer's personality and ideology could simultaneously tap into the cohorts' longings for both paternal and maternal care.

Loewenberg has skillfully used and seldom abused the psychological "code" in history.[25] The ensemble of his book testifies not only to the relevance of systematic, professional training by the psychohistorian in both the disciplines of history and psychoanalysis, but also to the creative possibilities of such new modes of investigation and knowledge about the past. Since there really is no history, only historians, each with a point of view, a polemicist might argue that all history is psychohistory, in that it involves the unconscious and conscious mind of the historian. Loewenberg addresses political conflict, ideological formation, and the apparently illogical contradictions in the historical process without the psychological blinders of most of his academic colleagues and with an historical consciousness which his psychoanalytic colleagues lack. In this sense, his psychohistory is profoundly modern, profoundly in touch with the temper of our post-Freudian era. His work is also a nuanced extension of the hand to all of us to understand the past by grasping the multiple psychic layers of meaning buried there, if we would only learn to look.

226 Cultural Theory and Psychoanalytic Tradition

Notes

1   Erik H. Erikson, *Young Man Luther: A Study in Psychoanalysis and History* (New York, 1958).
2   William L. Langer, "The Next Assignment," *American Historical Review*, vol. 63, no. 2, January, 1958, pp. 283-304.
3   Ibid., p. 303.
4   Peter Gay, *Freud for Historians* (New York, 1985). The two best known critical dismissals of psychohistory are Jacques Barzun, *Clio and the Doctors* (Chicago, 1974) and David Stannard, *Shrinking History* (New York, 1980).
5   Peter Gay, *Freud for Historians*, pp. ix-x, n. 1
6   Ibid., p. xiv.
7   Ibid., p. 7.
8   Ibid., pp. 75, 187, 187 n. 5.
9   Ibid., p. 51.
10   Ibid., p. xiii.
11   Peter Gay, *The Dilemma of Democratic Socialism: Eduard Bernstein's Challenge to Marx* (New York, 1952).
12   Peter Gay, *Freud For Historians*, p. 28.
13   Ibid., pp. 59, 61.
14   Ibid., p. 58.
15   Ibid., p. 48.
16   Ibid., pp. 441, 54-55, 66, 69.
17   Ibid., p. 89.
18   Ibid., p. 77.
19   For a competent, less restricted bibliography see Peter Loewenberg, "Psychohistory: An Overview of the Field," in Loewenberg's *Decoding the Past: The Psychohistorical Approach* (New York, 1983), pp. 14-41; for two brief introductions, see Rudolph Binion, *Introduction à la psychohistoire* (Paris, 1982) and Jacques Szaluta, *La Psychohistoire* (Paris, 1987).
20   Peter Gay, *The Bourgeois Experience Victoria to Freud*, vol. 1, *The Education of the Senses* (New York, 1984) and vol. 2, *The Tender Passion* (New York, 1986).
21   Peter Gay, *Freud: A Life for Our Time* (New York, 1988).
22   See Peter Loewenberg, "Love and Hate in the Academy," for a psychoanalytic appreciation of his experience as a junior, non-tenured member of the UCLA history department during his psychoanalytic training, in *Decoding the Past*, pp. 67-80.
23   Erik H. Erikson, *Gandhi's Truth: On the Origins of Militant Nonviolence* (New York, 1969), pp. 229-254.
24   Jeffrey Masson, *The Assault on Truth: Freud's Suppression of the Seduction Theory* (New York, 1984) and Paul Roazen, *Brother Animal: The Story of Freud and Tausk* (New York, 1969).
25   Frank E. Manuel, "The Use and Abuse of Psychology in History," *Daedalus*, Winter, 1971, pp. 187-213.

12

An Intellectual History of Crowds

Serge Moscovici's *The Age of the Crowd* (1985)[1] is a marvelous and disturbing book. Ostensibly, it is an accurate, chronological account of the main contributors to crowd psychology from the late nineteenth century to the present. But is it much more than an intellectual history of the major theoreticians of mass society; it is a reminder about the extent to which we remain dominated by the techniques of mass manipulation.

In summarizing the contributions of Gustave LeBon, Gabriel Tarde, and their "best disciple," Sigmund Freud, Moscovici argues that crowd psychology exists as a full-fledged discipline with an internal logic and coherence and a solid foundation in social reality. Moscovici is well equipped to take us on this journey; he is trained in Social Psychology and is a Director of Studies at the École des Hautes Études en Sciences Sociales in Paris. Those who devalue these ideas as irrational and unverifiable fail to recognize that mass psychology has made history as evidenced by modern nationalist movements and the rise of fascism. Major political figures have acknowledged their debt to crowd psychologists, figures as different in ideology and culture as Mussolini and Theodore Roosevelt, Hitler and Charles de Gaulle. Moreover, crowds continue to make history, particularly in Third World countries and in Eastern and Central Europe.

The trio, LeBon-Tarde-Freud, jointly established an analytical theory of mass society which focused on the nonrational and unconscious effects on politics and social struggle. Intellectual historians have traditionally dismissed LeBon and Tarde as mediocre, unrigorous, deductive, and profoundly conservative thinkers, with apparently no deeper understanding of social structure or sociopolitical change. Because LeBon wrote best selling books and pamphlets, he has been unfairly denigrated as a popularizer and trivializer. Two significant exceptions are Robert Nye's incisive intellectual portrait of LeBon, *The Origins of Crowd Psychology* (1975)[2] and George L. Mosse's synthetic *The Nationalization of the Masses* (1975)[3]. Marxist social historians reject the fundamental insights of LeBon and crowd psychology as ignoring the facts of history; they repudiate his writings as "overdrawn, tendentious, and misleading."[4]

Without glossing over the frequently banal and confused aspects of their thinking, Moscovici takes these theoreticians seriously, advising his readers to confront the unpleasant, even intolerable, truths of this body of literature. As modern political philosophers they are the Machiavellis of the crowd era. Crowd psychology posits a radical psychology of the masses while drawing conservative conclusions. Moscovici asks his readers to study these truths primarily because they "work," particularly in the realm of pragmatic power politics and in grasping the politics of social movements.

Historians point to the period 1890 to 1914 as the heyday of theorizing on collective psychology; its major proponents were French and Italian. Most crowd psychologists saw crowds as a threat to individualism, reason, and freedom; most feared that the rise of the industrial and democratic masses might jeopardize the traditional pattern of European life established in the pre-industrial age. The conceptual bias shared by these thinkers was a distrust for mass behavior. They described mass behavior with animal metaphors and with a language borrowed from nineteenth-century psychiatry and deviance. In effect, crowd psychologists pathologized the masses. Taming the masses was the central intent of their inquiries. Their efforts were designed to train governmental and administrative elites, including the army and the police, in the methods of crowd containment and control. If their thinking claimed to be oriented toward a social psychology, it was characterized by the primacy of psychological methods of analysis over the sociological and economic.[5]

It is not accidental that French thinkers played a pivotal role in the development of crowd psychology since *fin-de-siècle* France continued to react to the horrific outbreak and bloody repression of the Paris Commune of 1871, the last great nineteenth-century social insurrection. Furthermore, LeBon, who was trained as a physician and who regarded himself, somewhat pretentiously, as a man of science, was well acquainted with the researches and discoveries of Charcot at the Salpêtrière on hypnosis and suggestibility. LeBon skillfully displaced the hypnosis paradigm from medicine and psychiatry onto the political and cultural milieu. But he did so because of his own anxieties about a repeat of the Paris Commune and his dread of other radical forms of social unrest. He described the leader's functions as if he were a hypnotist whose evocative power could sway an audience and whose ability to convince could shape and color its opinions. Crowd psychology, then, was primarily a psychology of unconscious stimulation with a built-in prejudice against social upheaval and the political activism of the working class; it was explicitly anti-socialist, anti-revolutionary, and anti-parliamentary.

Moscovici praises LeBon for his courage and originality in accepting the phenomena of mass psychology and for describing the regressive process of the individual in the mass. The subject in the mass is reduced to the lowest common denominator of the group; he can be induced into acts of madness and impulsivity; he can be stirred by extreme and wildly fluctuating affective states. For LeBon, men in crowds are threatening, intoxicated, and overexcited; they often behave as if drugged or mesmerized. Yet LeBon also emphasized the conformist and conservative aspects of crowd behavior. The masses are easily overpowered by passion and strongly expressed beliefs. Having lost a sense of reality and a capacity to respond to events critically, crowd behavior is often riddled with unrealistic fears, illusory thinking, and magical longings. In crowds, LeBon observed, individual personality was blurred and intellectual capacity was diminished; these regressions occurred regardless of the educational or cultural attainments of the individual in the crowd. If certain mass behaviors contained a potential for heroic idealism, unselfishness, and altruism, they also pulsated with a potential for violence and barbarism.

LeBon's grasp of the relationship of leader and led turned on his

notion of the crowd's mental predisposition to suggestibility. The
crowd's psychic misery inclines its individuals to act or interact at the
level of children or savages, that is, at something less than adult or
civilized standards. Crowds long for a master because collective situations release primitive emotions, transforming the individual into a
social automaton. The robot-like subject in a crowd follows the
dictates and urgings of his unconscious, in the sense of falling prey to
emotional, cathartic, unreasonable, and ferocious strivings. Hence,
crowd behavior tends to be action oriented, devoid of a sense of limit,
and not circumscribed by moral responsibility; individual man in a
mass is easily influenced by words and images. Suggestion from the
leader determines the fusion of the individual with the mass; such
merger, however, debases the individual into a social mechanism
unable to be guided by will, reasoned judgment, reality testing, or
ethical demands.

If individuals in crowds are automatons, LeBon depicted the crowd
mind as analogous to primary process thinking; such thinking is indifferent to contradiction; it tends to be lively, repetitious, and vivid; it is
emotionally colored; it is condensed, easily displaceable, and represents itself in symbols and visual images. This accounts for the
stereotypic, clichéd, and concrete forms of crowd thinking. In crowds,
the fickle and credulous masses search for hope, happiness, and
certainty, all of which are absent in their everyday lives. Crowds long
for strong men who project themselves as if they were beyond doubt
and uncertainties; crowds are intolerant, dislike logical argument, and
are impatient with rational debate. The leader secures his status as
leader precisely because of the proven strength of his courage over
intelligence and the superiority of his activist leanings over a reflective
stance.

Charismatic leaders, those who have a sign of election or some
mysterious power of ascendancy, mobilize crowds by their power to
mesmerize, terrorize, and charm a collectivity. The eyes and gaze of a
leader have hypnotic qualities, the ability to arouse admiration and
fear. The degree to which consciousness and personality dissolve in a
crowd depends upon the way in which the leader is celebrated as a
godlike, awe-inspiring figure. The identity between crowd and leader
is finally cemented by the repetition of slogans and rhetorical formu-
las, the shrewd and theatrical use of music and choreography, all of

which works toward the obliteration of historical memory and toward the replacement of history with a shared mythology (of race, of country, of esprit de corps, of ideological affiliation).

Gabriel Tarde's seminal contribution to crowd psychology involved a theory of communication in mass culture. Tarde was trained as a jurist and a sociologist and at the end of his career was appointed a professor at the Collège de France. His writings are marked by analytical skills and the same anxieties about the rise and revolt of the masses as LeBon. Tarde advanced his own version of the leadership principle. Crowds, he declared, cannot do without a master. Effective leaders create the mass in their own image; they have authentic and strong convictions; they are intransigent and monomaniacal; and they are motivated by a desire to achieve prestige, the will to be famous. Because they are mentally impoverished and physically enfeebled, the crowd looks to the leader as a savior. In describing the dynamics of imitation between leader and followers, Tarde was actually sketching out a theory of narcissism, in which the leader is idealized. The crowd's admiration for the leader is actually only a split-off way of admiring itself, for they attribute their most precious and highly valued characteristics, ambitions, and ideals to the leader, including a view of their pure or grandiose self. Mass society accelerates the development of the individual's need to love, obey, imitate, and admire a superior being. This makes collectivities receptive to suggestion. Tarde astutely understood that submission is first learned and experienced in early family life, where the father and parents serve as prefigurations of the leader.

Tarde also depicted the ways in which mass communication serves to discipline the masses. The reader of a newspaper, he observed, becomes an excited or obedient automaton. Mass communication rarely attempts to educate or inform, but rather constitutes a subtle form of mental domination. For Tarde, this form of manipulation resembled drug dependency. Modern man is not only prey to passing fashions, but he is easily fascinated by the large-scale, intensified, emotional effects of sophisticated techniques of communication. Today's media, whether the press, television, video, or radio, dangerously threaten to incite and pacify the population, making serious contestation and political opposition extremely difficult. By inference, those who control the means of communication can exercise a hegemonic influence over how contemporary man thinks, feels, and acts. Tarde wrote that industrial man was social in his readiness to suggestion, conformity, and somnambulistic states; modern crowds live as if suspended in a waking dream.

In *Group Psychology and the Analysis of the Ego* (1921) and elsewhere, Freud demonstrated that he had read and integrated the writings of LeBon and Tarde. Freud provided a synthetic explanation for the motive power of collective behavior, thus elevating crowd psychology into critical theory. Throughout the course of his writings, Freud remained preoccupied with the unconscious underpinnings of cultural problems. As a theoretician of collective psychology, however, he transposed the phenomenology of hypnotic suggestion into the framework of a dynamic psychoanalytic theory. Like his predecessors, Freud posited that a science of unconscious mental life could shift the study of history into that of mass psychology.

To account for the psychic wretchedness of the masses, Freud posed questions about the origins and significance of the father in early psychosexual development. If the masses are regressed in crowds, if individuals demonstrate atavistic, childish, even momentary pathological characteristics, then the leader assumes a central and exclusive position. Love, wrote Freud, was the impulse which creates attachment and affective bonds between individuals in a crowd. Love, including homosexual attachment, allows the crowd soul to unite and give cohesion to an otherwise disorganized and amorphous mass.

By introducing the psychoanalytic concepts of narcissism, identification, and psychosexuality, Freud accounted for the antisocial and unstable aspects of the masses. The narcissism of the leader depends on his capacity to love only himself, to develop a heightened and unique confidence in his own ability, ideas, belief system, and in his own feelings of mission, self-importance, and superiority. A leader without narcissism would be tantamount to one devoid of power or prestige. For their part, the masses love and admire the leader, but are unable to love or esteem themselves. The leader of a crowd performs like a father who loves the members of his family equally. Crowds reenact their early developmental ties to their parents by incorporating and fusing with a leader. This reproduction of a model of identification explains how the leader serves as both superego and social ego for the masses, given the propensity of the masses for symbolic thinking.

LeBon argued that everything collective was unconscious. Freud turned that formula around by stressing that everything unconscious was collective. Freud also observed that the erotic was paramount in the individual's psychic life, while the mimetic dominated the psychic life of the crowd; for the group mimesis concludes what eros initiates. Freud's theory helps to account for the conformity, predictability, and pressure to identify in the masses; it also shows how the leader can shape a crowd's mental state, transforming passivity into activity, melancholia into mania; such transformations can also operate in the opposite direction. Charismatic leaders arouse love and hatred, often intensely. Such leaders dominate as the result of the strong transferences which they elicit. In insisting that society abhors the absence of the leader, Freud provides a crucial insight into the nature of social organization; he also underscores the affective dynamics of prestige which play such influential roles in contemporary politics, sports, cultural endeavors, even in the broadcasting of the news.

Moscovici imaginatively interprets Freud's late cultural texts and especially *Moses and Monotheism* (1939) as an elaboration on politics in the age of the crowd. With Moses as the paradigmatic spiritual mass leader, the prophet sets himself up as a mirror in which the masses see themselves and in which there is an idealized longing for a hero. The leader, then, is called upon to play the role of great man in history, while the mass plays the submissive part of mother, or the passive role of children. Such a theory approximates but perhaps oversimplifies how cultures achieve a focus and collective superego, with agreed upon laws, regulations, and interdictions. Moreover, the cult of the father, formed around Moses or any other visionary leader, can result in a canonization of texts, an arbitrary rewriting of history, and the gross dichotomizing of historical actors into categories of good and evil, saints and traitors.

Moscovici's excellent scholarly account of crowd thinkers triggers deep ambivalence on the part of the reader. To be sure, crowd psychologists did discover the potent and often destructive energy of the masses. Despite its disagreeable content and pessimistic underpinnings, it is foolish to dismiss this body of literature as antidemocratic, authoritarian, or elitist. Human scientists have to confront and express unspeakable truths about modern social and psychic reality, not take refuge in soothing solutions or old-fashioned illusions.

Moscovici is not dismayed by Freud's pessimism or conservatism regarding mass psychology, even though he remains skeptical about the view of history and truth embedded in this relatively new branch of knowledge. There is something chilling about these ideas which border on a terrifying modern mythology of domination and enslavement.

Moscovici presents a discerning critique of the major mass psychologists. Most crowd psychologists, including Freud, lack historical specificity in their discussion of collective thinking and behavior; they have disregarded particular and changing social and economic factors in group behavior. In pathologizing crowds, they have denigrated the potentiality for rational or progressive behavior, intellectual and humane values, and even the moral aspirations of the groups they study. They tend to see all crowd situations as identical, without factoring in the particularities of time, space, culture, and circumstance.

What remains powerful but troubling about this essay is its unrelenting emphasis on the nonrational and unconscious determinants of political life. This stance ought not disorient an audience of psychoanalytic practitioners and cultural critics, who comprehend unconscious transferences and resistances in their work.

Most social historians studying crowd behavior, or sociological historians researching popular struggle, do not differentiate between the masses and the individual; most tend to ignore the crucial affective importance of leaders; and most take only cognitive factors into account. Such scholars, whether consciously or not, traffic in a conservative, pre-psychoanalytic psychology, despite the progressive nature of their methodology and conclusions. Moreover, they tend to address a readership of academics or administrators.[6]

On the other hand, crowd theorists, including Freud, write in a manner accessible to a wide, literate audience, offering a body of ideas that could serve the masses not just the leaders. There is an entire body of literature consisting of distinguished thinkers like Theodor Adorno, Erich Fromm, Wilhelm Reich, and the Frankfurt School who have recognized the astuteness of Freud's diagnosis, while rejecting his conservative conclusions. I, myself, find the "scientific" basis of this discipline provisional; perhaps some solid empirical and historical research in the future might work toward verifying some of its chief hypotheses. I share Moscovici's mixed feelings about this subject; in fact, Moscovici's double feelings pervade the text with a strange kind of shadow. For this is a branch of learning that documents the ways in which man remains controlled and manipulated by man. The only way out of total domination is to increase our awareness of the exact mechanisms and unconscious dynamics of subjection.

Notes

1   Serge Moscovici, *The Age of the Crowd: A Historical Treatise on Mass Psychology* (New York, 1985), translated by J.C. Whitehouse.
2   Robert A. Nye, *The Origins of Crowd Psychology: Gustave LeBon and the Crisis of Mass Democracy in the Third Republic* (London, 1975).
3   George L. Mosse, *The Nationalization of the Masses* (New York, 1975).
4   George Rudé, *The Crowd in History, 1730-1848* (New York, 1964), p. 257.
5   Robert A. Nye, *The Anti-Democratic Sources of Elite Theory: Pareto, Mosca, Michels* (London, 1977), pp. 7-14.
6   Charles Tilly, *The Contentious French* (New York, 1984).

13

Narcissistic Themes in a Psychobiography of Isaac Newton

*While artists and scientists may indeed be acclaim-hungry,
narcissistically vulnerable human beings, and while their
ambitions may be helpful in prompting them toward the
appropriate communication of their work, the creative
activity itself deserves to be considered among the
transformations of narcissism.*

—Heinz Kohut
"Forms and Transformations
of Narcissism," 1966

Richard S. Westfall has written the standard biography of Isaac Newton's personal life and scientific career, *Never at Rest* (1980). Its author, an eminent historian and philosopher of science at Indiana University, and a prominent contributor to Newtonian scholarship, offers a strikingly mixed assessment of Frank E. Manuel's *A Portrait of Isaac Newton* (1968), a psychoanalytic biography. Westfall praises Manuel's description of the scientist's life and times, but doubts the evidence and empirical foundations of his "psychoanalysis of Newton." While discovering few if any factual inaccuracies and while

237

finding the text enlightening, Westfall remains unconvinced about the verifiability of Manuel's interpretations. In fact, he expresses deeply ambivalent feelings, including epistemological ambivalence:

> Manuel's analysis is subtle, complex, and ingenious. Is it also true? It appears to me that we lack entirely any means of knowing. It is plausible; it is equally plausible that it is misguided. I am unable to see how empirical evidence can be used to decide on it, one way or the other. I trust it is clear that I am not offering an alternative analysis. It would confront exactly the same problem of confirmation, and in any case, I have no qualifications to offer one. Manuel's portrait, as distinct from his analysis, is a vivid and insightful account of established facts of Newton's life. No biographer of Newton can afford to ignore it.[1]

In his bibliographical essay, Westfall again questions the psychoanalytical component of Manuel's approach, advising students interested in Newton to disentangle the narrative from the critical sections: "It also offers a Freudian analysis of the roots of Newton's character which may or may not be true, but can be separated from the portrait of Newton, on which it is empirically based."[2]

Westfall somewhat conversationally confessed that he objected to Manuel's "excessive psychologizing," in an essay called "Newton and his Biographer." Many of Manuel's perceptions into Newton's "tortured psyche" threatened Westfall's view of Newton's scientific achievements. "I wanted to believe in the autonomy of the individual and the autonomy of the intellectual realm." Several of Manuel's insights into Newton's character apparently undermined Westfall's ideals and perceptions of himself: "in discussing Manuel's view that Newton was tied to his mother's apron strings. Not only did I object to that view; I took offense to it. It seemed to attack my conception of Newton. Perhaps, more deeply, it seemed to attack my conception of myself."[3]

My chapter on Manuel's psychobiography of Newton will not enter into a prolonged polemic with Westfall, but rather will attempt to show the degree to which Manuel's psychoanalytic interpretive framework is integrally related to his portrait of Newton. Instead of seeing Newton tied to his mother's apron strings, a trivialization of the analytic approach, I will discuss the narcissistic dynamics at work. I hope to show how a psychoanalytically informed historian can deepen and enrich our appreciation of the life and contributions of a scientific genius.

Frank Manuel's "The Use and Abuse of Psychology in History" (1971) surveys recent psychological histories, mostly German and French. In this elegant essay, Manuel confronts the methodological problems of preparing a psychologically informed history, while never relinquishing his skepticism toward past and present practitioners. He states his "ambivalence respecting the modern uses of psychology in historical studies." Finding himself "standing midstream in rather shallow waters" regarding the cohabitation of history and psychology, he is struck by the "enormous strides" recently taken; he insists that such an approach can add dimension and strengthen our understanding of historical experience.[4]

Manuel has both the credentials and knowledge to survey and evaluate the attempts to apply psychological understanding to history. He, himself, has written a psychoanalytic biography of Isaac Newton, which I will discuss in the main body of this chapter. He is a prolific European intellectual historian with formidable education, learning, linguistic skills, and interpretive capacities. He has held important faculty appointments at Brandeis University and New York University, including chairs in those history departments. His writing is characterized by erudition, urbanity, cross-disciplinary expertise, verbal facility, as well as a careful, lively, and sophisticated style of composition. He is one of our finest craftsmen.[5]

As a critique of psychological schools of thought associated with Wilhelm Dilthey and Lucien Febvre, Manuel notes their conspicuous omission of anything "below the navel." The psychology of these psychological histories was limited to what was consciously thinkable, to mental structures which exclusively focused on the realm of rational and cognitive factors; these historians had inadequate, faulty, or polemical knowledge of Freud's writings, no understanding of the concept of the unconscious or of unconscious mental conflict, no grasp of psycho-dynamics. Thus, they were unable "to plumb the lower depths." These historians wrote on an "intellectualist plane of psychology," a psychology without interest in or access to hidden forces, to fantasy, to defense mechanisms, to madness, to psychic breakdown, to psychic recovery, to powerful, untamable urges and desires; they totally lacked a conceptual approach to the unconscious processes of individuals, groups, or past eras.[6]

For Manuel, Freud's revolutionary writings and novel perspective decisively changed the landscape of psychological history, opening its creative possibilities. Though not an uncritical worshipper of Freud,[7] Manuel clearly indicates his debt to Freud's understanding of unconscious motivation, of psychosexual development, of attachment, separation and loss, of narcissistic vulnerability and creativity, of the role of fantasy, affect, guilt, shame, and play in mental activity. He acknowledges Freud's seminal contribution by insisting that "the unconscious demands a hearing and will not be silenced."[8] Psychological interpretation mediated by Freud's psychoanalytic approach can throw new light on historical inquiry. Even if psychoanalytic perspectives cannot solve all problems of personality and motivation, they open up new problematics, new vistas for research.

Manuel criticizes those psychoanalytic historians who debase their disciplines by pathologizing their subjects, forgetting the adaptive, creative, and restitutional aspects of the personality; he dislikes those who overinterpret their scanty data or make sweeping claims based on fragmentary evidence; and he condemns those whose analysis is gross, voyeuristic, prurient, wild, or irresponsible. Notwithstanding these disclaimers, he ironically aligns himself with the psychoanalytically oriented historians: "I still cast my lot with the Freudian 'psychologizers.'" Whether they write narrative or critical history, conventional historians, he declares, employ some theory of personality to account for motivation and to explain patterns of continuity and change in their subject's lives. It would be self-defeating for historians to reject the interpretive tools of the most powerful psychological conceptual approach of their era. Manuel points to a modified, nondogmatic, nonjargon ridden Freudian and post-Freudian form of interpretive stance. "And thus, as I see it, there is no escape from Freud's conceptions in some form, orthodox, or heterodox."[9]

Freud's postulation of the unconscious, Manuel argues, implies that historians can detect and subsequently decipher "traces" of the unconscious of past epochs. They can perform reflective soundings on these fragmentary residues, frequently unraveling meaning and transmitting significant insight into these themes. Nor does the psychoanalytic historian have to adhere to rigid, metapsychological, or deterministic forms of psychoanalytic thinking; he can borrow insights that enhance an understanding of meanings on an unconscious level; he can permit himself to be "eclectic and pluralist." Psychoanalytic history need not accept nor presume to perform the tasks of psychoanalytic therapy: the goal, after all, is to comprehend historical actors, not to treat them as sick or to cure them through the strict application of therapeutic techniques.

Manuel advocates a psychoanalytical history which will be fertile both for the disciplines of history and psychology. He proposes that the historian use psychology "modestly," that is, descriptively and analogically, not as part of a grand totalizing or systematic structure. History writing and theory building are different activities. The historian should eschew technical psychoanalytic vocabulary and attempt to write in a prose style that is accessible to his nonspecialized yet literate audience. Abstract discourse can obfuscate as often as illuminate elusive psychological issues. Manuel rejects specialized terminology because it is "ugly and dogmatic" and usually has scientific pretensions. Psychoanalytic history ought not to posture as a new form of positivistic enterprise; ideally, it could be subtle, indirect, raising historical consciousness evocatively; it could radically expand the parameters of historical inquiry.

Such an historian would demonstrate new sensitivity to reading documents; he would appreciate the emotional resonances and varieties of psychic expression, including the fantasies, defensive maneuvers, evasions, and self-deceptions of living beings from the past; he would recognize the pervasive role of psychology in the everyday life of historical actors, not dismiss the everyday life as trivial or self-evident; he would be attuned to the dynamics of repression and sublimation, illness, and restitution, the easily blurred borders between the normal and pathological, genius and abnormality. History committed to a modest, nonmechanistic, nonreductionistic form of psychoanalytic theory, then, would "reject exclusive intellectualism" and could be "multifaceted, possible, and suggestive."[10]

Manuel calls for a concrete psychoanalytic history designed to study personal life histories as the actors lived their history. He is receptive to, even enthusiastic about, an integration of the insights of Marx and Freud; he is inspired by Sartre's ground-breaking preliminary study of Flaubert where an individual's class situation and psychological personality were studied dialectically, illustrating Sartre's view of the family as the crucial mediator between the social and the psychological. Sartre's approach philosophically allowed for freedom and individual choice, while it explicitly contained an "humanist emphasis on the role of personality in history."[11]

I should now like to turn to Frank Manuel's 1968 text, *A Portrait of Isaac Newton* to assess how well he has executed his own proposals for a psychoanalytic history. In "The Use and Abuse of Psychology in History," Manuel humbly refrained from discussing his own work. One passage summarizing psychobiographies by the followers of Freud is a veiled reference to his own study of Newton: "until very recently it has not been attempted with physical scientists—though some of us may be creeping up on them, casting doubt on the autonomous development of science itself."[12] Manuel prefaces his portrait by situating himself perilously between two difficult forms of knowledge, the psychological and historical, neither of which could be evaded: "on more than one occasion I steered my way between a Scylla of historians of science and a Charybdis of psychoanalysts."[13]

His approach to Newton's character explicitly presupposes the existence of an unconscious mental life. He intended to understand Newton's psychic life, both in terms of intrapsychic conflict and deficiency, from a point of view informed by contemporary psychoanalysis.

> The existence of an unconscious with a symbolic language different from that of conscious everyday life and of the great rational systems of the West is a fundamental assumption of this study. Should the unconscious perchance not exist, one of the underpinnings of the book collapses. I owe a huge debt to the psychoanalysts, psychologists, and sociologists from whom I have learned.[14]

In acknowledging Erik Erikson's receptiveness to early discussions about his biographical project of Newton, Manuel states that he has been "deeply moved by Erikson's works and thought." Manuel, however, is no card-carrying Eriksonian. His objections to Erikson address the latter's limitations as a professional historian and social thinker. He criticizes Erikson for not providing a theory of social change; for not advancing our understanding of the complex interrelationship of the figure and his age; for producing a topology of leaders or geniuses that is a return to an old-fashioned history of the "hero" in which the hero's life serves as some kind of "sacred drama"; for writing with a "prophetic quality," as if he were "heralding the next stage in world history"; and for the absence of a rigorous explanation for historical crisis.[15]

With these disclaimers in mind, Manuel situates himself ironically toward Erikson's psychohistory, declining allegiance and party membership in the orthodox psychoanalytic establishment. "Though I can by no means claim the privilege of true discipleship, perhaps he [Erikson] may allow me the more dubious epithet of fellow traveler."[16]

As a psychoanalytic *compagnon de route*, he will accept what is valid and penetrating in the method, but discard expressions of belief and uncritical faith in the theory. Manuel resists true belief, remaining self-reflective about his own method. Manuel's portrait of Newton is not exclusively a "psychologizing" biography. Skillfully interwoven into the narrative and analytic sections are expertly condensed pictures of Newton's circumstances. Three areas of Manuel's historical knowledge round out and fully contextualize his psychoanalytic perspective on Newton's personality.

Manuel is masterful in depicting the cultural role of English Puritanism in the seventeenth century, specifically its impact on family life, on styles of living, and on codes restricting individual morality and comportment.[17] He understands the convergence of religion and science in the seventeenth century; he repeatedly points out that there was no discrepancy in being a sincerely practicing religious person, while also being committed to scientific and empirical endeavors. In fact, he indicates how science was conceived of as an object of religious worship, even Newton's *Principia*'s fundamental goal was to combat atheism. The incompatibility of science and religion began only in the eighteenth century, paradoxically advanced by popularizers of Newton such as Voltaire.[18] Manuel's understanding of the intricacies of institutions, particularly of English university life and the role and structure of scientific associations, adds a complexity to his story of Newton's tenure at Cambridge University and his role as "dictator" of the Royal Society.[19]

Manuel's biography does not deal with the technical scientific aspects of Newton's career or with the internal intricacies of his mathematical discoveries. His project is aimed primarily at elucidating the ambiguities of Newton the person, with particular attention to his personality dynamics, his mental and emotional peculiarities, his world view, and his mode of living. His account focuses on the inter-play of Newton's creative personality with the favorable conditions and receptivity to scientific innovation in seventeenth-century England. This "sounding" into Newton's life history presupposes that the inception and development of Western science had a significant psychological component, and that a humanistic and humane portrait of a seminal genius can only deepen our knowledge of the foundations of Western science itself. The biography is not intended to glorify Newton or to celebrate science. Exploring the deeper meaning of Newton's actions and mental conflicts has neither been expanded into a grandiose attempt to penetrate the core of his genius, nor to lay bare all of his deepest secrets. Many aspects of Newton's mind may remain unknown and beyond the categories and scope of rational analysis:

> This is *a* portrait of Isaac Newton and it does not pretend to encompass the whole man and his multifarious works.... Without presuming to unlock the secret of Newton's genius or its mysterious energy, I aim to depict and to analyze aspects of his conduct, primarily in situations of love and hate, and to probe for the forces that shape his character.[20]

The psychoanalytic biographer of Newton is severely handicapped by the scarcity of sources for constructing his life history, especially of earliest childhood. Documents for the first twenty-six years of his youth in Lincolnshire and of his earliest years at Cambridge University do not exist. Nor have letters or private papers from his mother or from significant family members survived. Newton himself was profoundly suspicious of his subjective and emotional life, distrustful of imaginative, poetic, or fictional language, pedantically opposed to expressing himself with strong and vivid adjectives; he may have burned or destroyed personal data. He left behind no diary, no autobi-ography, and only scanty evidence from his early years.

Manuel confronts his methodological problem ingeniously, but also cautiously. Previous Newton scholars had not analyzed four of the surviving notebooks covering the Lincolnshire and early Cambridge years. Manuel also deciphered psychoanalytically the scattered marginalia in other texts that could be approximately dated because of Newton's distinct handwriting. He investigated these notebooks and manuscript fragments in terms of what they revealed about Newton's personality, as though they contained rich and inaccessible material from his inner world. As he put it: "They allow us to make conjectures about his temper, his moods, his emotions, his character. They may even be a window into his fantasy world."[21]

Manuel reads these documents as a psychoanalyst would approach an analysand's free associations, errors, and verbal slips; he remains particularly attuned to their randomness, to their emotional coloration, to the chance appearance of a word or idea, to dramatic shifts of feeling, to upsurges of impulses and of expressions of guilt, shame, and rage, which may indicate a hidden psychological truth. Always looking for patterns of meaning, for ways of grasping underlying psychic conflicts or signs of deficiency, Manuel selects, structures, and interprets his evidence; but he refrains from sweeping causal explanations and dogmatic assertions of truth. He warns the reader that his interpretations are hypothetical, speculative, and analogical. Manuel maintains his doubts about arriving at some definitive conclusion about Newton's mind, based on an analysis of these relatively free associations; yet he asserts that the expression of affects, mental states, and attitudes are quite evocative and revealing:

> When the word and phrase association in these documents are free, they can, *faute de mieux*, serve as a rather primitive objective personality test, even though the data would hardly lend themselves to refined quantification techniques. No single text in isolation is conclusive, and their evidence is proffered with a measure of skepticism; but in their total effect these records are compelling.[22]

Nor is Manuel inclined to assert the primacy of the psychoanalytic interpretation over the social. For instance in his discussion of the predominance of the color crimson in Newton's furnishings, he suggests that crimson may be indicative of Newton's bloody fantasies. Yet the biographer reiterates that crimson was simultaneously the color of the British monarchy and that Newton's lowly social origins may have motivated some of his wishes for aristocratic status and privilege. "Perhaps both elements were at play, and the rival claims of the psychological or sociological explanation can be conveniently adjudicated."[23]

Manuel constructs a plausible picture of Newton's character based on a psychological evaluation of the available documents; he does so with a nuanced appreciation of free association and of automatic writing. He is aware of how powerful wishes and desires can escape repression and may express themselves defensively. But he complements his audacious psychoanalytic reconstructions and his picture of character structure with disclaimers and a pronounced skepticism about arriving at a deterministic or reductionistic truth about Newton.

> While conscious of recent abuses in the interpretive extension of the boundaries of meaning in historical scholarship, a man of the late-Freudian era cannot put on blinders, refraining from an examination of psychological facts and from making hypotheses about them merely because they are not subject to traditional forms of verification.[24]

The biographer of Newton faces other formidable obstacles. Newton is remembered not simply as a genius in both experimental and theoretic science, but he is revered almost as if he alone shaped modern science. After his death, Newtonianism became adopted as a fundamental model of Western science, with Newton regarded as someone who single-handedly established the basic paradigm of modern science. It is daunting to suppose that one could grasp the mind of the man who made revolutionary contributions to optics, the experimental demonstration of the heterogeneity of light; to mechanics in establishing the laws of universal gravitation; to mathematics in forging the discovery of the calculus. In addition, Newton left behind an abundance of experiments and texts in alchemy, theology, and history.

Manuel's portrait is deliberated poised between pathography or hagiography; he does not denigrate Newton the man nor devalue his enormous scientific contributions. The biographer humanizes the life through empathically feeling and thinking himself into the inner struggles, the passions, and turmoil of the great scientific and mathematical genius. It is unfair and polemical to insist that Manuel's emphasis is primarily of "darkness" and not one which presents a vast palette of color, including gray. Throughout the text, Manuel acknowledges Newton's genius, creativity, strength, resilience, the awesome range of his intellect, and the universality of his scientific system. The task is never to debunk Newton, but "to bring the humanity of genius to us,"[25] while indicating the psychological dimensions of scientific revolution and institutionalization as it developed in the seventeenth and early eighteenth centuries in England.

Manuel repeatedly affirms Newton's passionate intellectual curiosity, his enormous vitality, his capacity for sustained concentration, his incredible memory, his sensory responsiveness, his visual imagination, and his ability to tap into his own primary process, to "symbolize, condense, and displace." He also underscores certain favorable conditions in the environment that validated and recognized his scientific discoveries. Manuel often seems in awe of the "grand universality of his inquiries."[26] He also refrains from any omnipotent claims about having fully captured Newton's personality; on more than one occasion, he calls Newton "enigmatic," a "mystery,"[27] and he honestly admits that his own attempts to comprehend him rely on speculations, metaphors, and inventive forms of verification of the data.[28]

In turning to the psychoanalytic dimensions of the portrait, Manuel is more deeply influenced by the Freudian than the Eriksonian school, and even closer to the English object relations schools and those theoreticians and clinicians who have studied the dynamics of narcissism, the mother-child dyad and the significance of themes of attachment, traumatic separation anxiety, and profound, nonrecuperative loss. Manuel's argument pivots around the device of reconstructing a rigorous picture of Newton's earliest personal history and signaling its lasting impact, its multiple reenactments, on Newton's personality.

In his dense and elusive essay, "On Narcissism: An Introduction," (1914), Freud initiated the modern psychoanalytic inquiry into the phenomena of narcissistic personality types. Although Manuel neither cites Freud's paper, nor any of the more contemporary analytic literature on narcissism, it is a safe bet that he is familiar with its contents and realizes that much of Freud's observations and theorizing apply, albeit in a modified form, to Newton.

Freud defined narcissism as a form of megalomania and of self-glorification. It was marked by a withdrawal of libido from attachments to other people to the subject's own person, more specifically to an idealized internal representation of that person. Because of this withdrawal of interest and investment in other people, narcissistic individuals are frequently self-absorbed, preoccupied with their self-image and body image, while presenting themselves as self-sufficient and inaccessible to others. Narcissistic personalities are often prone to believe in the omnipotence of thoughts, specifically of their own ideas, which they value immensely. They tend to subscribe to the arts of magic, to engage in magical forms of thinking—even when they have demonstrable cognitive abilities. They are prone to hypochondria and to perfectionism, and they crave recognition and fame. They are terribly disturbed by the admonitions of others, frequently experiencing mild rebuke or reprimand as severe criticism. They are extremely self-critical and judgmental of themselves. They often channel their considerable energies, intellect, or talents into the construction of ego-ideals, which become powerful symbols of ambitions, aspirations, and ideals; at times they worship these ego-ideals, or require that others revere them.

In seeing themselves as beautiful (or pure, or holy, or prophetic) and in taking themselves as love objects, Freud, following the descriptions in the Greek myths, saw these personalities being prone to a peculiarly narcissistic object choice; that is, they transform idealized or valued parts of themselves, or romanticized periods of their life, into memories or emotions of intense aggrandizement and exaltation. Narcissistic personalities are emotionally shallow and devoid of personal knowledge; they have difficulty in showing care and compassion for others, except as a form of manipulation. They often display paranoid characteristics and are subject to the defensive operations of inappropriately projecting their self-criticism and anger onto others, thereby becoming terribly sensitive to observation and scrutiny. They are easily slighted and easily enraged.

Freud also discovered that narcissistic object choice accompanied homosexuality; the homosexual may actually be falling in love with a reflection of himself, or an idealized version of himself as a child or a young man. Narcissists struggle with difficulties in maintaining the coherence of their internal picture of their selves and in maintaining their self-regard. They tend to have a distorted and exaggerated image of themselves, one lacking in insight. Freud observed that their chronic feelings of inferiority and impoverishment of the ego often gave rise to disturbances in the regulation of self-esteem, that primitive feelings of omnipotence served to offset severe experiences of depletion and emptiness of the personality.[29]

Newton's early history is easily sketched. He was born prematurely on Christmas Day in 1642. Being born prematurely and on Christmas meant that the infant Isaac was both extremely disadvantaged at birth and regarded as special, perhaps a prophet, a vehicle of "God's truths." Three months before his birth, his father had died. Earliest descriptions of Isaac underscored his littleness, his miraculous survival, his concern about nourishment, and his fear of suffocation. Anxieties about surviving may have meant particularly caring and nurturing attention from his mother and the formation of a deep affective attachment to her. His mother, Hannah, remarried when Isaac was three years old. Remarriage severed her tie with the child as she lived close by (approximately a mile and a half away) but separated from Isaac, who was placed in the care of a maternal grandmother. After the death of his stepfather eight years later when Isaac was eleven, Hannah returned home, bringing with her three siblings sired by her recently deceased husband.

From these critical facts, Manuel infers that Newton's mother was the central figure in his life, that his fluctuating and fragile self-esteem, his oscillations between omnipotence and severe forms of self-deprecation, stem from her early abandonment of him and from the "trauma of her departure."[30] Newton's lifelong patterns of anguish, aggressiveness, depression, and fear of abandonment can be related directly or indirectly to his earliest traumatic loss of his mother; Manuel also insists that the proximity of his mother in the community probably aggravated the infant's sense of deprivation, specifically the loss of continuity and reliability of maternal warmth, security, basic trust, and the sense of belonging in the world.

Newton never recovered from the sense of vulnerability and fragility caused by his abandonment by his mother. He experienced her remarrying and move as an act of betrayal. He became permanently distrustful, cautious, and suspicious of intimate relationships. "Ambivalence toward his mother colored his entire life."[31] That mixed feeling was marked by a recurring wish to fuse with or reunite with his mother, as well as an equally powerful wish to punish her and her husband, his stepfather, who had robbed Newton of the most precious person in his universe. His mother remained the one and only female in his life; Newton was sexually inhibited around women, avoided physical relationships, and died a virgin. Yet his mother's remarriage also left another indelible scar: he went through life suspicious and deeply hostile toward male elders. Being unable to identity with older male figures and unable to dis-identify with his mother, Newton made no father surrogates out of authorities, teachers, or older men. He projected his yearnings for a father figure outwardly and cosmologically, imagining a fusion with God the Father.[32]

As a way of protecting himself against future losses, Newton took flight from intimate ties with other human beings, male or female. He foreclosed abandonment by never engaging in close personal relationships and by regarding people as things, never as ends in themselves. Since his attraction to and love of his mother had resulted in so much hurt, Newton channeled his quite abundant energies away from people and toward work, which entailed little social contact and an austere work discipline. As an isolated and somewhat eccentric man, Newton focused his energy on abstract entities, like theorizing about time and motion. Theoretical knowledge was superior to the emotions and disappointments of love. Scientific knowledge could be used to outstrip, even humiliate, his rivals and to overcome his deep-seated sense of inferiority, loneliness, isolation, and his personal sense of insignificance. The uncertain and mistrustful Newton began to direct his vast reservoirs of curiosity and creativity toward finding absolute certainty, constructing a closed scientific system consistent with his own most recurring personal strivings.[33]

From the outset, Manuel designs his portrait to capture the swings between Newton's self-idealization and self-devaluation. The young Newton greatly admired his mother and praised her strength of character. In contrast, he described himself as small and his own survival on the order of a miracle. As a schoolboy, the little Newton, already "passive and fearful," gained a victory over the school bully, thoroughly enjoying the punishment he meted out to his rival. That pattern would characterize Newton's relations with competitors and enemies throughout his life.[34]

As a boy, Newton is reported to have lived a lonely and isolated life, where he sought refuge in solitary revery and activity. He retreated into his own private world. Living in such a reclusive, shut off private world may have psychologically prepared him for his receptivity to the secret language of numbers. The fearful and solitary Newton, when he was not preoccupied with his work, developed a powerful and insatiable desire for recognition and affirmation from others; he was fortunate that British society in the seventeenth century encouraged and rewarded the activities of scientists.[35]

Newton, of course, had an uncompromising devotion to work, a

Puritanical work discipline. Work served to ease his considerable anxieties about death and about his health; being compulsively busy could help restore a coherence to his self and protect him against his recurring annihilation anxiety. "The chronic hypochondria, a common symptom of narcissism, anxiety and fear of death, did not, however interrupt his work (he may even have sought to blot out his apprehensions in unremitting labor and busyness)."[36]

Newton suffered extreme swings of emotional states, from grandiosity to self-devaluation. He conventionally described himself and his achievements modestly, but occasionally there would be an upsurge of "self-maximization." He frequently expressed himself to his scientific critics with a tone of superiority and annoyance; at other times he was timid and afraid, even obsequious.[37] Newton developed a self-image as the perfect scientist, one incapable of making factual errors or misrepresenting his material; he had "fantasies of omnipotence and omniscience." Rather than regard his scientific colleagues as members of some collegial or professional association, he considered himself as continually under surveillance. They became opponents who particularly enjoyed tripping him up and discovering flaws in his research. Manuel connects the absolutism of Newton's loyalty to the rules of empirical science to the dynamics of suspiciousness, resentment, and infallibility. Thinking scientifically, he imagined, was his mission, a mission that Newton regarded as divinely inspired.[38]

Toward rivals and competitors, Newton behaved in a contemptuous and disdainful fashion. He was usually able to control his outbursts of rage for opportune moments, so as to better crush his enemies. This is particularly evident in his relationship with Robert Hooke.[39] Newton disliked competition and withheld publishing the results of his research. To publish was to achieve closure, to consummate a piece of work, to break away from the initial exhilaration of early discovery, when he was flooded with insight and excitement. The self-absorbed Newton never felt enjoined to share his discoveries with others and seemed to derive pleasure in retaining and not surrendering his creative efforts to the public. Moreover, publication meant the risk of exposure or criticism, which Newton experienced as a grave risk to his sense of self; it exposed him to the putative desires of others to trounce or crush him.[40]

In a superlative passage, Manuel described the narcissistic dynamics of Newton's character, even at a climactic moment of publishing *The Principia.* These dynamics revolve around a deep need for solitude and removal from the world and an upsurge of equally profound fury. What triggered this conflict was his anxiety that he might be accused of having plagiarized the solution to the problem of gravity. Newton's narcissism involved dangers because it might plunge him into a regressive, emotionally cut off world or it might lead to an explosion of murderous rage toward others:

> For a man of his character there was always the ultimate dangerous enticement of Narcissus, of sinking into a private world and contemplating only for himself and eternity. Through the long years in Cambridge he alternated between escapes into solitude and, when the dikes broke, violent outbursts when his rage overflowed.... It is not uncommon for men who are extremely sensitive to criticism to be blindly injurious to others.[41]

Manuel's portrait pivots conceptually around the dialectic of Newton's narcissism: his shifts from a chronic state of worthlessness, self-belittlement, inner fragmentation, and depressiveness (all symptoms of pathological narcissism) toward a grandiose project of unifying all knowledge in a grand synthesis (symptomatic of creative narcissism when combined with a powerful intellect, an ability to work, to endure long periods of solitude, and an intense capacity to concentrate). Newton's narcissistic injuries, his perpetual sense of himself as small, abandoned, inadequate, and fragile help to explain the persistent themes in his life of emptiness and internal fragmentation; they also illuminate the unresolved expressions of shame, guilt, distrust of others, and self-accusation throughout his life.[42] The intense separation anxiety of his earliest childhood, the internalized feelings of deprivation and deficiency, required a gigantic, compensatory leap— represented by his project of creating a systematic, precise, and assured way to grasp the laws of the universe. The utterly uncertain, internally fragmented inner world of Newton constantly strove toward complete, scientific certainty, an absolute certainty best expressed in his efforts to make knowledge mathematical.[43]

Manuel's description of Newton's narcissistic dynamics makes comprehensible the persistence of the great scientist's polarized sense of self, his swings from megalomania to lack of self-esteem. Like other narcissistic personalities, Newton lived a reclusive, secretive, retentive, emotionally cut off life.[44] He always needed to be perfect, or to be seen as perfect. His conscience was extremely punitive and perfectionistic. He saw failure as a sign of evil, as if he were possessed by the devil. He was easily slighted, terribly sensitive to criticism; he feared his critics and was reluctant to publish his work; and he held on to grudges for decades, even after a rival had been humiliated or died. He was uncharitable and aloof in his personal relations. He could not tolerate challenges to his theories and he refused to acknowledge the talent and merit of other scientists in his era. He had little capacity for empathy and no sense of humor. His thinking ability tended not to be self-reflective; he was philosophical in a theological sense, but had no taste for literature or for moral or social philosophy. His aggressivity was boundless; he had an enormous capacity to inflict pain on those who injured him or who contested or damaged the projects and theories he was invested in. His self-absorption coupled with his austere Puritan ethics and his ascetic existence meant in practice that he lived a monastic life of illusory autonomy and dubious independence: "He received nor gave anything to others."[45]

In 1693 Newton suffered a severe psychotic breakdown. Manuel's handling of that midlife episode of madness is as strikingly sensitive as it is psychologically astute; the biographer remains consistent with his method of offering plausible hypotheses, carefully qualified, not sweeping dogmatic generalization or wild pseudopsychoanalytic interventions. The reader learns of Newton's temporary fragmentation and restitution as a major crisis erupting around the unresolved issues of Newton's narcissistic dynamics. The interpretive passages deepen our sense of the complexity of his character, making palpable both his tenuous mental equilibrium and his enormous reparative resources.

At age fifty Newton, a middle-aged, severely inhibited, virginal bachelor decided to live together with Fatio de Duillier. The decision to cohabit with Fatio was a dramatic departure from a life of reclusiveness and asceticism, from a need to regulate distance with others and to preclude intimacy. Fatio, born in 1664, was a young aristocratic Swiss with precocious abilities as a scientist and mathematician, as well as a considerable degree of charm and seductiveness. Newton had been fascinated with him for a number of years, expressing affectionate feelings for Fatio that were quite rare and quite intense affectively. Although the exact nature of their relationship remains ambiguous,

Manuel argues that Newton's attraction appeared to have been narcissistic rather than homosexual: "the character and strength of Newton's inhibitions probably precluded both the cohabitation with women and inversion, though not feelings of tenderness toward a succession of younger men."[46]

Newton and Fatio had many common interests including a genius for science, a love of systematic experimentation, and an intellectual curiosity; they both tended to be hypochondriacal, depressed, secretive, and to oscillate between "megalomania" and "outbursts of rage." Fatio was around twenty-three when he first met Newton, approximately Newton's age at the moment of the *Annus mirabilis* of 1666— the year of his unequalled triumphs in scientific invention. Both shared an interest in apples in addition to theories about gravity; both were intrigued by mysticism, although Newton remained far more cautious and far less fervent than Fatio, for the "realm of mystical experience" was a dangerous heresy in the seventeenth century.[47]

For Fatio, friendship with Newton became his most dazzling social success; he vicariously experienced some of Newton's glory and enhanced his own fluctuating self-esteem through his ties to the great English scientist. In becoming Fatio's spiritual guide and mentor, Newton replaced Fatio's parents with whom he had strained relations. Fatio would subsequently lose contact with social reality, relinquishing any vestiges of discretion. He became swept away, possessed, by a mystical cult, The Prophets; he ultimately became socially disgraced because of his association with this sect and his fanatical views. He spent the latter years of his life in a tragically wasteful way, lost to science. At the exact moment of Fatio's humiliation, his conviction for blasphemy and his punishment of being publicly pelted in the pillory, Newton abandoned him, "never raised a finger to save him."[48] As an old man Fatio continued to live a fictive existence as Newton's "ape"; toward the end of his days he became a "crank living on the memory of Isaac Newton."[49]

Toward Fatio, Newton had expressed authentic feelings of attention, warmth, passion, even care; the expression of such feelings were exceptional for such a cold and self-absorbed individual. In 1693, Newton ultimately decided against having Fatio move in with him, preferring instead to not risk any further closeness or any further passionate attachment to him.

The documents are full of ambiguities, and the picture of their intimacy remains obscure, though it follows the pattern of a middle-aged bachelor's affection for a young replica of himself when a fixation upon the mother underlies his whole emotional structure.[50]

Manuel speculates that Newton's ties to Fatio revolved around a narcissistic attachment, primarily a mirroring bond. Fatio represented an internal picture of Newton as a fertile young man, bursting with ideas and brimming with excitement about scientific discovery. Fatio became a substitutive figure who allowed him to recapture a sense of himself as a boyish, vital, creative, perfect, and pure. In Fatio, Newton found a reflection of himself that he preferred to anything else in the world. He would love Fatio in ways that lifted the repression of his love for his mother. By identifying himself with his mother, he psychologically became his mother; thus he loved Fatio as he wished his mother could have loved him as a child. Newton's affection for Fatio recapitulated his intense need to love a grandiose image of himself.

In Fatio Newton witnessed a reenactment of his own prodigious youth. Newton liked talented young people; he sponsored them and toward them his affective being turned, though his favorites supplanted one another rather rapidly. The narcissistic element in his friendship for Fatio can be related to an early fixation upon his mother. If one adopts Freudian imagery, Newton first identified himself with his mother and took himself as the sexual object; then he found young men resembling himself and loved them as he would have had his mother love him. The maternal element in his nature found reinforcement.[51]

Manuel interprets Newton's break with sanity as overdetermined, but deeply motivated by the trauma of loving then discarding Fatio. "Although the significance of Fatio in the final critical episode is mere inference and might be disputed, the concatenation of events points to him as a major provocation."[52] Other factors influencing Newton's derangement many have been a delayed, postpartum depression after the publication of *The Principia* in 1687. *The Principia* represented the high point of Newton's genius, having enunciated the mathematical laws governing the universe; its publication may have resulted in some despondency about the inevitable waning of his creativity.[53]

The major symptoms of Newton's breakdown included a progressive withdrawal from society, delusional and confused thinking, unprovoked attacks on his loyal friends, violent outbursts, and paranoid attacks, for example in wishing that the philosopher John Locke were dead and in alleging that his friend Samuel Pepys was a papist. Newton resorted to the primitive mechanism of projection in suddenly seeing friends as objects of hostility. "He attacked them for evils with which he was himself possessed."[54]

For Manuel, Newton's psychotic crisis of 1693 can only be rendered comprehensible if it is seen as a result of a lifetime of suppressed narcissistic rage; his affection for Fatio threatened his fragile sense of self and his self-esteem. The sudden unleashing of this fury necessitated a harsh and severe repression which itself rendered Newton ill. Manuel points to a primitive and self-punitive form of guilt which erupted as Newton became conscious of something sinful or evil in his passion for Fatio, a tenderness that threatened his chastity, purity, and righteousness. Following his acute breakdown, Newton was burdened for over a year with severe depression, marked by disturbances of sleep, loss of memory, loss of pleasure, persistent states of sadness, chronic uneasiness, anguish, and a recurring sense of his own worthlessness. Manuel hypothesizes that Newton's prolonged depression may have resulted from a midlife recognition of the passing of both his youth and his scientific inventiveness.[55]

If Newton's mental breakdown indicates the degree to which his narcissism could have a shattering effect on the scientist's sense of self, the recovery from his mental illness demonstrates Newton's "strength," "recuperative powers," and "extraordinary resilience." Newton was a terribly complex man who could take flight from reality into illness, but who could also restore himself into a high degree of functionality.[56] To convalesce Newton relied on his enormous resources of concentration, on the healing aspects of solitude, and on the powers of confession and apology to purge himself of what he regarded as evil thoughts and fantasies. Confessing became a working through process of his guilt and his obsessive self-reproaches. Somehow or another he endured the crisis, gaining the cohesiveness to reorganize his personality so as to not fall apart again.[57]

Newton lived another three decades which were remarkably productive, especially as an administrator; these years were marked by the energy of his "rechannelled capacities." These last thirty years would witness the institutionalization and victory of his science, in addition to the awarding of honors, status symbols, and ultimately knighthood to him. Perhaps these tokens of acclaim were recompense to the elderly scientist for the passage of his youthful genius. Newton, however, never became a fully integrated social man, never responding to or reciprocating the emotional demands of a wife and children, never developing any close and empathic ties to any human being. He remained solitary, committed to preserving his tenuous sanity and to contributing to scientific knowledge and understanding of the natural world. Until the end of his life Newton continued to shun people, to avoid intimacy, and to not permit enduring loves in his life after the Fatio episode; his deeply ingrained feelings of guilt and unworthiness remained, as did his rage, reinforced by his feelings of disappointment and of living in a hostile world.

> The price he paid for his about-face [the transformation of narcissistic aggressiveness turned outward] was to cut himself off in large measure from the boundless inner world which had sustained him with new creations ever since his boyhood. To the extent that he became a successful manipulator of men he was alienated from himself.[58]

The ample evidence of hostility, envy, resentment, and fury in Newton's role as administrator both as warden and master of the Mint and as president of the Royal Society is also explicable in terms of narcissistic dynamics. This is particularly transparent in his nasty and prolonged quarrels with Flamsteed and Leibniz, with Newton's rage unleashed toward men who crossed him or who contested the priority of invention. Newton's seemingly inexhaustible aggression against his enemies was reactive, stemming from early deprivation and deep hurt; Newton's aggressivity flowed from the fragility of his self-esteem. When his theories were threatened or his idealized sense of self was challenged, he reacted with a combination of anger, suspiciousness, paranoia, and vengefulness.

The psychoanalytic insight into narcissism, balanced between an awareness of both its creative and pathological forms, illuminates Newton's internal struggle to restore and to regulate his injured sense of self-esteem. The personal history of cruelty and of insatiable anger, the exaggerated concern with autonomy and preserving his work from critical scrutiny, suggests poignantly that his deficient sense of self was never repaired; Newton persevered as a wounded man, despite his extraordinary intellectual conquests, his breathtaking discoveries, and the universal significance of his achievement. Work, not personal relationships, became the deepest source of his self-regard and personal fulfillment.

For Manuel, Newton's inability to repair this early deprivation and restore a coherence and basic trust to his internal sense of self extends far beyond Newton the man; it becomes symptomatic of modern science itself; the psychoanalytic biographer cautions us to remember the "Janus-like" face of science in terms of its impressive innovations and triumphant discovery as well as its equally horrific power and potentiality for destructiveness.[59]

We must remember that Manuel's *A Portrait of Isaac Newton* was written by a nonpsychoanalytically trained historian; nonetheless, he has arrived at a penetrating and profoundly empathic understanding of the subject. He has presented a picture that is suggestive, subtle, evocative, and plausible; his study is strikingly judicious and balanced, not judgmental toward the conspicuously abnormal features of Newton's character, respectful of his efforts to find personal fulfillment in his work and to recapture a precarious balance to his delicate sense of self. The portrait is not weighted toward the pathological, and the portraitist is mindful of Newton's creativity. He has neither tried to nor solved all the riddles of Newton's personality. Manuel adeptly reads documents as if they were relatively random free associations, thus providing us with a window into Newton's fantasy world and into his private inner realm of dominant fury and occasional tenderness. His depiction of Newton's attachment to and abandonment by his mother is a daring and innovative use of post-Freudian forms of thinking, applied to a world historical figure.

Not only does Manuel depart from instinctual drive theory and from an Oedipal explanation for Newton's psychic conflicts, but he grasps the pre-Oedipal dynamics of Newton's narcissism, the dialectic of Newton's grandiosity and fragile self-esteem; this helps to explain the recurring episodes of depression, isolation, anger, resentment, suspiciousness, and vengefulness throughout Newton's life; it also provides a conceptual clue to the psychotic collapse and recovery of 1693. Manuel's treatment of the themes of abandonment and separation offer a compelling insight into the intricacies of Newton the man. Such a view is opposed to a history of science perspective that tends to idealize the discoveries, or to maintain mythical versions of Newton as if he were a legend, prophet, and form-imprinter of a significant scientific paradigm without persistent internal conflicts or a damaged sense of self.

As a psychoanalytic biographer Manuel is deliberately tactful and restrained; this may inadvertently limit his inquiry because of the lack of candor in specifying the countertransference issues. He never spells out his own inner connection to Newton. Every biographer is engaged in some sort of autobiography, some inner quest to find himself. Manuel never alerts the reader to his own feelings, desires, anxieties, irritations, identifications and counteridentifications in living with Newton all these years, while writing three scholarly works about him. He might have emulated Erikson's openness and self-disclosure in *Gandhi's Truth*, where the psychohistorian allows his subjectivity, including his anger and disappointment with the Mahatma, to intrude into the text.[60]

Manuel does not sufficiently indicate how he, as a biographer, interacted with his subject; he still maintains a naive stance of objectivity or neutrality regarding his study, as if the author of a psychobiography had no unconscious conflicts, fantasies, subjective desires, or narcissistic needs that are played out and challenged in his study. In dealing so directly and sensitively with Newton's narcissistic issues, Manuel never indicates how maintaining a stance of empathic attunement to Newton may have placed demands on his narcissism, his self-esteem, and his own sense of himself, thus complicating the writing of this portrait. Nor does Manuel indicate how the biographer's awareness of his own narcissistic problems perhaps permitted him to elaborate sensitively and work through analytically some of his own subjective problems.

Manuel, for example, might have alerted readers to his own personal history of narcissistic injury. Manuel has gone through his entire adult life with an amputated leg. Living with and reflecting upon such a personal tragedy may have generated a nuanced awareness of the sense of helplessness, shame, humiliation, castration anxiety, and rage associated with bodily deficiencies and loss, perhaps making him more attuned to Newton's susceptibility to early abandonment and to compensating strategies. I know from personal acquaintance with Manuel, having studied with him at New York University from 1968 to 69, that he underwent a long and comprehensive course of psychoanalytic therapy. There is no doubt that Manuel's analysis enriched his portrait of Newton. He might have indicated how his own psychoanalysis sharpened his consciousness of narcissistic themes.

Despite the distinction and the quantity of his publications and his excellence as a teacher, the portraitist Manuel has suffered from an uneven and problematic academic career in America, especially in the early phase from 1933 to 1956. Perhaps his professional ambitions may have been closed to him because of his Jewishness and his early Marxist views; perhaps, because of certain difficult and disagreeable aspects of his character, including narcissistic features. In short, Manuel has personally experienced the pains of exclusion, persecution, and miscomprehension by institutions and by colleagues—in spite of real evidence of his powerful intellect, his own internal dynamic may have undermined his ambitions. Manuel was Craine Brinton's first successful doctoral candidate in history at Harvard University. Like Newton's relations with Isaac Barrow, he may have had a particularly distant and ambivalent relationship with his former mentor, at least in the first twenty-five years after receiving his doctorate.

Manuel offers no self-disclosure in his portrait; he may have rejected this strategy as if it were a gratuitous piece of self-inflation, or a deflection from his theme. In the middle and late 1960s most psychoanalysts were reluctant to reveal or discuss the ensemble of their feelings, fantasies, desires, and anxieties triggered by the transference reactions to their patients; this was deliberately kept out of the psychoanalytic process, as if it were an inappropriate residue of the analyst's neurosis, one which interfered with a scientific or objective understanding of the patient's dynamics. Manuel once again opts for a skeptical, middle road; he is audacious in his interpretive ideas about Newton's inner world and overly cautious in indicating any of his own conscious or unconscious reactions to his subject. He failed to realize that an examination of his own subjective conflicts was a legitimate way of grasping Newton's character.

Manuel's seventy-three pages of scholarly footnotes follow standard historiographical canons; he predominantly refers to primary and secondary sources on Newton's life and times. Nowhere in the footnote apparatus does he cite any psychoanalytic literature or authority. This robs his audience of the psychological knowledge which forms the core interpretive structure of the study. Manuel made a deliberate choice to exclude all references to psychoanalytic theory and practice. It is unclear why. It suggests a defensive return of his ambivalence about integrating psychological insights into historical scholarship. Perhaps he did so because he regarded the American or Anglo-Saxon academic culture of 1968 as ill-prepared or nonreceptive for such an approach. He might have risked indicating his theoretical and conceptual debt to Freud's writings on narcissism and mourning, to the English object-relations school, to psychoanalysts like Bowby[61] who stress attachment, separation, and loss, and to those like Spitz[62] dealing with issues pertaining to the infant's early trauma with the mother, to those theoretical and clinical studies of narcissism by Annie Reich[63] and Kohut,[64], and to those researching normal and pathological symbiosis like Mahler,[65] all of which he probably drew upon. This significant omission leaves his readers unnecessarily guessing at the conceptual foundation of the psychoanalytic framework of the book.

Manuel's fascination with latencies make his form of psychoanalytic biography an archeological form of inquiry, as well as a piece of detective work. Manuel had another agenda in writing his psychobiography of Newton, namely an attempt to demonstrate the possibilities of a nonintellectualized intellectual history. The author may have designed the Newton portrait to function as a form of therapy to those historians of ideas who have traditionally overvalued rational systems and under estimated the role of unconscious symbolization and ideation in Western thought.

The classic psychoanalytic formulation of intellectualization emphasizes how thinking operates to protect the individual from instinctual dangers or intrapsychic conflicts. Intellectualization is a defensive process whereby one masters intense emotions or exaggerated fantasies by concealing them in discursive, abstract, or highly theoretical forms. Intellectualization in treatment situations is always regarded as a resistance, usually designed to neutralize painful feelings, to distance forbidden affects, or to repress unpleasant memories. Intellectual historians may intellectualize or display a narcissistic investment in a given theory for similar reasons; they may fear taking a closer look at their subject's or their own narcissistic wounds, unconscious defenses, anxieties, fantasies, self-deceptions, and

desires. Manuel's psychoanalytic portrait of Newton subtly demonstrates the power, elegance, and plurality of meanings in a nonintellectualized version of intellectual history.

Deciphering the latent meanings and motivations of the dead is a
risky undertaking; Manuel's favorite skeptic, David Hume, might
comment ironically on his study: "There is much in what you say, but
not as much as you think." Hume would thus be underscoring the
importance of ambiguity and multiple meanings in every interpretative
activity, including an intellectual biography informed by psychoanalytic methods and insights. There is much in what Manuel says and
evokes in his portrait of Newton, but as a portrait it remains open to
further elaboration, elucidation, revision, and modification by subsequent historians. The true twentieth-century skeptic, then, combines
Hume with Freud: he may say what he thinks, often in a eloquent and
learned way as does Manuel, but still retain doubt and self-doubt as to
the essential correctness of his interpretations.

Notes

1   Richard S. Westfall, *Never at Rest: A Biography of Isaac Newton* (New York,
     1980), p. 53, n. 32.
2   Ibid., p. 877.
3   Richard S. Westfall, "Newton and his Biographer," in *Introspection in
     Biography: The Biographer's Quest for Self-Awareness* (Hillsdale, New Jersey,
     1985), pp. 175-189, eds., Samuel H. Baron and Carl Pletsch; for an appreciation
     of the "biographer inclined to see man psychoanalytically," see Peter Gay,
     "Secrets of a Genius," *Saturday Review*, 1 February 1969, p. 32.
4   Manuel, "The Use and Abuse of Psychology in History," *Varieties of
     Psychohistory*, eds, George M. Kren and Leon H. Rappaport (New York, 1976),
     pp. 38-62; The essay was originally published in *Daedalus*, Winter, 1971,
     Historical Studies Today, pp. 187-213. The title echoes Nietzsche's 1874 essay
     "The Use and Abuse of History," sometimes translated as "Of the Advantage
     and Disadvantage of History For Life."
5   Frank E. Manuel, *The New World of Henri Saint-Simon* (Cambridge, Mass.,
     1956); Manuel, *The Eighteenth Century Confronts the Gods* (Cambridge, Mass.,
     1959); Manuel, *The Prophets of Paris* (Cambridge, Mass., 1962); Manuel, *Isaac
     Newton, Historian* (Cambridge, Mass., 1963); Manuel, *Shapes of Philosophical
     History* (Stanford, California, 1965); Manuel, ed., *Utopias and Utopian
     Thought: A Timely Appraisal* (Boston, 1965); Frank E. Manuel and Fritzie P.
     Manuel, *French Utopias: An Anthology of Ideal Societies* (New York, 1966);
     Frank E. Manuel, *The Religion of Isaac Newton* (Oxford, 1974); Frank E.
     Manuel and Fritzie P. Manuel, *Utopian Thought in the Western World*
     (Cambridge, Mass., 1979).

6   Manuel, "The Use and Abuse of Psychology in History," *Varieties of Psychohistory*, pp. 43, 44, 46.
7   Manuel, *Utopian Thought in the Western World*, pp. 788-792, 795.
8   Manuel, "The Use and Abuse of Psychology in History," p. 41.
9   Ibid., pp. 49, 54, 58, 55.
10   Ibid., pp. 56, 57, 58.
11   Ibid., p. 52. This essay was written before the publication of Sartre's monumental biography of Flaubert, *The Family Idiot*.
12   Manuel, "The Use and Abuse of Psychology in History," p. 49.
13   Frank E. Manuel, *A Portrait of Isaac Newton* (Cambridge, Mass., 1968), p. ix. Out of print for years, the text has recently been reprinted by the Da Capo Series in Science (New York, 1990).
14   Ibid., p. ix.
15   Manuel, "The Use and Abuse of Psychology in History," pp. 50-52.
16   Manuel, *A Portrait of Isaac Newton*, p. x.
17   Ibid., pp. 54-55.
18   Ibid., pp. 125-132.
19   Ibid., pp. 68-69, 91-116.
20   Ibid., p. 2.
21   Ibid., p. 9.
22   Ibid., p. 57.
23   Ibid., p. 61.
24   Ibid., p. 10.
25   Ibid., p. 19.
26   Ibid., pp. 5, 47, 74, 86, 88, 279, 390.
27   Ibid., pp. 380.
28   Ibid., pp. 9-10.
29   Sigmund Freud, "On Narcissism: An Introduction," *The Standard Edition of the Complete Psychological Works of Sigmund Freud*, vol 14 (London, 1957), pp. 67-102.
30   Manuel, *A Portrait of Isaac Newton*, p. 25.
31   Ibid., p. 27.
32   Ibid., p. 28.
33   Ibid., pp. 18, 44.
34   Ibid., p. 45.
35   Ibid., p. 47.
36   Ibid., p. 70.
37   Ibid., p. 139.
38   Ibid., p. 141.
39   Ibid., p. 146.
40   Ibid., p. 156.
41   Ibid., 157.
42   Ibid., pp. 49, 52.
43   Ibid., pp. 65-66.
44   Ibid., p. 97.
45   Ibid, pp. 156, 279.
46   Ibid., p. 142; also see Anthony Storr, *Solitude: A Return to the Self* (New York, 1988), pp. 164-167, for a sensitive treatment of Newton's psychosis. For a neurological perspective, see Herold L. Klawan's, *Newton's Madness: Further*

Tales of Clinical Neurology (New York, 1990), pp. 30-39, who holds that Newton suffered from mercury poisoning and dismisses disdainfully any and all psychiatric explanations for his psychosis.

47   Manuel, *A Portrait of Isaac Newton*, pp. 194, 202, 205, 208.
48   Ibid., p. 210.
49   Ibid., p. 212.
50   Ibid., p. 196.
51   Ibid., p. 195.
52   Ibid., p. 201.
53   Ibid., pp. 218, 220.
54   Ibid., p. 219.
55   Ibid., p. 220.
56   Ibid., p. 223-224.
57   Ibid., pp. 216, 219.
58   Ibid., p. 225.
59   Ibid., p. 392.
60   Erik H. Erikson, *Gandhi's Truth: On the Origins of Militant Nonviolence* (New York, 1969), pp. 229-254.
61   John Bowby, *Attachment* (London, 1969).
62   René A. Spitz, *The First Year of Life* (New York, 1965).
63   Annie Reich, "Pathologic Forms of Self-Esteem Regulation," *Psychoanalytic Study of The Child*, vol. 15, 1960, pp. 205-232.
64   Heinz Kohut, "Forms and Transformations of Narcissism," *Journal of the American Psychoanalytic Association*, vol. 14, 1966, pp. 243-272.
65   Margret S. Mahler, *On Human Symbiosis and the Vicissitudes of Individuation* (New York, 1968).

Index

55, 57, 60, 65, 67, 68, 82,
85, 86, 94, 95, 99, 103, 110,
118, 124, 126, 131, 139,
146, 147, 149, 150, 151,
153, 154, 164, 200, 209,
215, 216, 221, 222, 224,
225, 229, 230, 232, 233,
234, 235, 239, 240, 242,
259, 260, 261
Underwood, Pamela, xliii
Universal (theories),
  universalism, 41, 114, 121,
  122, 125, 197

Vermorel, Henri, xliii
Vienna Psychoanalytic
  Society, 92, 93, 159, 168,
  223
Vienna, 31, 62, 145, 148, 168,
  169, 173
Vienna, University of, 32, 38,
  268, 277
Vivekanada, Swami, 49, 51

Voltaire, François-Marie
  Arouet, 243
Vulgar Marxism. *See* Marxism

Wagner, Richard, Wagnerian
  hero, 87
Weltanschauung, 54, 59, 126,
  132
Westfall, Richard S., 237-238
White, Hayden, 198-199
Winnicott, D.W., 180
Wisconsin, University of, ix, x
Wittkowski, Victor, 62, 63
World War One, xii, 91
World War Two, 91

Yale University, 210

Zionism. *See* Herzl, Theodor
Zurich, 36, 40, 81
Zweig, Stefan, 28, 30, 31, 32,
  33, 37, 38, 39, 53, 59, 67,
  69, 70, 71, 72